The Dynamics of Desista

INTERNATIONAL SERIES ON DESISTANCE AND REHABILITATION

Series editor: Stephen Farrall

Published titles

The Dynamics of Desistance: Charting pathways through change,
by Deirdre Healy

Criminal Behaviour in Context: Space, place and desistance from crime,
by Nick Flynn

The Dynamics of Desistance
Charting pathways through change

Deirdre Healy

Routledge
Taylor & Francis Group

LONDON AND NEW YORK

First published by Willan Publishing 2010
This edition published by Routledge 2012
2 Park Square, Milton Park, Abingdon, Oxon OX14 4RN
711 Third Avenue, New York, NY 10017

Routledge is an imprint of the Taylor & Francis Group, an informa business

ISBN   978-1-84392-783-9 hardback
ISBN   978-0-415-62805-1 paperback

British Library Cataloguing-in-Publication Data

A catalogue record for this book is available from the British Library

Project managed by Deer Park Productions, Tavistock, Devon
Typeset by GCS, Leighton Buzzard, Bedfordshire

Contents

List of tables and figures

Tables

Figures

General Editor's Introduction

The International Series on Desistance and Rehabilitation aims to provide a forum for critical debate and discussion surrounding the topics of how and why people stop offending and how they can be more effectively integrated into the communities and societies to which they belong. The books published in the series will be international in outlook, but tightly focused on the unique, specific contexts and processes associated with desistance, rehabilitation and reform. Each book in the series will stand as an attempt to advance knowledge or theorising about the topics at hand, rather than being merely an extended report of a specific research project. As such, it is anticipated that some of the books included in the series will be primarily theoretical, whilst others will be more practically focused on the sorts of initiatives which could be employed to encourage desistance. It is not our intention that books published in the series be limited to the contemporary period, as good studies of desistance, rehabilitation and reform undertaken by historians of crime have much to teach us and are also welcome. In terms of authorship, we would welcome excellent PhD work, as well as contributions from more established academics and research teams. Most books are expected to be monographs, but edited collections are also encouraged.

Deirdre Healy's excellent book is an ideal early contribution to the series. As she notes in the early sections of her book, her main aims were to explore the subjective factors associated with desistance from crime; how these interacted with the social context to produce change; the mechanisms responsible for the shift from criminal to conventional lifestyles; and the early stages of the change processes through which people move away from crime. In short, her aims were to explore the role of agency and its interaction with wider social contexts. This is particularly interesting set of questions in its own right, but set against a background of rapid social and economic change in Ireland (and at the time of writing it appears that Ireland may be in for more dramatic changes) they become all the more interesting. Healy finds that sudden, dramatic changes are not uncommon and that periods of reflection often 'kick start' processes of change. Among her sample (73 male probationers living in Dublin) Healy finds little evidence of the role of generativity in her desisters' accounts of their change (perhaps because, as she freely acknowledges, they were still at the early stages of leaving crime behind). Instead, redemption appears to be a result of desistance, and the role of generativity comes in supporting the process of desisting. Social processes (such as rebuilding damaged relationships) appear to develop slowly and iteratively alongside desistance.

All in all, this is a fascinating read which unpacks several recent theoretical developments in research into desistance and rehabilitation and explores them in the context of well-designed and executed empirical research. For those reasons, this book represents an auspicious start to what we hope and expect will be an important and stimulating series.

Stephen Farrall,
Sheffield

Preface

This book explores the nexus between social and personal forces in the desistance process. It was assisted in its development through ongoing dialogue, both formal and informal, with many colleagues. I would especially like to thank my PhD supervisor, Professor Ian O'Donnell, Director of the University College Dublin Institute of Criminology, for his guidance and support throughout this project. I am grateful to others who provided advice and suggestions about earlier drafts of this book and the various publications that have arisen from the study. In particular, I would like to mention: Anthony Bottoms, Ros Burnett, Steve Farrall, Shadd Maruna, Mick O'Connell, Joanna Shapland, and Glenn Walters. In addition, I would like to thank the Irish Probation Service and An Garda Síochána (the national Irish police force) for facilitating this research and the probation officers who participated in the study. I would like to extend special thanks to the probationers who volunteered their time to participate in this research and shared their wisdom and experience with me. I would like to gratefully acknowledge the Irish Research Council for the Humanities and Social Sciences for funding my post-doctoral research fellowship for two years. I am also obliged to the National University of Ireland, who provided me with a small grant. Finally, I would like to thank Cormac Behan, Angela Ennis and Seamus Healy for reading the manuscript.

When I began my research, desistance was still a somewhat novel research topic and little was known about the processes that engendered the termination of criminal careers. I spent many hours talking to men who were trying to move away from crime. They described lives that were characterised by social disadvantage, drug addiction, and limited vocational experience, and I was struck by just how difficult it would be for them to change direction. Yet, many had stopped or were reducing their offending. Coming from a background in psychology, I was particularly interested in discovering whether, and how, they used their inner resources to overcome the odds that seemed to be stacked against them.

My intellectual journey frequently led me beyond criminology into new territories. During one of these forays, I came across the story of a Sligo-born woman named Elizabeth Gilbert (1821–1861). Her story encapsulates many of the themes that appear throughout this book. Like many of the people I spoke to, she faced significant structural obstacles which led her to adopt an unconventional lifestyle, but later she forged a positive new identity which helped her to overcome these obstacles. Her 'fall' began when she left an unhappy marriage and began a public affair with another man. As a result, she found herself in difficult financial straits. Her family disowned her so she was unable to turn to them for assistance. She reinvented herself as a Spanish dancer and changed her name to Lola Montez. She gained international notoriety as a result of her many adventures, which included romantic liaisons with some of the most famous men of her time. She encountered widespread opprobrium but refused to bow to it. After moving to America, she became a highly successful actress, lecturer and author; and, by the end of her life, she had achieved financial independence and a measure of respectability. She attributed her success to a triumph of will in defiance of unjust social restrictions.

Many of the men I spoke to encountered significant external challenges on their pathway towards desistance. Few attained the level of success that Lola achieved or remained as unaffected by social censure. Nevertheless, there was clear evidence that they were beginning to muster their personal resources to help them embark on meaningful and productive lives. It is difficult to improve upon Lola's own words, which are taken from the dedication in her first book, published in New York in 1858:

> To all men and women of every land, who are not afraid of themselves, who trust so much in their own souls that they dare to stand up in the might of their own individuality, to meet the tidal currents of the world.

Chapter I

Desistance and reintegration

That the majority of offenders eventually terminate their criminal careers is a well-established finding in criminal justice research. For a long time, this phenomenon was dismissed as a function of maturation or 'ageing out' of crime (see Glueck and Glueck 1940; Gottfredson and Hirschi 1990) and little was known about the processes underlying it. As Maruna (1999: 1) concluded, 'few phenomena in criminology are as widely acknowledged and as poorly understood as desistance from crime.' Recently, this neglected and potentially valuable area of research has begun to receive increasing attention and there has been a renewed interest in studying the mechanisms, contexts and individual characteristics that are associated with reducing or stopping offending.

This book aims to contribute to this nascent area of enquiry by providing a phenomenological account of the psychosocial processes involved in desistance. It focuses on a number of key questions that have not yet been fully explored in desistance research. What prompts prolific offenders to periodically cease their criminal activity? Are there different factors involved in the onset and maintenance of desistance? What impact, if any, does desistance have on the minds and lives of ex-offenders? And finally, can probation supervision support individual efforts to change? Before addressing these questions, it is necessary to examine what existing theoretical perspectives and empirical findings reveal about desistance. The following review draws on a broad literature, including research into risk, recidivism and rehabilitation, in order to provide additional insights into the process of change.

Crime across the life course

Criminal career research has provided a wealth of information about pathways through crime. One of the best known and most methodologically stringent studies to explore the progression of criminal careers was initiated at Cambridge University during the 1960s (see Farrington *et al.* 2006). The Cambridge Study, as it became known, consists of a longitudinal survey of 411 eight-year-old boys from a working class area in London. The study, which is ongoing, uses a combination of self-report surveys, interviews and police records to measure offending and its correlates over time. Various techniques were used to minimise the loss of participants, resulting in an exceptionally good response rate, with over 90 per cent of the sample re-interviewed at age 48.

By that time, 41 per cent of the men had acquired at least one conviction and 93 per cent self-reported committing at least one offence during their lifetime. The study identified clear differences that reliably distinguished between individuals who offend and those who do not. Children who were most at risk of later offending were impulsive, lacked good parental supervision, experienced socio-economic deprivation, performed poorly at school, and had a family member who engaged in crime. Many of these differences began to emerge when the participants were children, and their influence remained evident well into adulthood. In particular, conduct problems in childhood predicted offending and antisocial behaviour in adulthood. As a result of these findings, Farrington (1997: 362) described involvement in crime as a feature of 'a larger syndrome of antisocial behaviour' that originates early in life and is evident over the life course. He observed, 'typically, a career of childhood anti-social behaviour leads to a criminal career, which often coincides with a career of teenage anti-social behaviour and leads to a career of adult anti-social behaviour' (ibid).

In the USA, three longitudinal studies of delinquency involving over 4,000 participants largely confirmed the findings of the Cambridge Study. The studies identified a similar set of risk factors for crime, which included individual (such as intelligence, hyperactivity, gender), family (such as poor parental supervision), and structural (such as low socio-economic status, parental unemployment) factors (e.g. Browning and Loeber 1999). These factors had a cumulative impact on offending; that is, the higher the number of risk factors, the higher the probability that the individual would engage in crime. In England and Wales, a survey of almost 5,000 youths aged 12 to

30 identified drug use, problems in school and the absence of pro-social bonds as the most important risk factors for offending among males (Flood-Page *et al.* 2000). Again, these factors were found to have a cumulative effect on offending. Over half of males who had at least four risk factors were involved in persistent or serious crime at the time of the survey. Of course, this also means that just under half were not committing serious crime despite being at high risk, suggesting that the criminal pathway is not inevitable. Taken together, these studies suggest that certain demographic, behavioural, social and psychological factors increase the likelihood that someone will engage in crime but their effects are not inescapable. As with many social phenomena, pathways to crime are rarely clear-cut and adult criminality is not necessarily presaged by childhood experiences.

The idea that certain factors are strong predictors of reoffending suggests a somewhat deterministic view of criminality, where individuals possessing certain characteristics are almost fated to play out a particular destiny. In reality, there is always the potential for change as well as continuity in human behaviour. Longitudinal research on criminal careers has revealed that changes in offending trajectories are possible and frequently occur. In Rutter's (1990) longitudinal study, children at risk often managed to circumvent troubled pathways if certain protective contingencies were present. These factors exerted a protective influence, shielding them from the damaging effects of early difficulties. For example, children who liked school tended to plan their futures better, and this was related to improved outcomes later in life, particularly in the areas of marriage and employment.

Furthermore, while a large proportion of adolescents engage in delinquent behaviour, few become involved in serious or sustained criminal activity. When Kyvsgaard (2003) examined the criminal careers of Danish offenders, she found that 6 in 10 desisted after their first conviction regardless of age, gender and employment status. In all, estimates suggest that fewer than 10 per cent of men become involved in serious or persistent offending although those that do are often highly prolific offenders (see Flood-Page *et al.* 2000). In the Cambridge Study, 7 per cent of the participants were responsible for more than half of all reported crime (Farrington *et al.* 2006). Nevertheless, even chronic or persistent offenders eventually move away from crime. In a longitudinal study of desistance among young offenders, Ezell and Cohen (2005) found that, despite evidence of continuity, there was variability in criminal activity among even the most persistent offenders. They described the juxtaposition of stability

3

and change in the criminal career as the 'paradox of persistence' (Ezell and Cohen 2005: 6).

Longitudinal studies reveal that criminal activity tends to peak in adolescence and then tapers off in young adulthood. This phenomenon, known as 'the age-crime curve', shows that by the age of 28, most offenders have ceased to be involved in crime (see Farrington *et al.* 2006). In other words, desistance from crime is the norm rather than the exception. In fact, once they stop, many ex-offenders manage to create conventional lifestyles that are often indistinguishable from those of non-offenders. In the Cambridge Study, a 'life success' indicator was created to measure success in key life domains, such as accommodation, relationships, employment, alcohol and drug use, and criminality. The sample was divided into three groups: desisters (who had received no further convictions after the age of 21), persisters (who were convicted before and after the age of 21) and a group who were never convicted. Overall, although persisters had achieved the least life success, the majority of participants in all three groups were considered successful by the age of 48. There was very little difference between desisters and the never-convicted group, suggesting that desisters in particular had transcended the negative effects of criminality to lead successful conventional lives (but see MacDonald and Marsh (2005) for an alternative perspective on life success among ex-offenders).

Some dispute the notion that offenders can desist and have sought alternative ways to explain attrition in criminal careers. Adopting a developmental perspective, Moffitt (1993) attempted to account for observed heterogeneity in criminal careers by differentiating between two groups of offenders: 'life-course persistent' and 'adolescent-limited' offenders. She observed that 'life-course persistent' offenders were more likely to begin their criminal careers at an earlier age, engage in a variety of offences, and terminate their offending later than the 'adolescence-limited' group. 'Adolescent-limiteds' were mostly involved in delinquency during adolescence and some antisocial behaviours during early adulthood (for example, alcohol and drug use), whereas anti-social behaviour among the 'life-course persistent' group was fairly stable from childhood to adulthood and, for them, continuity was more likely than change. According to Moffitt, the 'life-course persistent' group suffered from 'cumulative continuity' where the psychological and social dysfunction they experienced in childhood was amplified over time. Unlike chronic offenders, 'adolescent-limiteds' had adequate social skills and resources. They committed crime during adolescence to obtain access to coveted adult behaviours and lifestyles. As they aged, they began to use their resources and skills to find conventional ways to obtain the things they had previously acquired through crime. They subsequently re-evaluated their view of crime and came to regard it as a threat to their legitimately acquired lifestyles and, as a result, stopped offending. Essentially, Moffitt proposed that offending patterns were stable for just a minority of offenders and that most of the people who became involved in crime engaged in relatively minor offending, which petered out as they reached adulthood. Her conclusions are not supported by longitudinal research, which suggests that most offenders have the capacity to change their criminal trajectories.

Although there is evidence for continuity in behaviour between childhood and adulthood, 'the chain of adversity is far from inevitable' (Rutter *et al.* 1998: 31). While early criminal career theorists emphasised childhood experiences as the primary determinants of adult criminal behaviour, it is now recognised that experiences throughout the life course exert an equally important influence on development. Santrock (1999: 9) characterised the life span as 'lifelong, multi-dimensional, plastic, historically embedded, multi-disciplinary and contextual'. At birth, an individual is placed on a trajectory or path. This pathway may be interrupted by transitional experiences, positive or negative, and these can initiate turning points that alter the current life direction. While childhood risk factors show a strong and consistent relationship with crime, adult life events often exert a more important influence on behaviour (see Laub and Sampson 2003). While there is variability in the timing, nature and celerity of desistance, virtually all offenders cease to offend.

Different shades of grey

Pathways to desistance are rarely linear or straightforward but are better described as tumultuous, dynamic and uncertain. Desistance does not occur as an abrupt termination of offending but usually consists of a gradual reduction in the frequency, severity and versatility of offending (see Loeber and LeBlanc 1998). Even then, desistance is rarely absolute and many ex-offenders continue to engage in some form of antisocial activity. Nagin, Farrington and Moffitt (1995) found that some young men who had not been convicted since adolescence and were officially classified as having terminated their criminality, continued to participate in more socially acceptable forms of antisocial behaviour such as brawling, drinking and drug use. Nagin *et al.* (1995: 132), who endorsed the central tenets of social control theory, described this as 'circumscribed deviance'. They suggested that these offenders avoided crimes with a high risk of conviction to escape the possibility of losing work and family ties. Interestingly, their employment prospects and spousal relationships were similar to those of the group that had never been convicted, suggesting that they had superseded the negative consequences of their earlier brushes with the law.

Leibrich (1993) interviewed 35 people classed as desisters (i.e. who had no official police contact recorded against them since completing a probation sentence 3 years earlier) and found that almost half were still involved in crime. Not all were engaged in the type of crime they had previously committed, and some continued to commit minor offences such as small-scale shoplifting. To further complicate matters, many of them regarded themselves as going straight and described themselves as desisting. Leibrich (1993: 1) concluded that the pathway away from crime is 'curved'. She introduced the notion of improvement, where people were offending less frequently or less seriously. She noted the implications of her findings for policy, observing that 'decisions will continue to be made on black and white figures, whereas it is the shades of grey that matter' (Leibrich 1993: 42).

The distinction between persistence and desistance is frequently blurred and, for the majority of offenders, their identification with both categories is fluid. The offender 'transiently exists in a limbo between convention and crime, responding in turn to the demands of each, flirting with one, now the other but postponing commitment' (Matza 1964: 28). They belong to neither world and reside in both, depending on prevailing circumstances. It seems that criminal activity is intermittent rather than constant. Greenwood *et al.* (1978) discovered, contrary to their expectations, that persistent offenders actually committed relatively little crime. Overall, prisoners in their study reported committing violent offences at a rate of 4.6 per year and property crimes at a rate of 18 per year. Their analysis led Greenwood *et al.* (1978: 7) to conclude: 'the picture that begins to emerge from these empirical data is not one of a large number of dedicated criminals consistently pursuing a pattern of serious crime. Rather, the majority of incarcerated offenders appear to commit serious crimes at relatively low rates.'

Periods of temporary desistance in criminal careers are relatively common. Despite their prevalence, the 'zig zag' path of criminal careers (Glaser 1964: 57) has been subject to little theoretical or empirical scrutiny to date (but see Piquero 2004). One theoretical perspective offers a potential way forward. Maruna and Farrall (2004) proposed a useful distinction between two stages in the process of reform: *primary desistance*, defined as any hiatus in criminal activity; and *secondary desistance*, a more long-term process, which results in the reframing of personal identity into a new conventional self (see also Maruna, Immarigeon and LeBel 2004). Secondary desistance is treated as a long-term process during which individuals must gradually develop a new sense of identity as a non-offender. The process is complete when this new, non-criminal identity is internalised. In the language of social learning theory, these concepts might correspond with the distinction between the acquisition of behavioural change and its maintenance (Bandura 1977). While secondary desistance has generated much empirical interest in recent years, little is known about the processes involved in primary desistance.

The fact that pathways to desistance are not linear or straightforward creates difficulties for defining and measuring of desistance. There is currently no agreed approach. Desistance is variously regarded as an event (e.g. Weitekamp and Kerner 1994) or a process (e.g. Maruna 2001). Laub and Sampson (2001: 11) tried to resolve the dilemma by differentiating between the event of termination of a criminal career, that is, 'the time at which criminal activity stops', and the process of desistance, that is, 'the causal process that supports the termination of offending', claiming that both need to be studied. There is also disagreement among researchers about how long an offender must be crime-free before being considered a 'desister'. As already noted, many offenders experience lulls in their criminal activity, and it is important to be able to distinguish between 'true' and temporary desistance. Some researchers have argued that a year is sufficient to determine whether desistance has occurred (e.g. Graham and Bowling 1995), while others have observed that 'the true age of desistance can be determined with certainty only after offenders die' (Farrington 1997: 373). In the evaluation literature, it is generally accepted that a follow-up period of 2 years captures the majority of reconvictions, except in the case of sex offenders, who tend to take longer to reoffend (e.g. Cann, Falshaw and Friendship 2004).

The absence of a standardised definition of desistance means that research may generate inconsistent findings and make it difficult to draw accurate conclusions (see Kazemian 2007). Dichotomous measures may obscure the important changes in offending behaviour that occur as offenders progress towards reform. A purely quantitative approach may miss some of the important subjective changes that accompany

7

behavioural change. A limited follow-up period may not capture all episodes of reoffending. These issues have elicited increasingly sophisticated methodological responses, and researchers now often use advanced statistical techniques to capture nuanced changes in offending behaviour. In their longitudinal analysis of criminal career trajectories, Bushway *et al.* (2001: 500) defined desistance as 'the process of reduction in the rate of offending from a non-zero level to a stable rate empirically indistinguishable from zero'. This definition was based on findings from Laub, Nagin and Sampson's (1998) longitudinal study, which described two groups as desisters because their rate of offending was so low as to be indistinguishable from that of non-offenders.

Bottoms *et al.* (2004: 383) hypothesised, 'rather than a steady progression, we suspect that, whilst moving generally in a conformist direction, people oscillate on what we might visualise as a dimension, or continuum, between criminality and conformity. On such a continuum, complete criminality and complete conformity are for the vast majority, points never likely to be reached.' It is important to be cognisant of these issues when attempting to research desistance.

Understanding desistance

Desistance research is fairly new and, although several models have been advanced to account for the termination of criminal activity, few have been subject to stringent empirical testing and several key questions remain unanswered. There is, for example, disagreement about the roles played by the various factors in the desistance process. Early explanatory models fell into three broad categories: those that attributed desistance to maturation, those that prioritised informal social control, and those that stressed the importance of personal agency (see Maruna 1999). Most researchers now endorse an interactive perspective, where maturation, agency and structural factors are seen to play a role.

Adult transitions, self-control and maturation

One of the best known and most stringently tested models of desistance was proposed by Laub and Sampson (2003). They reanalysed longitudinal data on 500 delinquent boys who had been incarcerated in a reformatory school during the 1940s. The authors subsequently contacted and reinterviewed 52 of the original participants, who were by then aged 70. Over their lifetimes, the men's criminal careers were characterised by both stability and change. While childhood events and individual characteristics encouraged stability in offending behaviour, adult life events were capable of altering their criminal trajectories in either a positive or negative direction. Two factors consistently emerged as having strong correlations with desistance – employment and marriage. However, it was not employment or marriage alone that facilitated desistance, but it was their *strength* and *quality* that was important. Only jobs and relationships that the men had invested in emotionally were capable of prompting desistance. The authors proposed an age-graded theory of informal social control to account for these findings. In their view, desistance was linked to the acquisition of social bonds during the transition to adulthood. They argued that individuals gradually acquire social stakes in work and family, which add structure to their lives and act as a source of informal monitoring and emotional support (see also Laub, Nagin and Sampson 1998). Although they described desisters as active participants in the change process, Laub and Sampson (2003) prioritised structural factors in their account.

A challenge to social control theory is posed by Gottfredson and Hirschi's general theory of crime, which prioritised internal and maturational factors in offending and desistance. They took as their starting point the finding that age and prior criminality show stable associations with crime over time. Observing that research has not found a consistent link between marriage or employment and crime, they contended that any correlations between social institutions and delinquency are actually artefacts of an underlying personality trait, namely low self-control. In their view, people who lack self-control are 'impulsive, insensitive, physical (as opposed to mental), risk-taking, short-sighted and non-verbal' and, as a result, are more likely to engage in criminal and analogous behaviours (Gottfredson and Hirschi 1990: 90). Individuals with low self-control are not only more likely to engage in crime but are also more prone to experiencing difficulties in other life domains, including work and relationships. According to this perspective, low self-control develops in childhood through ineffective family socialisation. To account for desistance, they distinguished between the propensity to commit crime, which remains relatively stable throughout life, and actual criminality, which can change over time.

There is some evidence to support the contention that low self-control influences offending behaviour. Farrington *et al.* (2006) reported that 'high daring' (similar to impulsivity), measured during

9

childhood, was one of the strongest predictors of adult criminality to age 48. A meta-analytic review of studies testing the relationship between low self-control and criminality also revealed a significant link between the two, which was particularly apparent among males and youths (Pratt and Cullen 2000). The authors concluded, however, that other explanations could not be discounted. While it is likely that self-control is involved in criminal behaviour, empirical tests show that it typically accounts for only a small proportion of offending behaviour (Longshore 1998).

Self-control theorists do not recognise the role that adult life events and wider social circumstances can play in criminal behaviour. Furthermore, the theory cannot account for other, more recently documented, subjective aspects of desistance, such as identity change. Self-control might best be viewed as one dimension of criminality which operates alongside social and other subjective factors to encourage or inhibit offending behaviour. Brannigan *et al.* (2002) tested the interaction of structural, control and self-control variables in generating misconduct and aggression among children aged 4 to 11. They found that the most significant factors were individual (especially hyperactivity), followed by control (especially hostile parenting) and, lastly, structural (especially family). A model comprising all three sets of factors performed better than any of the individual models.

Identity, rational choice and cognition

What is missing from social or maturational explanations is the individual. According to Maruna (1999), the correlates of desistance, such as age and employment, must be studied alongside subjective changes in offenders' world views to provide a more complete picture of the reform process. Many ex-offenders attribute desistance to subjective changes, including shifts in identity associated with becoming a parent (Burnett 1992), the re-evaluation of life choices following a negative experience with the life of crime (Cusson and Pinsonneault 1986), and feeling shame at past behaviours (Leibrich 1993). Various subjective theories of desistance have been proposed but the role of the individual in desistance remains under-theorised.

In his influential ethnographic study, entitled *Making Good: How Ex-offenders Reform and Rebuild Their Lives,* Maruna (2001) used narrative theory to explore the psychology of desistance. According to this perspective, people create meaningful narrative identities through the medium of personal life stories. Maruna interviewed 55 men and

10 women and found that the narratives of offenders and desisters differed in several important ways. Ex-offenders used particular cognitive strategies to help them to put their criminal pasts behind them and build positive new futures. They developed a 'redemptive script' in which they claimed that their criminal pasts were due to external events beyond their control (Maruna 2001: 87). Aided by an outside force, they escaped the cycle of crime and punishment and attempted to 'make good' by engaging in generative pursuits. Persistent offenders, on the other hand, lived by a 'condemnation script' (Maruna 2001: 73). They held fatalistic outlooks on life and were uncertain about their ability to change. Although this study provided important insights into how ex-offenders perceived themselves and their place in the world, it did not reveal how or why people change. It is not clear, for example, whether the redemption narrative is the cause or the outcome of the desistance process. The study has generated substantial interest in ex-offenders' change narratives (e.g. Presser 2008), but has not yet been replicated.

Shover (1996) adopted elements of rational choice theory in his perspective on desistance. He found evidence that offenders make a sort of cost-benefit analysis in relation to the commission of crime, which he termed 'the criminal calculus' (Shover 1996: 140). He proposed that desistance occurred when ageing and experience meant that the costs of crime began to exceed the benefits (for example, a higher number of previous convictions increases the likelihood of a longer prison sentence on conviction). In his research, successful offenders (defined either as those who expect financial gains or who are successful at avoiding imprisonment) were more likely to commit crime (Shover and Thompson 1992). Many within his sample initially offended in order to fund a hedonistic lifestyle involving drink, drugs and partying. Over-indulgence, however, resulted in increasing difficulties, such as addiction or loss of employment. This prompted a re-evaluation of values and a determination to change, which engendered a new perspective on the self and on delinquent behaviour. They began to distance themselves from youthful behaviour and reformulate their goals from an emphasis on partying and building a reputation to more conventional pursuits. Shover (1996) concluded that the determination to abandon crime operated alongside the development of conventional social bonds and rewards in the process of desistance.

Generally speaking, cognitive appraisal may be compromised for offenders. Everyday decision-making, while rational, is subject to error, bias, and distortion. Since most people evaluate situations quickly and subjectively, with incomplete information, they may misjudge outcomes (Kahneman, Slovic and Tversky 1982). While this is true for all individuals, certain cognitive factors associated with criminality and delinquency may augment the probability for error among offenders. Research has shown that extraversion (Eysenck and Eysenck 1977), sensation-seeking (White, LaBouvie and Bates 1985) and impulsivity (Farrington *et al.* 2006) are disproportionately present among offenders. These traits militate against a considered evaluation of the costs and benefits of a particular course of action. Research has shown that little planning is involved in the decision to commit a crime or in the actual commission of an offence. Studies of armed robbers, for example, have suggested that the majority of those arrested are either opportunists or engage in minimal planning prior to committing their crime (Morrison and O'Donnell 1994). Studies of offender decision making have also shown that recidivists may be less likely than non-recidivists to consider the potential negative consequences, such as imprisonment, when faced with an opportunity to commit a crime (Zamble and Quinsey 1997). They are more likely to focus on the potential benefits such as money (Shover 1992).

Although originally developed in addiction research, Prochaska, DiClemente and Norcross' (1992) trans-theoretical model can also be applied to desistance from crime. The theory consists of a six-stage model of the cognitive processes involved in recovery from addiction. At first, individuals are unaware of the extent of their problem and have not yet begun to think about change (*pre-contemplation* stage). Then, they realise that a problem exists but do not yet make a commitment to change the behaviour (*contemplation* stage). At this point, they begin to weigh up the pros and cons of both the problem and the potential solution. Next, they make a decision to change (*preparation* stage) and begin to address the problem behaviour (*action* stage). Finally, they consolidate the changes they have made, a process which can take considerable time (*maintenance* phase). Over time, feelings of self-efficacy increase and vulnerability to temptation decreases. Recognising that relapse is often part of the reform process, Prochaska *et al.* (1992) added a final *relapse* stage. The model envisages change as a spiral process where individuals can recycle back to an earlier stage after a failed attempt.

This model is widely influential in addiction theory and practice but has received some criticism (see West 2005). Some question the idea that the variety of human experiences can be slotted into discrete and somewhat arbitrarily defined stages. Others have pointed out that many of the psychological processes involved in addiction are habitual and often operate outside conscious awareness. In addition, because it focuses exclusively on the cognitive processes involved in behavioural change, the model has been criticised for failing to take account of the social influences on behaviour (Barber 2002). Finally, the model reveals little about how people make the transition from one stage to another. Nevertheless, it has a number of positive features. It is empirically based and has been successfully applied to a wide range of behaviours. It represents change as a process rather than an event and is therefore capable of capturing the dynamic nature of desistance. This model is also one of the few that can accommodate unsuccessful as well as successful desistance attempts. This is particularly important since pathways to change inevitably contain relapse experiences.

Integrated perspectives

Most theorists now accept that it is some combination of individual, social and psychological factors that brings about desistance. Bottoms *et al.* (2004) proposed an integrated perspective that attempted to take account of the roles played by background factors, structure and agency. They proposed that certain innate characteristics (such as age) increase or decrease the likelihood that someone will commit crime. These individual characteristics interact with the social context, which can also promote or hinder desistance (for example, an offender in employment is less likely to reoffend). The prevailing culture and its associated assumptions, values and norms also influence whether change will occur. When a specific opportunity to commit crime presents itself, situational factors come into play (for example, the availability of a target). The final component in their model is agency, which they conceptualised as a socially situated and subjectively interpreted process of choice (see also Wikstrom 2006). They stress that focusing on any of these elements in isolation can never provide a complete picture of desistance.

Another attempt to draw the various strands together was proposed by Andrews and Bonta (2006), who developed an empirically based personality and social psychological theory of criminal conduct. They considered criminal attitudes to be one of the 'big four' risk factors that played a strong role during the 'psychological moment' of crime (Andrews and Bonta 2006: 137). According to their theory, antisocial attitudes generate the rationale for engaging in antisocial behaviour. Attitudes are influenced by antisocial peers, who model criminal behaviour and control how the benefits and costs of such behaviour are meted out. Under such circumstances, individuals with a history of criminal behaviour are more likely to engage in crime because they are more confident that they can successfully commit a crime. Personality traits are also involved in determining whether crime will occur. Impulsive people, for example, are more likely to be attracted to the thrill of crime and are therefore more likely to offend.

In their theory of cognitive transformation, Giordano, Cernkovich and Rudolph (2002) assigned weights to the various cognitive and social processes behind desistance. They prioritised cognitive processes in their account, arguing that the wider social environment plays a secondary role. According to their perspective, the individual must first experience a readiness to change. He or she must then encounter an environmental 'hook' for change. If this is perceived as both meaningful to and accessible by the offender, it constitutes an opportunity for reform and may trigger the creation of a new pro-social identity. More recently, Giordano, Schroeder and Cernkovich (2007) added an extra component to their theory by highlighting the role that emotions can play in desistance. They suggested that emotional states can affect the actor's ability to benefit from desistance opportunities. Individuals with negative emotional states, such as depression or anger, are less able to avail themselves of 'hooks' for change.

Rehabilitation and reintegration

So far, the review has concentrated on the social and subjective influences on desistance. The final element that will be considered is the criminal justice system, which can also affect the course of an individual's criminal pathway. Labelling theorists propose that, when people experience a negative social reaction to their criminal activities, they may internalise this label. In an effort to cope with the ensuing stigma, people may augment their offending behaviour and move deeper into the criminal lifestyle (see Lemert 1972). In fact, mere contact with the criminal justice system has been shown to increase the likelihood that individuals will be charged again in the future, irrespective of their actual level of offending. McAra and McVie (2007: 337) observed that a 'filtering process' was at work in the Scottish youth justice system. In their study, a group of the 'usual suspects' was identified by youth justice agencies and repeatedly recycled through the system, even when they reduced their offending. One of the strongest predictors at all stages of the process was having been charged in the past, and this was independent of the level of self-reported offending. In addition, the deeper the young people went into the system, the less likely they were to desist.

Studies of offender populations frequently illuminate lives of chronic drug use, poverty, deprivation, and long histories of unemployment as well as extensive criminal histories (see O'Mahony 1997), but the relationship between these factors and crime is not clear-cut. Several studies have identified biases in sentencing practices, which suggest that certain people are more likely than others to be arrested, convicted, and imprisoned. More often than not, these groups constitute vulnerable members of society, who are drawn into a cycle of disadvantage and crime that is difficult to escape. People residing in economically deprived areas in Ireland are more likely to be imprisoned (Bacik *et al*. 1997). In the USA, young, black men have a higher risk of receiving a custodial sentence than other groups (Steffensmeier, Ulmer and Kramer 1998). McAra and McVie (2007) found that Scottish teenagers who lived in economically deprived areas were more likely than those from more affluent areas to come to the attention of the authorities. This should be borne in mind when interpreting findings from studies using reconviction rates as a proxy for reoffending.

Over the last two decades, the drive towards accountability in criminal justice systems in the Western world has precipitated an 'era of evidence-based practice' (McGuire 2002: xiv) and a wealth of data about recidivism among convicted offenders. Although this research exists largely in a theoretical vacuum, it provides important information about the factors associated with reconviction and what can reduce it. Certain factors have been found to increase the likelihood that people who have become involved in the criminal justice process will be convicted again. Risk factors can be categorised into static and dynamic risk factors (see Andrews and Bonta 2006). Static factors, which include age and criminal history, consistently emerge as the strongest predictors of recidivism. In a large-scale national study of reconviction in England and Wales, Lloyd, Mair and Hough (1994) found that the most significant predictors of reconviction were age, number and frequency of prior court appearances, offence type, number of previous convictions and gender. Younger offenders with longer criminal histories were more likely to be reconvicted. (Of course, this may be partly explained by the fact that people with prior contact with the system are more likely to be rearrested (see above).) Lloyd *et al*. (1994) were aware that their model of recidivism was limited, given the lack of data on dynamic variables. This deficiency was addressed by a further Home Office study, conducted by May (1999). Although many dynamic factors were related to reconviction, inclusion of these only slightly improved prediction of reoffending. The most important were employment and drug use.

Other studies suggest that both static and dynamic factors play important roles in reoffending. Cottle, Lee and Heilbrun (2001) examined the factors associated with recidivism among juvenile offenders. They found that the most significant predictors were offence history, social and family problems, physical or sexual abuse, poor use of leisure time, and delinquent peers. In a meta-analysis of 131 studies, criminal attitudes, criminal history, socio-demographic and family factors emerged as the strongest predictors of recidivism (Gendreau, Little and Goggin 1996). Generally speaking, although static factors are better predictors of reoffending, it is the malleable dynamic factors that practitioners are most interested in, as these can be targeted for change.

Interestingly, the sentence received, whether custodial or community-based, does not appear to have a significant impact on reoffending. Kershaw, Goodman and White (1999) found little difference in reconviction rates between prisoners and probationers, both averaging over 50 per cent. The difference between the groups was further reduced when standard risk factors (such as age and criminal history) were controlled, leading the authors to conclude that there was 'no discernible difference' between the two sanctions (Kershaw *et al.* 1999: 1). Similar results have been observed in other countries, such as Canada (Gendreau *et al.* 2000) and New Zealand (Triggs 1999). Imprisonment inflicts several serious consequences on offenders, including disruption of family and work ties, the very factors that have been shown to promote desistance. Since community sanctions are at least as effective as custodial options in reducing reoffending and do not disrupt social bonds to the same extent, it is worth examining them in more detail.

Firstly, there is a lot of evidence that rehabilitation programmes can help people to move away from crime. Meta-analysis, a powerful technique that can be described as a kind of statistical literature review, enables researchers to analyse hundreds of evaluations of offender treatment programmes at once and to draw conclusions about their overall impact on reoffending. In one study, Lipsey (1995) reviewed 443 programmes for juvenile offenders and found an average reduction in recidivism of 10 per cent. His findings were supported by a number of similar investigations, leading researchers to conclude that treatment has a weak but positive effect on reconviction.

Researchers have also identified a list of factors that increase programme effectiveness. The so-called 'what works' principles are described extensively elsewhere (see McGuire 2002) and need only be briefly reiterated here. According to these principles, programmes should target moderate to high-risk offenders (the risk principle), address criminogenic needs such as employment, antisocial attitudes or substance abuse (the need principle), and match teaching styles to the learning style and abilities of the clients (the responsivity principle). Treatment type is also important. Multi-modal programmes with an emphasis on cognitive behavioural techniques have been identified as being among the most promising approaches, although no single approach is effective in all settings. Community-based programmes tend to be more effective than programmes delivered in custodial settings. Finally, programme integrity must be maintained. This means that programmes should be properly implemented and regularly evaluated.

These guidelines were enthusiastically embraced by criminal justice practitioners around the world, most notably in Canada, the USA and the UK, and rehabilitation interventions based largely on cognitive behavioural principles were introduced. Early evaluations suggested that these interventions could significantly reduce reconviction, but subsequent studies revealed that the impact of these programmes was not as strong as expected (see Merrington and Stanley (2004) for a review). The positive effects of treatment begin to fade after 2 years (Raynor and Vanstone 1997) or when risk factors are controlled (Taylor 2000). In other words, efforts to address criminal cognitions can significantly depress criminal activity in the short term but not the long term. This suggests that focusing exclusively on the cognitive processes behind desistance may not be sufficient to encourage permanent behavioural change. A number of other explanations for this lack of success have been proposed. Some have questioned the lack of debate or empirical testing of the central tenets of the 'what works' approach and critiqued the poor methodological quality of many of the primary studies on which its principles are predicated (e.g. Mair 2004). The 'what works' initiative also faced significant implementation and organisational challenges. Mair (2004) documented the difficulties of working in a managerial culture, where staff must maintain a balance between integrity in practice and the need to achieve government targets. The speed of change and a perceived lack of consultation left many probation officers feeling disenfranchised. It is more likely that the narrow focus of the 'what works' approach meant it failed to address the impact of wider personal and social circumstances that influence offending behaviour (see Haines and Case 2008). Practitioners themselves were concerned about the reliance on a single approach (i.e. cognitive behaviourism) to address a multi-faceted problem (i.e. crime and its consequences). Atkinson (2004: 248) described how traditional techniques had been 'hijacked by a method that is being marketed as a panacea to supersede all rival methods'.

In one of the few large-scale and well designed investigations of the impact of probation supervision on desistance, Farrall (2002) concluded that probation supervision had little impact on the resolution of the obstacles probationers faced. He found that extra-therapeutic factors, such as individual motivation and social circumstances, were more important for desistance than the work probation officers undertook with their clients. Similarly, released prisoners generally do not consider re-entry programmes as being of much assistance and are more likely to cite support from family and friends as being instrumental in easing their paths back to the community (see Visher, LaVigne and Travis 2004).

Some researchers have spoken directly to probationers to find out which elements of probation practice are most helpful in promoting desistance. Probationers appreciate having someone independent to talk to about their problems (see Mair and May 1997). They frequently mention the importance of receiving help with personal difficulties but prefer to receive advice about how to resolve their problems rather than direct intervention (see Rex 1999). This is in line with the view that personal agency is important in change. Probationers who attribute changes in their behaviour to supervision often refer to the 'active and participatory' nature of these experiences (see Rex 1999). This approach is characterised by empathy, respect and the ability to listen, combined with professionalism. Offenders are more likely to follow pro-social examples they find credible and compelling (Trotter 1995). Given this, it is worrying that the traditional welfare-oriented practices of many probation services have been supplanted by a new 'managerialist' approach, which emphasises risk management, evidence-based practice, punishment and public protection. As Barry (2000) notes, the key message of the Probation Service in England and Wales has shifted from 'advise, assist and befriend' to 'confront, challenge and change'.

The 'what works' literature provides a sophisticated account of the ingredients a programme must contain in order to create the conditions for change, but it cannot account for the personal nature of change and the power of choice as revealed by the desistance literature. Interventions operate alongside personal agency and social mechanisms in a larger process of desistance. Researchers are coming to realise the importance of studying the interactions between programme processes, contexts, individuals and, of course, outcomes. Scientific realists believe that programmes are 'social systems ... [composed] of the interplay between individual and institution, of agency and structure, of micro and macro social processes' (Pawson and Tilley 1997: 63). In the words of Maruna (2000: 12), 'by concentrating almost exclusively on what works, offender rehabilitation research has largely ignored questions about how rehabilitation works.'

While important, the influence of the criminal justice system operates at the periphery of desistance while subjective, social and individual factors play a more central role. It is better to view reintegration as a long-term process rather than the outcome of a single intervention. A comprehensive analysis should take account of individuals' circumstances prior to imprisonment or probation supervision and their experiences during their sentence in addition to their post-sentence experiences and long-term adjustment (see Visher and Travis 2003).

Chapter 2

Issues and challenges

There are a number of key theoretical, conceptual and methodological issues that have not yet been fully addressed in desistance theory and research. This chapter outlines four of the most pressing challenges and establishes the extent of existing knowledge about each of them. First, it draws together information about the subjective factors associated with desistance. It continues with an investigation of how these factors interact with the social context to generate change. Next, it examines what is known about the mechanisms underlying the shift from a criminal to a conventional lifestyle. Finally, it focuses on the early stages of change and what occurs in the minds and lives of ex-offenders as they make the often turbulent transition from criminality to desistance.

Agency, cognition and identity: the psychology of desistance

The concept of 'agency' is frequently invoked in contemporary discourse on desistance yet, despite recent theoretical and empirical advances, the role of the individual remains poorly defined and under-researched. Researchers use different definitions and a variety of measures, making it difficult to establish a clear picture of the psychology of desistance. In addition, several theories attempt to address the subjective aspects of desistance. Some implicate stable personality traits (e.g. Gottfredson and Hirschi 1990), while others prioritise transient cognitive processes (e.g. Giordano *et al.* 2002).

The 'what works' literature provides a useful starting point for an exploration of the subjective dimensions of change. Although this strand of research is frequently criticised by desistance researchers for its neglect of the wider social and structural influences on offender behaviour, it sheds some light on the cognitive factors associated with reoffending and desistance. Pro-criminal attitudes are among the strongest predictors of reoffending (see Gendreau et al. 1996). People's attitudes towards offending, their level of victim empathy, and estimates about their likelihood of reoffending are related to subsequent offending (see Frude, Honess and Maguire 1994). Social psychological research also shows broad support for a link between attitudes and behaviour (see Ajzen and Fishbein 1980).

It may not only be *what* offenders think but also *how* they think that has implications for whether they engage in offending behaviour. Walters (1990) identified eight criminal thinking styles that support the criminal lifestyle, including power orientation (a desire to control or manipulate others), cognitive indolence (lazy thinking) and discontinuity (a tendency to become distracted from goals). These have been correlated with both past and future criminal behaviour (Walters 1995; 1996). Based on his findings, Walters (1990) developed a lifestyle theory of criminal conduct. He proposed that three influences – conditions, context and choice – interact in a complex, dynamic and multi-directional way to generate the criminal lifestyle. Internal and external conditions set the context for behaviour and establish the individual's vulnerability to future criminal opportunities. The individual then makes a choice about whether to offend and alters his or her cognitions to support the resulting lifestyle. Walters' work is supported by earlier research on criminal thinking, which suggested that offenders employ certain cognitive strategies to rationalise their behaviour and neutralise their feelings of guilt (see Maruna and Copes (2005) for a review).

High levels of motivation and self-belief appear to be essential for successful behavioural change and have been implicated in a number of desistance theories. Among them, Giordano et al. (2002) suggested that 'readiness to change' is a critical component in the desistance process. Addiction researchers also claim that strong motivation is crucial for recovery (e.g. Prochaska et al. 1992). Nevertheless, many offenders are ambivalent about change. Although most express a desire to stop offending, many believe that they lack the inner resources to bring about successful behavioural change. In a landmark study, Ros Burnett interviewed 130 prisoners prior to release and followed their progress over a 10-year period (Burnett 2004). While

21

80 per cent claimed they wanted to avoid further crime, almost half felt it was probable that they would reoffend on release. Participants who expressed confidence in their ability to change were less likely to reoffend than those who were ambivalent about desistance. Their predictions were borne out in the 10-year follow-up, by which time 82 per cent had reoffended (Burnett and Maruna 2004).

Poor coping skills may impede an individual's ability to desist. In a study of recidivism among ex-prisoners, Zamble and Quinsey (1997) found that reoffenders tended to perceive more problems in their lives than desisters. They experienced low self-awareness and negative emotional states and displayed poor coping skills. Earlier work by one of these authors (Zamble and Porporino 1988) found that the problems faced by offenders were no more challenging than those most people encounter. They concluded that the problem lay in offenders' inability to recognise or resolve their problems. Offenders who are highly motivated tend to report fewer problems in their lives and seem to cope with them more easily (Farrall 2002). Perceived self-efficacy, which refers to a person's beliefs about his or her personal capacity to achieve desired goals, is important in desistance. Bandura (1997), who introduced the concept, reported that individuals with high self-efficacy feel more in control of their lives, enjoy better psychological well-being and are equipped with superior decision making capabilities. They embrace challenges and remain committed to their goals even when they encounter obstacles. A strong sense of self-efficacy can reduce the likelihood that an individual will engage in problem behaviours, such as drug use and crime (Ludwig and Pittman 1999).

Although developed with non-criminal populations, Côté's (1997) work on agency is relevant for desistance research. He contended that, as a consequence of the individualisation of the life course in late modern society, people must increasingly rely on their own resources to assist them in negotiating their paths through life. Those who take a 'default' individualisation route are inclined to allow external circumstances and immediate impulses to govern the course of their lives. In contrast, individuals who follow the 'developmental' individualisation pathway reflect carefully on available alternatives before making decisions and actively pursue opportunities for self improvement. In other words, they exercise agency. Using a composite indicator of agency, which included measures of self-esteem, sense of purpose, resilience and locus of control, Côté found that agency predicted the extent to which young adults were able to establish a coherent adult identity and achieve their life goals. University students who scored higher on these attributes experienced more life success at a 2-year follow-up, as measured by job satisfaction, personal development and goal attainment. Similarly, desisters must play an active role in shaping their lives if they are to successfully make the transition to adulthood and a crime-free lifestyle. Pawson and Tilley (1997: 36) recognised the crucial role of individual choice, describing it as 'the very condition of social and individual change.'

There is growing evidence that several key personality traits are involved in offending behaviour. In particular, negative emotionality, which is characterised by a tendency to experience negative emotional states such as anger, and weaker control (similar to impulsivity) have been linked to offending. These findings have been replicated in Scotland (Smith *et al.* 2001), Pittsburgh (Browning and Loeber 1999) and New Zealand (Caspi *et al.* 1994). People who experience negative emotional states may be more likely to interpret interpersonal events as threatening. In conjunction with weaker controls, these negative emotions may be acted upon more readily (see Caspi *et al.* 1994). Emotional states also appear to play a role in desistance. Giordano *et al.* (2007) found that people who reported higher levels of anger and depression were more likely to reoffend. They posited that these emotions can reduce motivation to change and limit an individual's capacity to take advantage of desistance opportunities. A negative mindset can exacerbate social problems (see LeBel *et al.* 2008).

The role of identity

Criminologists have long been producing vivid accounts of criminal identities, such as the 'dope fiend' and the 'hustler' (e.g. Shover 1996), yet knowledge about desistance identities remains limited and nebulous. Burnett (1992) derived a typology of desistance identities from prisoners' accounts of their motivation to change. 'Non-starters' identified with a non-criminal identity and claimed their criminality was an aberration. 'Avoiders' were motivated to change by a desire to avoid incurring further costs of crime. 'Converts' claimed their values had changed and had adopted new conventional identities. They were committed to desistance and disapproved of offending. In a follow-up of this sample, LeBel *et al.* (2008) found that prisoners who endorsed an identity as a 'family man' prior to release from prison were less likely to reoffend, even after 10 years.

Narrative theory has added a temporal dimension to the study of desistance and identity. Vaughan (2007: 396) noted, 'human agents constitute their identity by plotting their lives within a narrative that exists between a past that is denounced and a future ideal towards which they strive.' Similarly, Presser (2008) describes narrative identity as a dynamic account of the lived experience which integrates the subjective past and present and the desired future. Self-stories are not just concerned with the past. They are purposive and can be used to guide future behavioural choices. Maruna (2001) suggested that the generative and spiritual goals in the narratives of desisters acted as a strategy for making amends for their past as well as promoting their new non-criminal identities. He found that ex-offenders often reframed their negative pasts into a new positive life story. They lived by a redemption script, which presented their past mistakes as a necessary prelude to a worthy and productive life.

The redemption script is characterised by generative concerns, high levels of agency and reframing of criminal pasts (see Chapter 1 for an overview of Maruna's theory). In later work, he argued that identity change was the outcome of the desistance process (see Maruna, Immarigeon and LeBel 2004). Giordano *et al.* (2002) agreed that the creation of a pro-social identity was an integral part of desistance. Others dispute the notion that identity change is a prerequisite for desistance and argue that behavioural change can occur in its absence. Bottoms *et al.* (2004) pointed out that offenders can remain crime-free for lengthy periods of time without adopting a new identity; for example, because of a change in circumstances which favours desistance (such as forming a strong relationship). Similarly, Laub and Sampson (2003) proposed that desistance arises indirectly through a series of 'side-bets' in employment and relationships rather than through cognitive transformations or identity shifts.

Possible selves theory offers a useful way to conceptualise identity in criminological research. Markus and Nurius (1986: 954) defined possible selves as 'the cognitive components of hopes, fears, goals, and threats'. In other words, they are representations of the selves that a person might become, would like to become, or is afraid of becoming. According to this theory, individuals generally endorse several projected future selves, both feared and desired, at any given time. A balance between positive and negative possible selves increases motivation to achieve the desired self and ability to avoid the feared self. Applying this theory to criminology, Oyserman and Markus (1990) found that, while delinquent youths feared becoming 'criminals', they were unable to envision possible alternative conventional selves that could have provided them with a template for an alternative lifestyle. The extent of the imbalance between their feared and desired selves predicted their subsequent criminality. Conversely, it suggests that offenders who can conceive a conventional alternative identity may be more likely to desist.

When examining the role of identity in desistance, it is important to consider the influence of local cultures. Often, offending behaviour is reinforced by membership of a powerful street culture. Jacobs and Wright (1999) interviewed a group of active offenders who provided an insightful account of the nature and effects of street culture, which ingrains itself into the individual's sense of identity. It calls for the constant pursuit of pleasure through drugs and partying, and a philosophy that espouses freedom from responsibilities. Fleischer (1995, quoted in Jacobs and Wright 1999: 168) concluded, 'getting offenders to go straight is analogous to telling a lawful citizen to relinquish his history, companions, thoughts, feelings and fears and replace them with something else.' In the pilot interviews for the Sheffield Desistance Study, Bottoms *et al.* (2004) discovered that an important habitus, or culture, involved assumptions about gender roles and masculinity, which guided individual lifestyle choices and influenced levels of offending.

Overall, existing evidence suggests that criminal cognitions, such as attitudes and thinking styles, may play an important role during the early stages of desistance, but their long-term impact on behaviour is less certain. As explained in Chapter 1, teaching offenders cognitive skills does not appear to have an enduring impact on recidivism. Cognitive behavioural programmes have a highly significant short-term effect but do not reduce reoffending in the long term (see Merrington and Stanley 2004). Lipsey (1995) found that psychological change (which included self-esteem, attitudes and personality) was not correlated with changes in offending. There is some evidence to suggest that people who engage in criminal thinking are more likely to reoffend (Walters 1996) but the findings are inconsistent (Palmer and Hollin 2004). In a recent review, Maruna and Copes (2005) suggested that the neutralisation techniques associated with criminal thinking are unlikely to be involved in primary deviance but may be important for maintaining involvement in crime over time. This does not necessarily mean that cognitive factors are not important. Because dynamic risk factors can change, they are less likely to have a long-term impact on behaviour (Gendreau *et al.* 1996). As such, subjective factors are likely to be found at the forefront of change but, given their unstable nature and liability to change, they are unlikely to be strongly associated with long-term desistance.

Social bonds, society and culture: the contexts of change

It is clear that a range of subjective factors, some durable, others evanescent, are involved in desistance. Their impact is, however, always mediated by wider social and structural forces. The social factors involved in desistance have received considerable theoretical and empirical attention. In particular, desistance has been linked to structural factors associated with the transition to adulthood, most notably by Laub and Sampson (2003) in their age-graded theory of informal social control. However, the world has changed significantly since the Glueck men entered the Boston reformatory school in the 1940s. In late modernity, pathways to adulthood have become more fluid, unpredictable, individualised and complex. The key developmental transitions, such as finding a career, getting married and having children, that traditionally marked entry into adulthood are frequently delayed. The transformed social landscape led Arnett (2000) to postulate the existence of a new intermediate life phase situated between adolescence and adulthood, which he called emerging adulthood. During emerging adulthood, young people explore a variety of possible identities, experiment with risky behaviours, and rarely form ties to social institutions.

This raises the question as to whether social bonds can still exert as powerful an influence on individual behaviour as they did in the past. Giordano et al. (2002) found that neither job stability nor marriage predicted levels of criminality in their sample. However, only a minority (8 per cent) were classed as having above-average levels of marital happiness and job stability. Although numbers were low, participants with what they called the 'respectability package' were more likely to be desisting than participants without it (Giordano et al. 2002: 1013). The authors speculated that, because transitions to adulthood are delayed in contemporary Western society, their impact on desistance is reduced. In fact, the evidence suggests that the opposite is true and that social ties continue to play an important role in desistance but their impact may be gradual and slow to emerge (Laub et al. 1998).

Being involved in a steady romantic relationship increases the likelihood that someone will desist. Savolainen (2009) found that both cohabitation and marriage reduced the rate of offending among a sample of Finnish men with a history of criminality. Horney, Osgood and Marshall (1995) found that marriage, but not cohabitation, significantly reduced the likelihood of offending. Marriage may facilitate desistance, not by increasing ties to social institutions, but by disrupting friendships with delinquent peers (Warr 1998). Although dissociation from delinquent peers has been linked to desistance, few studies have investigated the impact of pro-social peers on desistance. There is some evidence to suggest that developing bonds with pro-social co-workers can disrupt antisocial peer relationships and reduce recidivism (see Wright and Cullen 2004). Among young people, strong bonds with pro-social peers can protect against criminality and reinforce positive behaviour (Catalano and Hawkins 1996). Gaining employment also increases the likelihood of desistance. In Savolainen's (2009) study, employment emerged as the most significant predictor of desistance. A meta-analysis showed that gaining employment had the most significant impact on subsequent offending behaviour (Lipsey 1995). Other studies show more mixed results. In Horney *et al.*'s (1995) research, having a job was only weakly associated with reductions in crime. In fact, the odds of committing a property crime actually increased during periods of employment.

Although frequently implicated in the move away from crime, evidence regarding the impact of parenthood on desistance is mixed. For example, Savolainen (2009) estimated that having a child reduced convictions among recidivist Finnish offenders by 15 per cent. Others have suggested that having children does not reduce, and may even increase, offending (Thornberry *et al.* 2000). Giordano *et al.* (2002) found that, although attachment to children was not associated with desistance, children featured strongly in participants' desistance accounts. This led the authors to conclude that, while exposure to parenthood (or indeed any hook for change) could induce a lifestyle change, it did not inevitably lead to desistance. Social bonds alone do not facilitate desistance; it is their strength and quality that are important (Laub and Sampson 2003). Using data from the National Youth Survey, Ganem and Agnew (2007) discovered that high-quality parent–child relationships significantly reduced the likelihood of offending. While a successful transition to adulthood appears to be associated with desistance, maintaining strong ties with one's family of origin is also important. Graham and Bowling (1995) found that the only factors predicting desistance from crime among young men aged 14 to 25 were having a good relationship with parents and remaining in the family home. Similarly, bonds with parents and parents' commitment to school have been associated with early desistance among young offenders (Smith 2006). Farrington and Hawkins (1991) showed that fathers' participation in leisure activities with their sons was associated with desistance even after parental criminality was controlled.

There may be gender differences in the impact of adult transitions. Graham and Bowling (1995) discovered that, for women, the termination of criminal careers was influenced by forming relationships, finishing school and becoming financially independent. Men tended to make these transitions later in life with the result that these factors were not as influential for desistance. Even among those who did make the transition, desistance was not significantly linked to these transitions but was more likely to be affected by risk factors, including past criminal history, continued association with other criminals and drug or alcohol abuse. As Graham and Bowling (1995: 64) observed, young men may be more likely to be 'dependent rather than independent, to have an absence of responsibility for themselves and others and to remain with their family of origin rather than forming a family of their own'.

The timing of social events is important and desistance may be influenced by different factors at different points in the lifecourse. Morizot and LeBlanc (2007) found that, while social control factors had a small but important impact on long-term outcomes, they were only significant during certain developmental windows (for example, having pro-social friends was important but only during adolescence; employment stability was important but only during emerging adulthood). Others have found similar time-varying effects. Uggen (2000) discerned no overall relationship between employment and desistance but further analyses revealed that gaining employment had reduced offending among men aged 26 and over. Desistance among pre-adolescents has been linked to social withdrawal, criminal attitudes and family factors, while later desistance is influenced by levels of depression and parental supervision (see Loeber *et al.* 1991). Younger desisters tend to consider the potential negative consequences of offending and begin to realise that offending is morally unacceptable, while older desisters cite their increasing maturity and family responsibilities as their primary reasons for desistance (Jamieson, McIvor and Murray 1999).

It is important to account for cognitive, as well as demographic, aspects of the transition to adulthood. When Arnett (2000) asked young people to define 'adulthood', they frequently referred to cognitive changes such as accepting responsibility for themselves, making their own decisions, and developing consideration for others. Demographic transitions, such as getting married or becoming a parent, were rarely mentioned. He concluded that, as adult transitions have become more individualised in contemporary society, traditional demographic markers of adulthood are less salient. Most, however, believe that the transition to adulthood is best described with reference to both social and cognitive criteria (e.g. Shanahan *et al.* 2005). Summarising the literature on the social factors associated with desistance, Farrall (2002) concludes: 'Most of these factors are related to acquiring "something" (most commonly employment, a life partner or a family) which the desister values in some way and which initiates a re-evaluation of his or her life and, for some, a sense of who they are.'

Although most regard desistance as a psychosocial process, theorists variously prioritise subjective and social factors in their accounts (see Chapter 1). Several studies have attempted to disentangle their effects but have failed to provide conclusive evidence for either side. Nagin and Land (1993) discovered that variations in criminal trajectories could be predicted by variations in social bonds over and above stable criminal propensities. In contrast, Wright and Cullen (2004) controlled for prior criminal history and found that the effects of marriage and employment became insignificant when prior criminality was controlled. It is difficult, if not impossible, to establish causal order between cognitive and social processes. Important life events may instigate positive cognitive changes but it is equally possible that individuals with favourable cognitive profiles may self-select into conventional social roles. As Kazemian (2007) notes, the interdependency of situational and cognitive events militates against attempts to unravel their effects on the desistance process. Taking on this task, LeBel et al. (2008) studied the interaction between prisoners' subjective states prior to release, their experiences of social problems and their levels of recidivism. Their research suggested that a positive mindset guided ex-prisoners towards positive social opportunities and helped them to cope with difficulties, thus reducing the likelihood of recidivism. Nonetheless, the nature of this interaction is still disputed, particularly with regard to the role played by the individual. A critical task for desistance research is to determine the relative weight of each of these elements in the change process.

Community, culture and social capital

Theories of crime frequently implicate wider community and societal factors in criminal behaviour (e.g. Merton 1938). Neighbourhood characteristics, such as levels of social exclusion and socio-economic deprivation, can influence levels of crime. Numerous studies show that the majority of young people who become involved in crime come from communities with high levels of social disadvantage and limited access to sources of social capital (e.g. Kemshall *et al.* 2006). Little and Steinberg (2006) found that community characteristics were among the strongest correlates of adolescent drug dealing. In their study, adolescents who were alienated from sources of pro-social opportunities and had low expectations for conventional success were more likely to be involved in criminality. The level of collective efficacy in an area (defined as informal social control and social cohesion) has been found to significantly predict crime rates above and beyond individual differences in neighbourhood composition and prior levels of violence (see Sampson, Raudenbush and Earls 1997).

Braithwaite (1989: 100–101) proposed that communitarian societies, which have high levels of interdependency between individuals and prioritise group loyalties above personal interests, would have lower crime rates because they engage in reintegrative shaming, defined as 'shaming which is followed by efforts to reintegrate the offender back into the community of law-abiding or respectable citizens through words or gestures of forgiveness or ceremonies to decertify the offender as deviant.' However, Baumer *et al.* (2002) reviewed studies of reimprisonment rates in a range of countries and found that, while communitarian countries had lower crime rates, they did not experience lower rates of reimprisonment. In fact, the rates were surprisingly uniform, oscillating between 45 and 50 per cent across all countries surveyed. Baumer *et al.* suggested that reoffending may constitute a different process to the onset of offending and may operate independently of societal factors.

In order to desist, young people must first encounter and then act upon opportunities to acquire and spend social capital (Barry 2007). McNeill (2006) argued that the odds of desistance improve when offenders develop social links with people in different social hierarchies, which enable them to access wider social resources. Most young people have only limited access to conventional sources of social capital, and this may encourage them to attempt to accumulate capital through crime, at least temporarily (Barry 2007). This is particularly true for young people living in marginalised areas, who often lack social capital, but it also applies to ex-offenders, who frequently encounter significant social obstacles to desistance. The Social Exclusion Unit's (2002) *Reducing Re-offending by Ex-prisoners* report identified nine key barriers to (re)-integration for prisoners returning to the community. These were: education, employment, drug and alcohol misuse, mental and physical health, attitudes and self-control, institutionalisation and poor life skills, housing, financial difficulties, and family problems. High levels of social difficulty can significantly interfere with motivation to change (Bottoms *et al.* n.d.). The more problems experienced, the more likely it is that the person will engage in crime (Browning and Loeber 1999).

An individual with low levels of social capital must exercise more agency than someone with high levels of social capital in order to desist (Healy forthcoming). Successful ex-offenders often display high levels of personal agency, while people who commit crime tend to hold less optimistic outlooks on life (Maruna 2001). As Giordano *et al.* (2002: 1026) observed, 'on a continuum of advantage and disadvantage, the real play of agency is in the middle.' It is possible to exercise agency even in structurally constrained circumstances. Evans (2002) found that young people recognised the structural constraints on their lives but attached considerable importance to agency irrespective of their situation in life. Although people from more disadvantaged backgrounds felt they had to be realistic in their goals, almost none felt hopeless about their futures. Evans (2002: 262) introduced the concept of bounded agency, defining it as a 'socially situated process, shaped by the experiences of the past, the chances present in the current moment and the perceptions of possible futures'.

Others paint a less positive portrait of agency among disadvantaged youths, particularly those who are involved in crime. MacDonald and Marsh (2005) interviewed 186 young people living in deprived communities. Ironically, while their connections to local social networks helped them to cope with social exclusion, these bonds also limited their ability to escape it. Bound by a fatalistic outlook on life and strong bonds to a limited social group, young people who offend may feel unable or unwilling to leave their present situation. Kemshall *et al.* (2006) found that young people regarded their incentives to change as limited and unrewarding, while the disincentives to change were seen as high. While the social context provides an important framework for action, individual factors appear to play a more significant role. Studies of the interactions between neighbourhood factors and individual characteristics reveal that young people can exercise agency when confronted with a criminogenic environment. For example, Oberwittler (2004) found that adolescents with extremely deviant attitudes committed fewer serious offences in socially organised neighbourhoods than they did in socially disorganised neighbourhoods, while adolescents without deviant attitudes did not offend very much in either context. He concluded that the effect of structural disadvantage was mediated by the attitudes of peers and the intergenerational social ties within the neighbourhood.

Opening the 'black box'

The quest to identify the causes and correlates of offending has a long history, which traces its origins back to the pioneering work on criminal careers initiated by Sheldon and Eleanor Glueck in Boston during the 1930s and continued by David Farrington in Cambridge during the 1960s. Criminological interest in identifying risk factors gained further momentum during the 1990s with the rise of the managerial approach to justice. Advocates of the risk factor approach believe that if they can identify a consistent set of risk factors, this information can be used to design interventions to address these problem areas, and this will, in turn, lower participants' risk of reoffending. Case (2007) characterised the search for universal risk factors as the 'holy grail' of criminological research, and, to date, it has produced an embarrassment of riches. Researchers have discovered a multitude of risk factors, operating on multiple levels, which span individual, family, school and community domains.

While certain factors consistently emerge as correlates of recidivism, the ability of these factors to predict behaviour is less evident when measured prospectively, particularly in the long term. In a longitudinal study, the Youth Level of Service Inventory, a well-known risk assessment tool, made correct predictions in only half of cases after a 5-year follow-up period (Schmidt, Hoge and Gomes 2005). Furthermore, many of those who experience risk factors during childhood do not become involved in crime as adults. Flood-Page *et al.* (2000) found that children who experienced multiple risk factors were more likely than their peers to engage in antisocial activity, yet only 4 in 10 actually engaged in such behaviour. There are several possible explanations for this lack of predictive success.

One explanation concerns the predominantly quantitative methods used in this type of research (see Case 2007). It is difficult to ascertain whether the factors that show a statistical relationship with reoffending are the causes or merely the symptoms of crime. Risk factors often accumulate in the lives of offenders, making it harder to disentangle their individual effects. The role of protective factors is equally unclear. It is not known whether protective factors are simply the opposite of risk factors or whether they operate independently to mediate or block the effects of risk factors. In addition, the sheer numbers of risk and protective factors that have been identified limit their utility as an explanation of crime. As a result, risk factor research offers only a shadowy glimpse into the black box of desistance. While it is capable of providing sound information about the correlates of reoffending, it cannot provide insight into the mechanisms and contexts through which these relationships are generated. In other words, it cannot tell us how or why people change.

The risk factor approach is unable to accommodate the complexity of the social world, making it very difficult to make accurate long-term predictions about behaviour. Humans act within an interconnected arena where multiple variables, both internal and external, must interact in order for a given behaviour to manifest. Long-term prediction must necessarily be incomplete because it can never take account of the full range of variables that can influence behaviour or the wide variety of possible interactions between them (Williams and Arrigo 2002). Chance and random events also play important roles in behaviour (see Bandura 1997). As Webster, MacDonald and Simpson (2006) observed, reoffending and desistance often come about, not as a result of changes in predictable risk factors, but through 'intermittent crises, contingent and chance events and choice operating in a structural context'.

Involvement in crime is often erratic and uneven, with people moving towards and away from crime at various times in their lives (see Greenwood *et al.* 1978). If people can switch back and forth between crime and conformity, there may be corresponding changes in their minds and lifestyles. This has been found to be the case with social circumstances. Using a retrospective design, Horney, Osgood and Marshall (1995) found that the likelihood of engaging in criminal activity increased or decreased depending on month-to-month changes in local life circumstances. There is also some evidence that offenders can alter their cognitions to suit their current circumstances (see Walters 2003). Social and cognitive processes are also highly dynamic and complex, a fact that renders the process of prediction even more difficult and raises questions about its utility.

Desistance theories are frequently stratified according to whether they endorse maturation, social or psychological processes (see Chapter 1). Gadd (2006: 191) argued that there is a need to move beyond 'the dichotomy between agency and determinism' in order to increase knowledge about the dynamic processes that occur at the psychosocial frontier. The boundaries between these traditions have recently begun to dissolve and most researchers now agree that behavioural choices are always influenced by the structural, situational and cultural contexts in which they are made as well as the background characteristics of the individuals who make them. Farrall and Bowling (1999: 261) observed that desistance arises from 'an interplay between individual choices and a range of wider social

33

forces, institutional and societal practices which are beyond the control of the individual'.

These issues are difficult to address using the standard quantitative methods favoured in risk-factor research. Case (2007) proposed that the predominantly quantitative methods used in risk-factor research should be supplemented with qualitative approaches in order to expand knowledge about the processes, mechanisms and contexts behind desistance. Qualitative approaches offer an opportunity to investigate the processes behind desistance and to explore the significance of events to those that experience them. Phenomenologists, for example, aim to gain insight into the people's subjective understanding of the world, to describe their lived everyday world (*Lebenswelt*) and to 'make the invisible visible' (Kvale 1996: 53). Narrative psychologists use personal narratives to explore people's subjective understandings of their lived experience as it is reflected through the prism of their past, present and future selves. A number of desistance researchers have begun to draw attention to the importance of exploring the hidden subjective meanings that people impose on important life events (e.g. Gadd and Farrall 2004). As a result, qualitative research has experienced a revival in criminology, with several studies employing it either exclusively (e.g. Maruna 2001) or in conjunction with other methods (e.g. Farrall 2002).

Several recent longitudinal studies have begun to explore the dynamic interactions between social processes, individual characteristics and their impact on offending behaviour over time. The Edinburgh Study of Youth Transitions (Smith and McVie 2003) is a longitudinal study involving secondary school boys and girls, who were aged about 12 years at the onset of the study. It aims to examine the interaction between the neighbourhood context, individual factors and the criminal justice system and their relationship to offending and desistance. Similar studies have been initiated elsewhere; for example, the Pathways to Desistance Study in the USA (Mulvey *et al.* 2004), the Tuebingen Criminal Behaviour Study in Germany (Mischkowitz 1994), and the Sheffield Desistance Study in the UK (Bottoms *et al.* 2004), and many include qualitative components.

Desistance pathways are complex social processes with multiple causes and outcomes (Kemshall 2008). The processes involved are dynamic, multi-faceted, complex and difficult to predict. In order to increase understanding about what occurs during the transition to desistance, new approaches must be devised that are capable of capturing the complex nature of the social world, the role of personal characteristics, and the wider structural circumstances that constrain or facilitate offenders' ability to change their lives. In other words, researchers must delve further into the black box of desistance and study the processes behind the termination of crime as well as its statistical correlates.

Liminality and change: offenders on the threshold

Despite widespread recognition that pathways to desistance are rarely straightforward and are usually preceded by temporary cessations and decelerations of activity, few studies have examined primary desistance in depth. In fact, Maruna, Immarigeon and LeBel (2004) argued that the early stages of change were not worth studying, proposing that researchers should focus their attention on long-term desistance. Others suggest that, given their frequency and the potentially interesting theoretical questions they raise, the study of short-term changes in offending behaviour should form 'an integral part of the study of desistance' (Bottoms *et al.* 2004: 371). While it is important to shed light on the process of secondary desistance, it is also necessary to understand the factors that precipitate the decision to change, particularly since there may be different processes involved in primary and secondary desistance. Lemert (1972) proposed that primary deviance was caused by negative life events while secondary deviance was engendered by the societal reaction to the deviant behaviour. Given this, it is important to develop a framework for conceptualising what occurs in the minds and lives of individuals on the threshold of change. Liminal theory (Turner 1970) offers a useful starting point.

In *The Forest of Symbols*, Victor Turner (1970) explored the rich landscape inhabited by individuals who exist in the liminal space 'betwixt and between' two social worlds (the word 'liminal' is derived from the Latin 'limen,' which means 'threshold'). Inspired by van Gennep's (1977) seminal work on rites of passage, Turner proposed a tripartite model of social transitions. During the separation phase, individuals begin their withdrawal from obsolete social roles and discard old values, thinking patterns and behaviours. The liminal or middle period is characterised by introspection, ambiguity and social withdrawal, but it is also a time of 'fruitful darkness' when personal transformation and growth can occur (Turner 1970: 18). During this time, liminal beings distance themselves from their past selves and begin to construct desirable new identities. The final stage, aggregation, denotes the individual's passage into the new role. In

35

traditional societies, rites of passage are often marked by symbolic ceremonies or rituals. Although reintegration ceremonies are known to encourage desistance (see Braithewaite 1989), the transition to desistance is rarely recognised in a formal way by the criminal justice system. In their absence, recognition and acknowledgement of change by significant others may be equally influential (Maruna and Roy 2007).

According to Turner, rites of passage are initiated by important life transitions or as a response to personal adversity. Similarly, desistance is often precipitated by important life events associated with the transition to adulthood, such as marriage or employment (see Laub and Sampson 2003) or by negative life experiences, such as a lengthy prison sentence, a shock event, or damage to relationships with significant others (see Cusson and Pinsonneault 1986). While it is widely accepted that adverse life experiences can provoke inner turmoil, even positive life transitions can induce psychological and social upheaval. Thomas, Benzeval and Stansfeld (2005) found that people who experienced transitions to or from formal employment were significantly more likely to experience challenges to their psychological well-being, compared to people who did not undergo such transitions. Studies of first-time fathers also reveal that many experience negative emotional states, use more alcohol and suffer deterioration in their social relationships during the transition to parenthood (e.g. Condon, Boyce and Corkindale 2003).

The transition from criminality to conformity may be equally tumultuous. In order to desist, individuals must often separate themselves from existing social networks, roles and environments. They must leave behind established lifestyle choices and entrenched cognitive and behavioural patterns. Maruna and Roy (2007) referred to this process as 'knifing off' from crime. This term refers to the severing of opportunities, whether positive (for example, avoiding old friends to reduce opportunities to commit crime) or negative (for example, losing conventional opportunities because of ongoing criminality). As a result, liminal beings generally 'have' little in terms of status, responsibilities or possessions. Barry (2007) suggested that, given their lack of social capital, this aspect of liminality was appropriate for discussions regarding young people on the threshold of adulthood. This is also true of offenders in general, many of whom come from disadvantaged backgrounds and have low levels of social capital.

Early-stage desisters begin to experiment with new pro-social identities but, at this point, these new identities are still at a distance and must compete with established criminal identities (see Giordano *et al*. 2002: 1000). Embryonic pro-social identities consist of 'skeleton scripts', which provide only fragmented guidance that must be fleshed out, rehearsed and modified (Rumgay 2004: 410). Turner (1970: 97) observed that 'transitional beings are neither one thing nor another, or may be both; or neither here nor there; or maybe even nowhere.' Many of the ambiguities of the liminal phase are also recognisable in the early stages of desistance. As Maruna (2001: 44) observed, 'the only thing more difficult than finding "pure desisters" is finding "pure criminals".' Research has found that the criminal identity may be fluid and that offenders often adapt their identities to suit the current situation. For example, Walters (2003) discovered that the criminal identities and cognitions of first-time prisoners increased during the first 6 months of their sentence.

Would-be desisters often express ambivalent attitudes towards crime and desistance. In her research, Burnett (1992) identified a subcategory of 'waverers', which comprised men who expressed a desire to desist but kept criminality as a reserve plan either because they felt unsure of their ability to cope with difficulties, were vulnerable to the temptations of crime, or had a low tolerance for failure. She concluded that the offender sits 'on a pendulum of ambivalence moving first towards desistance and then towards persistence as his or her orientation is swayed by the weight of alternative desires and rationalisations' (Burnett 2004: 169). In her view, offenders did not react passively to social events but had 'opposing desires and drives in relation to crime' (Burnett 2004: 168). During the chaos of the liminal phase, offenders begin to weigh up the costs and benefits of criminal and conventional lifestyles (Shover 1996). Some suggest that this internal cognitive reorientation may be more important than the external event that prompted it (e.g. Giordano *et al*. 2002).

The liminal phase may take considerable time to complete. According to Prochaska *et al*. (1992), would-be desisters must first traverse several preparatory stages before finally reaching the point at which they make the decision to change. During this time, they must develop an awareness of their problem and consider the costs and benefits of both continuing and changing their behaviour. Many people remain in the contemplation stage for years (see Prochaska and DiClemente (1984), cited in Prochaska *et al*. 1992). Failure to progress beyond this phase may have serious negative psychological consequences (see Noble and Walker 1997). The majority of desistance attempts do not succeed on the first try, highlighting the need to incorporate the potential for relapse into models of the change process. Sustaining desistance requires a repository of personal and social resources, including optimism, determination, good problem-solving abilities and strong social support networks (Rumgay 2004).

In sum, a range of subjective and social factors is associated with desistance. Desistance arises out of a complex and dynamic interaction between subjective factors, which include criminal cognitions and attitudes, motivation, self-efficacy, personality traits and identity, and social factors, which include social bonds, social capital, neighbourhood characteristics and culture. When researching the termination of criminal careers, it is important to focus not just on identifying the factors that show a relationship with desistance but also, on uncovering the processes underlying these relationships. There is growing evidence to suggest that the onset and maintenance of desistance may constitute distinct phases in the process and both phases should be afforded sufficient attention. The remainder of this book will attempt to address these issues and try to contribute to knowledge in these areas.

Chapter 3

Person and place

The characteristics of a society can influence the level and nature of crime. Social cohesion is known to reduce crime, while relative deprivation can increase it (see Chapter 2). Even affluent societies can conceal pockets of disadvantage so it is important to consider structural characteristics not only from a macro perspective but also from the perspective of the individual. This is particularly important since people who commit crime typically reside in areas that are characterised by high levels of disadvantage, and Ireland is no exception (see O'Donnell *et al.* 2007). This chapter describes some of the key features of Irish society that might impact on crime and desistance and provides a socio-demographic profile of the areas that were home to the men who took part in the study. It also outlines the research design and data sources that were used in the study and explains how the participants were selected and recruited.

Setting the scene

Traditionally, Ireland has been characterised as a predominantly rural and somewhat impoverished society with a populace that embraces strong religious tendencies and communitarian values. Until the 1980s, economic prospects were bleak and many young people were forced to emigrate. Between the mid-1990s and 2006, however, Ireland experienced dramatic and rapid economic, social and cultural change. The population, which had been in decline since the 1840s, has grown steadily since 1991 and was estimated at just over 4 million in the

2006 Census (Central Statistics Office (CSO) 2007a). The economy also experienced unprecedented economic growth during this period (although this trend began to reverse during 2006). Unemployment rates of just under 9 per cent were recorded in the 2002 and 2006 Censuses. There was a substantial increase in Irish wealth, and incomes reached parity with other OECD countries (Nolan and Maitre 2007). As Irish émigrés returned home and foreign nationals flocked to fill labour shortages, there was a shift in the balance from net emigration to net immigration for the first time since the 1970s (CSO 2007a). Ireland's previously homogeneous population expanded to accommodate a variety of new nationalities, who accounted for approximately 10 per cent of the total population in 2006. Ireland also metamorphosed from a rural into an urban society with two-thirds of the population living in urban areas by 2006.

Nevertheless, Ireland continues to experience high levels of inequality, and deprivation and disadvantage are still facts of life for many. Whelan, Nolan and Maitre (2007) estimated that around 20 per cent of the population could be classed as economically vulnerable. People in this category tend to experience higher levels of income poverty, economic strain (i.e. are unable to afford two or more basic lifestyle items) and subjective economic stress (i.e. feel unable to meet unexpected expenses). The impact of the so-called Celtic Tiger on Irish life was reviewed in a series of essays edited by Fahey, Russell and Whelan (2007). These analyses revealed that the transition to almost full employment was accompanied by better job quality, including shorter hours, better wages, more job security and upward social mobility. In spite of massive social change, Ireland still ranks high in international terms on indicators of family cohesion and community participation. Although the influence of the Catholic Church has waned, the majority of Irish people are still at least nominally Catholic and rely on Catholic ceremonies to mark significant life events, such as marriage and death. Divorce was introduced under the 1996 Divorce Act and, while the numbers seeking divorce are rising, the rate of marital breakdown is still low by international standards. Irish people also report higher subjective levels of well-being than their European counterparts.

Crime in Ireland

In an international context, Ireland has long been regarded as a country with a low crime rate (Kilcommins *et al.* 2004). Adler (1983) studied 10 countries, including Ireland, in an effort to understand how they managed to maintain low crime rates. She concluded that Ireland experienced low crime rates because of its culture of strong familial controls, slow urbanisation, and high emigration rates, which, she argued, depressed population growth, particularly among the crime-prone youth and poor. Adler's view of Ireland resembles Braithewaite's (1989) notion of a communitarian society. He claimed that these societies, which have high levels of social control, tend to have lower crime rates.

Figure 3.1 shows trends in officially recorded crime for the 10-year period between 1996 and 2006. Indictable/headline offences increased during this period from 100,785 in 1996 to 103,177 in 2006. Headline offences generally include more serious offences such as homicide, sexual offences, burglary, robbery and drugs offences. In contrast, there has been a significant and consistent decline in less serious crimes. Non-indictable/non-headline prosecutions during this period fell from 451,267 in 1996 to 302,986 in 2006 (before 2003, information relating only to the prosecution, but not the incidence, of non-indictable/non-headline crimes was published).

Whatever the nature of crime in Ireland, it is clear that a large proportion of it is drug-related. Of individuals apprehended in 1995-96 in the Dublin Metropolitan Area, over 40 per cent were identified by the Garda as known hard drug users (Keogh 1997). This group accounted for two-thirds of all detected crime. The majority involved small amounts of money. A subsequent survey which covered the whole of Ireland (Furey and Browne 2003) found that only 13 per cent of those surveyed had engaged in criminal activity to fund a drug habit. The authors suggested that better employment opportunities and the increased availability of drug treatment contributed to the

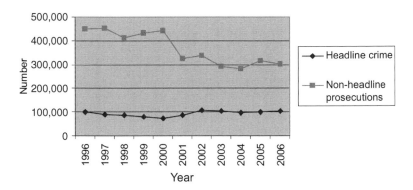

Figure 3.1 Crime in Ireland 1996 to 2006

decline in criminal activity among drug users (see also O'Donnell and O'Sullivan 2001). This finding may also be due to regional variations in drug use. Most cases of opiate use are concentrated in the Eastern Health Board regions, which includes Dublin city (Health Research Board 2003). Outside the Dublin area, cannabis is the most common drug used (50 per cent), followed by Ecstasy (18 per cent) and opiates (15 per cent).

The total number of problem drug users in Ireland is currently unknown. In the absence of these figures, the numbers seeking treatment for drug use has been used as an indicator of actual levels. Comiskey, Saris and Pugh (2007) estimated that there were 15,000 opiate users in Ireland, of whom approximately 12,000 live in Dublin. A report on national trends in treated drug use between 1996 and 2000 revealed that, while the numbers accessing drug treatment rose steadily, the number of new cases dropped (Health Research Board 2003). Overall, Irish drug users who present for treatment tend to be young, male, poorly educated and unemployed (Bellerose *et al.* 2009). In general, younger people are more likely to seek treatment for cannabis and inhalants, while older teenagers are being treated for opiate and Ecstasy use (Health Research Board 2003).

Responding to crime

Since the late 1990s both politicians and the media have been paying more attention to the problem of crime and how to reduce it. Despite declining crime rates, government policies underwent a 'punitive shift' during the 1990s, which began with the then Minister for Justice, John O'Donoghue's 1997 declaration of a 'war on crime' (O'Donnell and O'Sullivan 2003). This was prompted by two high-profile murders that occurred in June 1996. Garda Jerry McCabe was killed during a failed robbery attempt in County Limerick. Two weeks later, Veronica Guerin, an investigative journalist whose work aimed to expose high-profile drug dealers, was shot dead by two men on a motorcycle while her car was stopped at traffic lights on a busy junction in Dublin. As a result, the criminal justice landscape, which had remained largely unchanged since the Victorian era, underwent major changes, both legislative and ideological. These include the promotion of the crime issue to the forefront of the political agenda, an increasing prison population, harsher sanctions, and a more punitive political rhetoric (O'Donnell 2004).

The criminal justice infrastructure expanded greatly after the 1997 general election. Over 1,200 new prison places were created between

1996 and 2001 as part of the government's prison-building programme (Irish Prison Service 2001). Funding for An Garda Síochána increased significantly during this period. Harsher and innovative measures were introduced to deal with those criminals rarely apprehended by the law. The Criminal Assets Bureau (made up of officers from Revenue Commissioners, An Garda Síochána and the Department of Social Welfare) was established by the Criminal Assets Bureau Act 1996 to address, among other areas, the problem of drug trafficking. Presumptive sentences of 10 years for those caught in possession of drugs worth £10,000 (€13,000) were also introduced under the Criminal Justice Act 1999. Although there is evidence of a more punitive approach to crime in Ireland, the changes may not be as extensive or as invasive as they first appear (O'Donnell and O'Sullivan 2003). For example, the 10-year sentence for drug trafficking was used in only 5 of 130 eligible cases that came before the court between its introduction in 1999 and 2002 (Dáil Debates, 12 November 2002, see also Kilcommins et al. 2004). Furthermore, Ireland still has one of the lowest imprisonment rates in Europe (O'Donnell 2008).

The crime problem does not feature prominently among public concerns. Kilcommins et al. (2004) documented the shifts in the public feeling towards crime since 1981 in relation to public opinion polls taken at general elections. The crime problem hardly featured among concerns until 1997 when it was listed as the most important issue. This coincided with the murders of Veronica Guerin and Jerry McCabe and the government's declaration of a war on crime. By 2001, the issue returned to the bottom of the list. Surveys suggest that the Irish public prefer to see rehabilitative measures used with young offenders and offenders who have addiction or mental health problems, and have little faith in the ability of prison to reduce crime (Irish Penal Reform Trust 2007).

Criminology in Ireland could be described as an 'absentee' discipline (Kilcommins et al. 2004). The first national recidivism study of Irish prisoners, which concerned individuals released from prison between 2001 and 2004, has just recently been published (O'Donnell, Baumer and Hughes 2008). There are no comparable statistics available for probationers. Little is known about offenders, the factors associated with crime or desistance, or the impact of criminal justice interventions. Given the dearth of high-quality research on crime in this country, an empirical investigation of the dynamics of desistance among Irish offenders is germane. Finally, since the bulk of desistance research has been conducted in the UK and the USA, the study provides an opportunity to examine whether desistance findings are relevant in a different socio-cultural context, namely the Republic of Ireland.

Exploring psychosocial pathways

The first task involved selecting an appropriate methodology for the study. The study aimed to investigate key aspects of the journey towards desistance that are under-researched (see Chapter 2). It was essential to develop a study design that was capable of investigating the role of agency and social factors in desistance as well as disentangling the underlying processes by which the individual and the social context interact. The approach also had to capture what occurred during the early, or liminal, period of desistance. Ultimately, it was decided that the optimal design for this type of study would involve a mixed methods approach, where qualitative analysis would be supported by traditional quantitative techniques. This approach seemed to offer the best means to look at offending behaviour and desistance in depth and to investigate what goes on inside the 'black box' of change.

Quantitative methods are considered capable of accessing reliable, valid and objective knowledge about the world. The findings can be replicated and, if the sample is large enough, may be generalised to the population as a whole. One of the main disadvantages of this approach is that, while it can provide sound knowledge about the associations between key variables and criminality, it cannot tell us how or why such relationships exist. As explained in Chapter 2, many variables show a statistical correlation with desistance, and it is important to also explore the processes behind these relationships. Qualitative data, on the other hand, can provide rich insights into respondents' understandings of important life events. One of the strengths of the qualitative approach is its ability to facilitate access to the mechanisms and contexts behind change that would otherwise remain hidden from the researcher's view.

Qualitative approaches are characterised by small-scale, in-depth research aimed at eliciting insights into respondents' interpretations of their social world. This research tends to produce complex, data-rich accounts of the phenomenon of interest. Meanings and interpretation are prioritised over prediction and quantification. Key elements include the generation of 'thick' descriptions and the preference for depth over breadth in explanations. Kvale (1996) argued that research interviews should not be treated as either objective or subjective records of reality but are characterised as 'inter-subjective interaction' where meaning is constructed and verified through dialogue. Phenomenology is one such approach and aims to describe the lived everyday world (*Lebenswelt*) of participants. By studying an object from a variety of perspectives, phenomenologists believe that they can access objective information about reality, which they describe as the 'essence' of the phenomenon. As Kvale (1996: 53) explained:

> Phenomenology ... studies the subject's perspectives on their world; attempts to describe in detail the content and structure of the subjects' unconsciousness to grasp the qualitative diversity of their experiences and to explicate their essential meanings. Phenomenology attempts to get beyond immediately experienced meanings in order to articulate the pre-reflective level of lived meanings, to make the invisible visible.

Despite its advantages, it is hard to define what constitutes a good qualitative design, although a set of recommendations is currently under development by the Campbell Collaboration, a non-profit organisation which undertakes systematic reviews of evaluations of interventions. Some of the common criticisms of qualitative research include its susceptibility to researcher bias, difficulties associated with replication, inability to generalise, lack of transparency, and the risk of 'going native'. Suggestions have been offered to augment the reliability and validity of a qualitative study (e.g. Mays and Pope 1995). Some of these have been employed in the current work in an effort to strengthen the design.

The final research design consisted of three main elements. The first component was quantitative and aimed to produce a multivariate model of the psychosocial factors associated with desistance. Three psychometric tools were employed: the PICTS, CRIME-PICS and the LSI-R. Participants' scores on the three instruments were examined in relation to their self-reported involvement in crime at two points in time: (a) the past year and (b) the past month. This component aimed to explore the shifts that occurred in offending, cognitions and social circumstances at both stages of desistance.

The second element of the research was qualitative in nature. Careful questioning generated a series of 'thick' descriptions of important events and the motivation behind them. The interviews provided data-rich accounts of participants' attitudes towards crime and desistance, their reasons for persisting with or desisting from crime, their social circumstances, and the challenges of reintegration. Interviews were transcribed and coded by hand. Pseudonyms are used throughout to protect participants' identities.

The third element involved a follow-up study of participants and used police records. Participants' criminal records were reviewed over a period of time in order to establish whether the changes they reported were temporary or enduring. It also constituted a valuable check on the validity of the qualitative findings. Two aspects of reconviction were examined:

1. *Reconviction rate*: a dichotomous measure, i.e. reconvicted/not reconvicted.
2. *Time to reconviction*: a continuous measure of the percentages reconvicted (cumulative), calculated at regular intervals throughout the follow-up period.

Participants were followed for over 4 years. Reconviction for the majority of offenders tends to occur within the first 2 years of release (Lloyd *et al.* 1994) so this time frame should be more than adequate to capture subsequent offending behaviour.

Measuring the process of desistance

The primary method of data collection was semi-structured face-to-face interviews, designed to elicit from the participants narrative accounts of their involvement in crime. Qualitative data can provide rich insights into respondents' understandings of their social worlds and, as a result, are ideally suited for collecting information about processes underpinning change. A range of methods was employed to make the session more interesting. Many of the questions were open-ended to facilitate the collection of in-depth information about the participants' experiences. Other questions required participants to select an answer from a range of alternative responses. The list of answers was printed on a laminated card and presented to the participant.

It was decided to draw on existing questionnaires in the design of the main interview schedule. Experiences of probation were measured with standard evaluation questionnaires such as that created by Mair and May (1997) as a guide. The interviews used by Burnett (1992) and Farrall (2002) also featured strongly in the design of the schedule. Questions about the particulars of participants' most recent offence were partly taken from Zamble and Quinsey's (1997) work, which focused on understanding the process behind the commission of an offence. Another strong influence was McAdams's (1995) life-story interview, used by Maruna (2001), which focuses on key experiences and turning points in the life history. The questionnaire addressed the following areas:

- Perception of probation supervision, including its impact on their lives.

- Past involvement in criminal activity. This covered patterns, frequency and nature of previous offending.

- Current status and attitudes towards offending. The factors that are involved in both recidivism and desistance from crime were examined.

- Lifestyle indicators and future plans. This covered areas such as employment/education status, drug use, accommodation, and anger management.

Interview responses may be affected by bias, forgetfulness, social desirability and the level of rapport with the researcher. People's recollections of past events are coloured by post hoc rationalisations, unconscious distortions and memory failures (Farrall 2006). Some have suggested that the very act of articulating an experience alters it (e.g. Reddy 1997). Ex-offenders' explanations of desistance are, of course, also vulnerable to these biases. Despite this, interviews remain one of the most popular research methods and are ideal for use in a study that is concerned with the investigation of the mechanisms behind crime and desistance. The mixed-method approach helped to bolster objectivity and reduce bias. Validity was increased through the use of multiple data sources (for example, comparing offenders' reports with probation officer reports) through a practice known as 'triangulation'.

Probation officers also completed questionnaires about each of the participants. Their survey addressed topics similar to those on the participant questionnaire and was designed to provide an element of cross-validation. It covered areas, such as offending history, details of the current offence, the current supervision order, including work undertaken and progress; level of motivation to change; and potential obstacles to change.

Measuring the correlates of desistance

An important aim of the research was to explore the psychological and social circumstances that support desistance and to examine their relationship with offending behaviour. Only validated psychometric instruments, which have shown significant relationships with offending behaviour, were used. Three psychometric instruments were selected for this task, having been extensively tested and used in other jurisdictions. These were the Psychological Inventory of Criminal Thinking Styles (PICTS: Walters 1995), CRIME-PICS II (Frude, Honess and Maguire 1994), and the Level of Service Inventory-Revised (LSI-R: Andrews and Bonta 1995). The first two questionnaires were self-administered during the interview while the LSI-R was completed by the particpants' probation officer. Where literacy was an issue, the questionnaires were read to the respondents.

The Psychological Inventory of Criminal Thinking Styles v4.0 (PICTS: Walters 1995) is an 80-item questionnaire which measures eight thinking styles that support criminal behaviour: Mollification, Cutoff, Entitlement, Power Orientation, Sentimentality, Super-optimism, Cognitive Indolence, and Discontinuity. There are also two validity scales (Confusion and Defensiveness), which measure test-taking attitude. Respondents are asked to indicate on a 4-point Likert scale whether they agree or disagree with each statement. Higher scores indicate a more active thinking style. Two content scales (Current Criminal Thinking and Historical Criminal Thinking) have recently been added (Walters 2002c). These measure, respectively, whether the respondent has engaged in criminal thinking either currently or in the past.

The PICTS has been shown to be reliable, whether measured by levels of internal consistency or test–retest trials (Walters 2002a). Scores on the PICTS scales have also been related to past criminality, as measured by the number of prior arrests and convictions, in both North American (Walters 1995) and British (Palmer and Hollin 2003) studies. While its concurrent validity appears adequate, it is less accurate at predicting future criminal behaviour. Controlling for age, Palmer and Hollin (2004) found that Super-optimism was the only scale to significantly differentiate between those who had been reconvicted and those who had not. There were no observed differences between the groups on the Current and Historical scales.

CRIME-PICS II (Frude, Honess and Maguire 1994) consists of two parts. The first is a 20-item questionnaire, which measures the presence of criminogenic attitudes. Higher scores indicate more favourable attitudes towards crime. The second section is a problem inventory, which asks respondents to indicate whether they have problems in 15 areas, including employment, relationships, and boredom. While Frude *et al.* (1994) reported that CRIME-PICS II demonstrated good reliability and validity, Raynor and Vanstone (1997) found that the problem inventory, but not the attitudinal scale, predicted whether reconviction occurred within 2 years.

Finally, the Level of Service Inventory (LSI-R: Andrews and Bonta 1995) is a 54-item risk assessment instrument that was designed to assist with the assessment of risk of reconviction and criminogenic needs of offenders. It includes 10 sub-components and has a section on criminal history, as well as seven sections focusing on structural (employment/education, financial, family/marital, accommodation, leisure, companions and drug/alcohol use) and two on individual (mental health, attitudes towards crime and sentence) needs. Scores can be used to categorise offenders into low, medium and high risk of reconviction. Forms are completed by probation officers through file review and interviews with the offender. Research has shown that the instrument has good interrater reliability and adequate levels of internal consistency (Andrews 1982). Its predictive validity is quite high (see Kroner and Mills 2001).

Measuring offending behaviour

Information about offending was collected through a combination of self-report questionnaires and file-based information.

Self-report questionnaire

Information about criminal activity was obtained with a 17-item self-report instrument based on the work of Hindelang, Hirschi and Weis (1981) and modified to ensure that it was representative of offences recorded by An Garda Síochána (Ireland's national police force). Participants were asked to indicate whether they had committed any of the offences on the list, including minor (for example, Have you pickpocketed anything from someone?) and serious (for example, Have you beaten someone up so badly that they probably needed a doctor?) offences. Participants also completed a 'lifeline' based on the responses they gave to the self-report questionnaire. They were asked to specify: (a) the age they were when they first committed each offence type and (b) the most recent occasion that they had engaged in each offence. The lifeline was designed to provide an overview of participants' criminal activity throughout their criminal careers. In practice, it proved a successful method of eliciting this information from participants, who were capable of recalling very detailed information about the timing and nature of their criminal activity. The lifeline also acted as a useful introduction and supplement to participants' narrative accounts of their criminal careers.

Concerns have been raised about using the self-report method to access accurate information about criminality. Self-reports are vulnerable to self-presentation biases, particularly among offenders who may be inclined to obfuscate their results in criminal justice settings (see Harrison and Hughes 1997). In this study, the majority of participants were interviewed in probation offices, which may not be the ideal setting to ask people to report recent, undetected crime. Nevertheless, despite the sensitive nature of the topic, previous research has suggested that self-reports can be both valid and reliable measures of actual behaviour. Test–retest reliability can be as high as 0.85 to 0.99 (Huizinga and Elliott 1986).

Concurrent and predictive validity of self-reports is considered acceptable. West and Farrington (1977), for example, found that at age 18, 94 per cent of boys who had convictions admitted to having a conviction (53 per cent reported accurately, 34 per cent reported but minimised, 7 per cent exaggerated). Farrington *et al.* (1996) also found that self-reported offending predicted later contact with the criminal justice system among currently unconvicted boys. Self-reported drug use is a related area, which has more acceptable external criteria against which to test honesty (for example, urinalysis). Here, findings are less promising. Almost half of respondents involved with the criminal justice system or treatment programmes do not admit recent drug use in confidential settings (Harrison and Hughes 1997). While efforts were made to cross-check participants' accounts against actual behaviour (using probation officer reports and police records), it is important to be aware of the potential shortcomings of the self-report method when interpreting the results.

Police records

The Garda Criminal Records Office extracted anonymised data on the criminal offences committed by the participants from the PULSE [Police Using Leading Systems Effectively] computer system. Details of convictions, arrests and charges were made available, including information on dates, type of offence, and sentence received. Data on arrests and charges pending were only available from 2000 onwards (since the introduction of PULSE). The system does not provide information on juvenile histories, or convictions received abroad.

Also, in Ireland, individuals can be found guilty of an offence but not receive any official conviction (for example, offenders can be discharged without conviction under section 1(1) of the Probation of Offenders Act 1907), and cases can also be struck out for various reasons. This means that this measure is likely to underestimate participants' level of official contact with the criminal justice system to some extent.

Selecting and interviewing participants

Given the emphasis on discovering why people reoffend or desist from crime, it was decided that the focus of the study should be on persistent adult offenders. One of the major difficulties encountered was obtaining a sample size that was large enough to draw meaningful conclusions. With small samples, it is difficult to detect a statistically significant difference between conditions unless the effect is very large (Cunningham 2002). The criteria were kept as broad as possible to ensure that sufficient numbers could be obtained. Participants had to:

- Have a history of offending: defined as a minimum of two court appearances leading to convictions, where the interval between these appearances was at least 1 year.

- Be aged between 18 and 35: this is the peak time during which offending and desistance occurs.

- Be currently under supervision by the Probation and Welfare Service (those on community service were not included): this would facilitate an examination of the impact of probation supervision on desistance.

- Those convicted of sex offences were excluded.

Data collection began in September 2003 and was completed in August 2004. The sample was drawn primarily from the client lists of five probation teams in Dublin. As probation records are paper-based and there are no published statistics relating to those currently under supervision, it was not possible to select participants randomly, or to obtain a representative sample. Instead, each team was asked to provide details of all eligible individuals under their supervision. The search of their files resulted in a total of 98 men, of whom 84 attended for a regular appointment with their probation officer during the fieldwork period and were invited to participate in the research. Eight refused and three participants were excluded, as their interviews were incomplete. This left a final sample of 73. As sufficient numbers of female probationers who matched the criteria could not be found, it was decided to focus exclusively on male probationers.

The majority of interviews were conducted in probation offices ($n = 35$, 47 per cent). Efforts were made to meet the participants at the same time as their routine probation appointment to increase the likelihood of attendance and minimise inconvenience. Unless participants had not attended appointments for a long time, several attempts were made to interview them. Eleven participants whose cases had been re-entered following a breach of their probation order were subsequently interviewed in prison. This helped boost the representativeness of the sample, as it meant some of those who were not attending appointments or who had reoffended were interviewed. The average number of appointments arranged before an interview was achieved was 1.6. A full briefing session was done by the researcher before the interview began, and informed consent was obtained, in writing, from all participants. Participation was voluntary and no inducements were offered. Permission to tape-record the interview was given by participants in 76.2 per cent of cases ($n = 48$), where recording was allowed (tape recorders were not allowed in prisons). Although full transcripts of all interviews would have been useful, the issue was not pursued if a participant refused, as it was felt that it might affect disclosure. The interviews lasted an average of 72 minutes (range: 35 to 180).

Profiling offenders in transition

Research has revealed that certain structural factors, including economic disadvantage, social exclusion and social cohesion set the context for desistance by either constraining or facilitating change. Neighbourhood characteristics, such as levels of socio-economic deprivation and social cohesion, show a small but consistent relationship with offending behaviour (see Chapter 2). The prison population in Ireland is very homogeneous. Most people who are imprisoned come from a limited number of, mostly disadvantaged, areas (see O'Donnell *et al.* 2007). Given this, it is important to examine the type of neighbourhoods in which participants lived. Dublin is divided into four county council areas, Dublin City, South Dublin, Fingal and Dun Laoghaire-Rathdown. As can be seen from

Table 3.1, participants' addresses spanned the four council areas. The three most common were Dublin City, South Dublin and Dublin Fingal. Although all participants were recruited from Dublin probation offices, two lived outside the Dublin region. One of these was a Traveller (an indigenous minority group).

Table 3.1 Area of residence

Area	Number
Dublin City	37
South Dublin	18
Dublin Fingal	5
Dun Laoghaire-Rathdown	1
Outside Dublin	2
No fixed abode	10

The level of socio-economic disadvantage in these areas was measured with a deprivation index developed by Haase and Pratschke (2008). They used census data to generate deprivation scores for each region, county and electoral division in Ireland. Their deprivation index encompasses three dimensions: demographic profile, social class composition and labour market indicators. It was possible to use this information to develop a socio-economic profile of the areas in which participants resided. A search engine created by the Central Statistics Office was used to identify the electoral division (ED) in which each participant lived. This is the smallest geographical unit for which statistics are publicly available. In total, 63 participants provided home addresses that could be assigned to an electoral division. The remaining 10 had no fixed address. There was a wide dispersion, with participants located in 48 different electoral divisions. Figures from the 2002 census sweep, which correspond most closely to the research timeframe, were used to estimate levels of deprivation in participants' neighbourhoods.

Participants typically lived in areas that were classified as experiencing multiple deprivation. Scores ranged widely from –27 to +22, with a median score of –4.2. Overall, their areas were significantly more deprived than the Dublin region as a whole ($t = 6.9$, $p < .001$). Disadvantaged areas are characterised by poor physical environments, services shortages, and lack of infrastructure, which place their populations at increased risk of social exclusion. A recent report (Urban II Initiative Ballyfermot n.d.: 2) described

Ballyfermot, a community located in the Dublin City Council area and home to seven participants, as a 'bleak physical environment, which lacks community infrastructure' (Urban II Initiative Ballyfermot n.d.: 2).

Looking at the indicators in more detail reveals a more comprehensive picture of disadvantage in these areas. Despite significant decreases in overall unemployment rates during the study time frame, these areas continued to experience high levels of unemployment. Over half of participants (n = 41) lived in areas with male unemployment rates above 10 per cent. This compares to an average of 9.3 per cent in the Dublin region as a whole. Members of these communities who were in work were more likely to be employed in low or semi-skilled jobs. Over three-quarters (n = 48) of participants lived in areas with proportions of low skilled workers above the Dublin average. These patterns may have been influenced by higher rates of educational disadvantage. Compared to the Dublin region, the populations in the study areas were more likely to have primary education only (n = 42). Finally, 37 participants resided in areas that had above average proportions of local authority housing. All of these differences were statistically significant (p < .001). In other words, the majority of participants came from economically disadvantaged areas, which experienced above average levels of unemployment, low educational attainment and a higher prevalence of social housing compared to the Dublin region as a whole. Socio-economic deprivation is often accompanied by higher crime rates (see Sampson *et al.* 1997).

Multiple disadvantage tends to be concentrated within certain lower-working-class areas, particularly where housing is provided by the local authority. This creates a vicious cycle, where a combination of poor educational and employment skills results in cumulative disadvantage for the individual. The study, *Against All Odds* (Combat Poverty Agency 2001), highlighted the long-term impact of living in such communities. The research linked poverty to other risk factors, such as early school leaving and exposure to drug use and crime. It showed that the risk of income poverty associated with being unemployed was high (19 per cent of households headed by an unemployed person were living in poverty compared to a national rate of 5 per cent), although this figure had more than halved since 1994. Being in full-time employment substantially reduced the risk of living in poverty. The RAPID (Revitalising Areas through Planning Investment and Development) programme was introduced by the Irish government in 2001 to promote social inclusion and has improved the quality of local services and infrastructure in disadvantaged areas.

It is also important to highlight the fact that 10 participants, all from Dublin, were classified as having no fixed abode at the time of the interview. The links between homelessness, drug use and crime have begun to receive attention recently. A survey of prisoners found that a quarter had been homeless prior to their current period of incarceration (Seymour and Costello 2005). This was compared to 1.6 per cent of all people referred to the courts in Dublin. Those who were homeless were more likely to be young, male, have a history of mental illness, and lack family support, educational attainment and employment. Drug use and crime were strongly related to homelessness. In a survey by Merchant's Quay Ireland of 190 problem drug users in Dublin, 63 per cent reported having been homeless at some point in their lives (the definition included both those sleeping rough and those who did not have proper accommodation, who were, for example, staying in hostels or with friends (Cox and Lawless 1999). Around two-thirds attributed their homelessness to drug use. Those sleeping rough were significantly more likely to report engaging in risky behaviours (for example, injecting heroin in public places) than those experiencing other forms of homelessness. Homelessness, in general, was associated with risk-taking, criminality, and economic deprivation.

Criminal history

Many of the participants began to offend while they were quite young. The earlier individuals begin their criminal career, the more likely it is that they will develop into persistent offenders (Blumenstein *et al.* 1986). On average, participants reported having committed their first offence when they were 12 years old (SD = 2.7 with a range of 7 to 18 years). Participants also had had their first contact with An Garda Síochána at a relatively early age. The average was 14 (SD = 3.5), with a range of 7 to 29 years. According to their criminal records, the average age at which they received their first adult conviction was 18 years (SD = 3.0) with a range of 10 to 25 years. This is close to Farrington's (1997) estimate that most offenders are first convicted between 13 and 16 years. Given that persistent offenders typically begin their criminal careers earlier, it is surprising to note that 23 per cent (*n* = 16) were first convicted at 21 years or over (see Figure 3.2). It is possible that this subgroup may have begun offending earlier but been particularly good at evading detection.

Participants were engaged in serious criminality, as evidence by the sanctions they received. Around a quarter reported that they

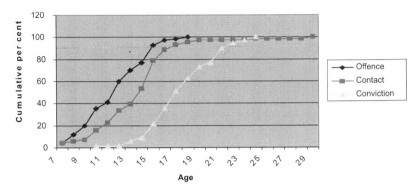

Figure 3.2 Age at onset

had been detained in a special school as children. Special schools were detention centres for young people who were convicted of an offence committed while under the age of 18, and they have since been replaced by 'detention schools'. The most common sanction handed down on the first adult conviction was a custodial sentence, with nearly one in four (37 per cent) receiving an immediate prison sentence or period of detention. A further five received suspended prison sentences. In total, 69 per cent served a prison sentence at some point during their adult criminal careers. The ratio of immediate custody to community sanctions received over the course of their criminal careers was calculated. Non-custodial options were broadly defined to include suspended sentences, community service orders and probation (fines were excluded). The average ratio was 2.11 in favour of immediate custody, suggesting that custodial options were by far the most common sanction handed down by the courts. In general, custodial sentences appear to be used more frequently than probation and community service by Irish courts (O'Donnell 2004).

Participants' criminal careers varied in length from 1 to 19 years. Frequency of convictions was calculated by dividing the number of court appearances which led to a conviction each year (including current offence) by the total number of years during which convictions occurred (career duration). Participants accumulated a total of 461 court appearances over 462 years, leaving an overall conviction rate of almost exactly one per year (M = 1.2, SD = 0.6). This is higher than the rate estimated by Tarling (1993) for a UK sample, who averaged about 0.5 convictions per year. A higher rate of offending among a sample of persistent offenders is, however, to be expected.

The number of previous convictions was defined as the number of previous court appearances resulting in at least one finding of guilt. Participants acquired an average of 6.8 previous court appearances (SD = 6.2; median = 5) prior to the interview (see Table 3.2). Using the number of court appearances as an indicator of previous convictions under-estimates the total number of convictions received by the sample. The majority of participants were convicted of more than one offence at each court appearance. Looked at this way, the average number of convictions appears much higher at 11.5 (SD = 8.3). As the number of court appearances is the standard unit of measurement in the literature, it is this statistic that will be used when referring to previous convictions.

All participants were under the supervision of the Probation and Welfare Service (PWS) at the time of the study. Table 3.3 shows the type of offences for which they received a supervision order. As can be seen, a wide variety of offences were committed by the sample and

Table 3.2 Number of previous convictions

	No.	Percentage
5 or fewer	38	52.1
6 to 10	18	24.7
11 to 15	7	9.6
16 and over	7	9.6
N/a	3	4.1
Total	73	100

Table 3.3 Offence type

	No.	Percentage
Robbery	15	20.5
Drugs offences	14	19.2
Larceny/theft	13	17.8
Assault	8	10.9
Unauthorised taking of car	6	8.2
Burglary	4	5.5
Motoring	3	4.1
Other	10	13.6
Total	73	100

most were at the more serious end of the scale. The most common were robbery, drugs, larceny and assault.

Probation supervision

Two-thirds (n = 48, or 65.7 per cent) of participants were on probation orders. Under the Probation of Offenders Act 1907, an offender may be made subject to a probation order for a maximum period of 3 years. Conditions may be attached to the order (for example, an offender may be required to attend a drug treatment programme). If the conditions of a probation order are breached, the case is re-entered and a warrant will be issued for the arrest of the offender. A further 11 participants were on adjourned supervision. In such cases the judge defers sentence until the offender has had an opportunity to demonstrate a willingness to respond to a specified intervention. This may involve the payment of compensation to the victim, participation on a drug or alcohol course, or engagement in victim–offender mediation. The understanding is that if the offender complies, and the progress reports prepared by the PWS are favourable, a prison sentence will not be imposed. This practice was developed by the judiciary and has no statutory basis.

Three participants were serving suspended prison sentences. A judge may impose a custodial sentence and suspend it on condition that the offender enters into either a bond or a recognisance, or agrees to be bound to the peace (Rottman and Tormey 1985). Alternatively, offenders may be ordered to serve a portion of the custodial sentence, and then come back to court for a review. If the review is favourable, the remainder of the sentence may be suspended. This practice was discontinued in 2000 when the Supreme Court ruled in the case of Finn that it interfered with the power of the executive to commute sentences (cited in Kilcommins *et al.* 2004: 148). If an offender breaches the conditions of a suspended sentence, the judge may activate the custodial sentence and the offender may be obliged to serve the full prison term. Two participants were on temporary release from prison. Temporary releases are governed by the Prisoners (Temporary Release) Rules 1960. In the past, this practice was often used to relieve prison overcrowding, creating what became known as the 'revolving door syndrome' (see Kilcommins *et al.* 2004). However, it is now unusual for prisoners to be granted unplanned, unsupervised release. A breach carries a maximum sentence of 6 months in prison.

Probation files showed that 34 participants were on orders of 12 months' duration or less, four had received supervision orders of 13 to

23 months, and 17 received supervision of 24 months and over. There was no information available in 10 cases, and a further eight were classified as 'ongoing', with no fixed termination date. Nationally, 33 per cent of those under supervision were on orders of 12 months or less in 1999. Only 7.4 per cent of the population was on orders of at least 24 months' duration. This cursory review indicates that the current sample tended to be under supervision for longer periods.

Chapter 4

Thinking, attitudes and social circumstances

A wide range of factors has been implicated in desistance, encompassing individual, psychological, social and neighbourhood domains, but there is little consensus concerning their relative importance in the process. Some theories prioritise maturation (e.g. Gottfredson and Hirschi 1990), others emphasise social factors (e.g. Laub and Sampson 2003), and yet others attribute change to cognitive or internal change (e.g. Giordano *et al.* 2002). Existing theories indicate that it may be helpful to distinguish between the onset and maintenance of desistance, as different factors may be relevant at different stages of the process. Maruna and Farrall (2004) distinguished between two stages in the process of desistance. The first consists of any hiatus in criminal activity (primary desistance) while the second comprises a more permanent state of non-offending (secondary desistance). Although knowledge about long-term behavioural change is growing, the early stages of desistance have received little theoretical or empirical attention. This chapter presents the results of an investigation of the psychosocial factors involved in desistance. It aims to identify whether the factors that are involved in the early stages of change (primary desistance) differ from those involved in the later stages (secondary desistance).

Defining desistance

The first step was to categorise participants into offenders or desisters, according to their level of involvement in crime. This proved to be a more complex procedure than was initially envisaged. It is difficult to fit individuals neatly into dichotomous categories as these may mask variations in offending behaviour. It is more accurate to conceptualise offending behaviour as a spectrum where 'the two groups (desisting and persisting offenders) represent similar individuals in different stages of the change process' (Maruna 2001: 74). In this study, some participants were still involved in crime, others were desisting, while others were situated somewhere in between. After much consideration, it was decided that anyone reporting the commission of a crime at whatever frequency or seriousness would be considered still involved in crime for the purpose of this analysis. While this would mean that participants who reported committing occasional minor offences would be in the same category as those reporting involvement in frequent or serious offending, it was felt that, if there were genuine differences between offenders and desisters, these should be discernible at all levels. Participants who reported drug use that was not supported by criminal activity were counted as desisters.

The next step was to define how long a person had to be crime-free before he could be regarded as a desister. Bushway *et al.* (2001) argued that many researchers actually study 'temporary non-offending' rather than genuine desistance. It is not always possible to verify whether an episode of desistance has endured, especially when a short follow-up period is used. Shorter measurement periods increase the likelihood that a study will capture temporary interruptions in participants' criminal careers rather than the early stages of true, or permanent, desistance. Researchers usually have access to only a snapshot of the entire life course of participants (although there have been some excellent longitudinal studies, such as Laub and Sampson (2003)). Secondary desistance was operationalised as 'no self-reported offending for at least a year' and primary desistance was operationalised as 'no self-reported offending for at least a month'.

Preliminary profile

Research suggests that desistance may be facilitated by a wide range of factors. A comprehensive analysis must therefore include measures of demographic, criminal history, social, and subjective factors. The following variables were selected because they consistently show strong relationships with offending behaviour. The selection process was also influenced by current theoretical perspectives (see Chapter 1). Age and criminal history are considered to be two of the most important predictors of crime (see Gendreau, Little and Goggin 1996). In order to take account of their influence, the following four variables were included in the analysis:

1 'Age' refers to the age of participants at the time of the interview, which took place over a 1-year period from 2003 to 2004. According to the literature, younger offenders are less likely to desist.

2 'Age at onset' is the age at which participants self-reported committing their first crime, irrespective of whether it came to the attention of the police. This indicator was incorporated because research suggests that the earlier individuals embark on an offending career, the more likely it is that they will continue their offending into adulthood.

3 'Number of previous convictions' was calculated from police records and refers to the number of court appearances made by participants up to the time of the interview. In general, people with more extensive criminal histories are more likely to reoffend.

4 'Number of previous prison sentences' refers to the number of prison sentences handed down to participants up to the time of the interview. This measure can be treated as a proxy for offence seriousness and was an important predictor in the only Irish study of offender recidivism (see O'Donnell, Baumer and Hughes 2008).

Three validated psychometric instruments were used to measure levels of thinking, attitudes and perceived social problems (see Chapter 3 for full details). These instruments were the Psychological Inventory of Criminal Thinking Styles (Walters 1995), CRIME-PICS (Frude, Honess and Maguire 1995), and the Level of Service Inventory-Revised (Andrews and Bonta 1995). A profile of the sample was generated from their scores on the three psychometric instruments. A brief summary of each instrument and participants' scores is provided next. (Tables showing the mean scores, standard deviations and t-scores for each scale can be found in Appendix 1.)

CRIME-PICS measures the presence of pro-criminal attitudes and perceived problems among offenders. It consists of four attitudinal scales, which measure General Attitude to Crime, Anticipation of Reoffending, Victim Hurt Denial, and Evaluation of Crime as Worthwhile. In addition, a Problem Inventory measures self-reported problems in 15 areas, such as employment, addiction, boredom, temper and relationships. The sample as a whole had high scores on the General Attitude scale and the Problem Inventory. These were in line with the scores reported in the standardisation studies (Frude *et al.* 1994) but were significantly higher than the scores obtained by a sample of offenders on Community Service Pathfinder projects (Rex *et al.* 2003), suggesting the presence of more pro-criminal attitudes.

The PICTS measures the presence of belief systems that support criminal behaviour, termed criminal thinking styles. As described in Chapter 3, it consists of eight subscales, which measure eight thinking styles. There are two validity scales, which check the honesty of participants' responses. More recently, two content scales (Historical and Current Criminal Thinking) have been added. Overall, the Irish sample scored higher than English (Palmer and Hollin 2003) and American (Walters 1995) prisoners, indicating higher levels of criminal thinking.

The LSI-R is a classification tool originally created to assist probation officers in their assessment of offenders. It includes a criminal history component, as well as seven structural (employment/education, financial, family/marital, accommodation, leisure, companions and drug/alcohol use) and two individual (mental health, attitudes towards crime and sentence) components. Scores are used to categorise offenders into low, medium and high risk of reconviction. Participants had an average risk of reconviction score of 24.97 (SD = 8.82), which places them in the 'high' to 'very high' risk of reconviction category. Their risk level was higher than a sample of English prisoners (Hollin, Palmer and Clarke 2003) but similar to a sample of Canadian prisoners (Loza and Simourd 1994).

Overall, the sample had relatively high levels of criminal thinking, pro-criminal attitudes, social problems and risk of reoffending. The next step was to discover whether there were any observable differences between participants who were classed as 'desisters' and those who were categorised as 'offenders' on these attributes. A two-stage procedure was used to identify the factors that were associated with primary and secondary desistance. For each type of desistance, a series of bivariate analyses was conducted with the data in order to establish whether there were any significant differences between the groups. The significant variables were then entered into logistic regression models to ascertain which of them explained desistance. Although all scales are considered in the bivariate analyses, just five subscales from each instrument were selected to represent each indicator in this stage of the analysis: the CRIME-PICS General Attitudes to Crime and Problem Inventory, the two PICTS content scales, Current Criminal Thinking and Historical Criminal Thinking, and the LSI-R risk of reconviction score. All of these are designed to be used as stand-alone indicators of, respectively, pro-criminal attitudes (see Raynor and Vanstone 1997), criminal thinking (see Walters 2002c), and risk level (see Andrews and Bonta 1995).

Secondary desistance: a psychometric analysis

Forty-nine participants reported that they had been involved in crime in the past year, while the remaining 24 stated that they had been crime-free for at least this period. Their reports were checked against official records of An Garda Síochána. Ten participants had convictions in the past year but did not self-report any involvement in crime. Arrest records, however, showed that, of these, only one participant had actually committed the offence for which the conviction was received within the past year. This was a relatively recent arrest for burglary so it is unlikely that the participant forgot about it. For the remainder, the divergence was the result of delays between arrest and conviction. It was deemed appropriate, therefore, to regard participants' self-reports as accurate. Almost one in three (29 per cent) reported committing crime in the past year that was not officially recorded. This is to be expected given the nature of self-reports. The most common self-reported crimes were buying stolen goods ($n = $ 30), shoplifting ($n = 26$), sale of drugs ($n = 21$), sale of stolen goods ($n = 23$), and car theft ($n = 14$). Nine reported committing one offence in the past year, while 31 reported committing three or more.

The groups were compared on age and three indicators of previous criminal history, as these factors are known to be associated with reoffending. At the time of the interview, participants had a mean age of 25.4 (SD = 4.4). Significant age differences ($t = 2.16$, $p = .04$) were found between participants who had committed crime in the past year (M = 24.63, SD = 4.05) and those who had not (M = 26.96, SD = 4.88), with younger men more likely to be involved in active criminality. The groups also differed on age at first offence. Secondary desisters (M = 13.29, SD = 2.7) were significantly younger than offenders (M = 11.33, SD = 2.5) when they initiated their criminal careers ($t = 2.97$, $p < .005$). There were no significant differences between the groups regarding the number of previous convictions or the number of previous prison sentences.

T-tests were used to test for differences between the current offenders and secondary desisters on the CRIME-PICS scales. Significant differences between the groups were found for three of the five scales with offenders scoring higher. This indicates the presence of more positive attitudes towards crime (G scale), a stronger belief that they might reoffend in the future (A scale), and the view that crime is worthwhile (E scale). Similar levels of victim empathy were reported by both groups. Each achieved low scores on this scale, indicating good awareness of the impact of their crimes on victims. There were no significant differences between the two groups on the Problem scale, which suggests that perceived problems were not associated with desistance.

The first two PICTS scales, Confusion and Defensiveness, measure the honesty of the participants' responses. There was a significant difference between the two groups with regards to Confusion, but not Defensiveness. These results indicate that both were equally likely to adopt a defensive test-taking style, but offenders were more likely to attempt a 'fake good' response. Next, differences between the groups on the eight thinking styles were examined. Scores differed on three of the eight PICTS thinking styles. These were Cut-off, Cognitive Indolence, and Discontinuity. In other words, secondary desisters were significantly less likely to demonstrate impulsive thinking, engage in lazy thinking and become easily distracted from their goals. There were no observed differences on the Mollification, Sentimentality, Power Orientation or Super-optimism scales, while Entitlement approached significance. Differences between the two groups on the Current and Historical Criminal Thinking scale were also calculated. The results suggest that those who had offended in the past year were significantly more likely to have currently active criminal thinking styles. There were no differences on the Historical thinking scale.

The two groups were compared on their overall risk score and their scores on each of the 10 sub-components of the LSI-R. The groups differed significantly with regards to their overall risk of reconviction scores, but differed on only two of the 10 need domains: Financial and Alcohol/drug use. This suggests that, while offenders had significantly higher levels of risk than secondary desisters, the groups did not differ much with regards to their overall criminogenic needs but had more financial and substance use problems.

In sum, these initial analyses suggested that secondary desisters were less likely to be currently engaging in criminal thinking, had fewer pro-criminal attitudes and had a lower risk of reconviction.

Secondary desistance: a psychosocial model

The significant variables were entered into a series of logistic regression models in order to discover which factors were important for secondary desistance. Because of the small sample, the number of individual variables that could be tested at any one time had to be restricted. As explained earlier, five subscales from the psychometric instruments were chosen to measure pro-criminal attitudes, criminal thinking and risk level in the multivariate analysis. The bivariate analysis showed significant differences between offenders and secondary desisters on three of these: CRIME-PICS General Attitude to Crime, the PICTS Current Criminal Thinking Scale, and the LSI-R Risk of Reconviction Score. Logistic regression analyses were performed to explore the relative influence of these factors on secondary desistance. Because of the small sample size, two separate logistic regressions were conducted.

The first model tested the three psychometric scales. Only one, the CRIME PICS General Attitude to Crime Scale, made a significant contribution ($ß = .17$, $p < .01$). The PICTS Current Criminal Thinking Scale ($ß = .04$, $p = .44$, ns) and the LSI-R Risk of Reconviction Score ($ß = .004$, ns) did not emerge as significant predictors. The CRIME-PICS General Attitude to Crime Scale was then entered into a second model alongside age at time of interview and age at onset, which had also differentiated between secondary desisters and offenders. The final model (shown in Table 4.1) explained 40 per cent of the variance. As can be seen, age at time of interview and the CRIME-PICS General Attitude to Crime made a significant contribution to the model while age at onset did not. Desisters were older and less likely to endorse pro-criminal attitudes.

Table 4.1 Predictors of offending (past year)

	ß	Wald	p	Exp (ß)
Age at interview	−.154	4.162	.041	.857
Age at onset of offending	−.209	2.384	.123	.811
CRIME-PICS General Attitude	.139	7.815	.005	1.149
Constant	1.745	.303	.582	5.724

Primary desistance: a psychometric analysis

Sixty-two per cent of the sample (n = 45) was classed as primary desisters. The remainder (n = 28) self-reported committing at least one offence in the previous month. Of these, 12 had committed one crime in the past month, while 11 had committed three or more. Their principal offences were handling stolen goods (n = 20), dangerous driving (n = 9), selling drugs (n=8) and violent crime (n = 7). Current offenders (M = 23.43, SD = 3.65) tended to be younger than primary desisters (M = 26.62, SD = 4.48) when interviewed (t = 3.17, p = .002). Only one of the three criminal history variables, age at first offence, proved significant (t = 2.63, p = .01). Primary desisters (M = 12.6, SD = 2.5) were older than current offenders (M = 10.9, SD = 2.6) when they began their criminal careers.

There were significant differences on four of the five CRIME-PICS scales (G, A, E scales and Problem Inventory). Primary desisters were significantly less likely than current offenders to endorse pro-criminal attitudes, to anticipate future offending, or to evaluate crime as worthwhile. They also reported experiencing fewer problems on the Problem Inventory compared to current offenders. The differences were significant. In spite of this, they tended to have good awareness of the impact of their crimes on their victims. Differences between the groups on the Victim Empathy scale remained insignificant, although desisters scored slightly, but not significantly, higher (indicating lower levels of victim empathy). Similar results were found for secondary desisters. This scale may be especially vulnerable to social desirability effects. The items are quite blunt (e.g. 'I have never hurt anyone by what I've done' [item 2]), and it would be difficult for someone to admit to not caring about victims without seeming callous. Overall, the results suggest that, compared to current offenders, primary desisters were less likely to endorse criminal attitudes or to experience problems in their lives.

As there were very significant differences between offenders and primary desisters on the Problem Inventory, the problems reported by participants were examined in more depth. The most common problems reported by both groups were boredom, lack of money and employment. T-tests showed that the groups differed significantly on 7 of the 15 factors. The most significant differences were found for relationships, employment/prospects, controlling temper, boredom and drink/drugs (all p < .001). There were no differences in self-esteem, self-confidence or depression. Meta-analytic studies have also found that self-esteem is not linked to criminal activity (e.g. Andrews 1995).

The differences between the two groups on six of the eight PICTS thinking styles were highly significant, suggesting that those who were currently involved in crime tended to have thinking styles that supported criminal behaviour. These were Cut-off, Power Orientation, Super-optimism, Discontinuity, Entitlement and Cognitive Indolence. There were no observed differences between the groups on the Sentimentality or the Mollification scales. Primary desisters were therefore less likely to attempt to cognitively eliminate deterrents to crime, use a sense of entitlement to justify criminality, feel a need to control others, believe that the costs of crime could be avoided, engage in lazy thinking, or become distracted from goals. Participants who were currently involved in crime scored significantly higher than primary desisters on the Current Criminal Thinking scale. The differences between current offenders and desisters on the Historical Criminal Thinking Scale were also significant.

The differences between current offenders and primary desisters on the LSI-R risk of reconviction were tested. There was a highly significant difference between the two groups in relation to their overall risk of reconviction. Participants reporting current involvement in crime had a significantly higher risk of reconviction than those who reported no involvement in crime in the past month. They also had higher scores on all 10 sub-components. Five of these reached significance: Criminal history, Leisure/recreation, Companions, Alcohol/drugs, and Attitudes. Differences approached significance on the Education/employment scale and the Accommodation scale. These results suggest that the criminogenic needs of participants who reported committing crime in the past month are more pronounced. The profile of reported problems was similar to that reported by participants on the CRIME-PICS Problem Inventory, where the most common problems were boredom, money and employment.

In sum, the bivariate analyses suggested that primary desisters were significantly less likely than current offenders to engage in criminal thinking, express pro-criminal attitudes, experience social problems or to be rated as high risk. They tended to start their criminal careers later in life and were older at the time of interview.

Primary desistance: a psychosocial model

Significant differences were found between current offenders and primary desisters on the five scales: CRIME-PICS General Attitude to Crime, CRIME-PICS Problem Inventory, the PICTS Current Criminal Thinking Scale, the PICTS Historical Criminal Thinking Scale, and the LSI-R Risk of Reconviction Scale. Logistic regression analyses were conducted to identify the relative influence of these factors on primary desistance. Again, because of the limited sample size, two separate logistic regression models were performed.

The first tested the five psychometric scales. Only the PICTS Current Criminal Thinking Scale made a significant contribution to the model (β = .16, p < .05), while the CRIME-PICS General Attitude to Crime approached significance (β = .15, p < .06). The CRIME-PICS Problem scale (β = .01, p = .88, ns), the PICTS Historical Criminal Thinking Scale (β = .04, p =.44, ns), and the LSI-R Risk of Reconviction Score (β = .06, p = .30, ns) did not explain primary desistance. The PICTS Current Criminal Thinking scale was then entered into a second model with age at time of interview and age at onset, as the groups differed on these factors. The final model (shown in Table 4.2) explained 60.9 per cent of the variance. All three variables were significant.

These findings suggest that pro-criminal thinking styles continue to play an important role in primary desistance even after age and age at onset are controlled. However, criminal attitudes and the presence of social problems (whether measured by the CRIME PICS Problem Inventory or the LSI-R Risk of Reconviction Score) do not appear to be important for primary desistance (see also Healy forthcoming).

Table 4.2 Predictors of offending (past month)

	β	Wald	p	Exp (β)
Age at interview	−.35	8.66	.003	.70
Age at onset of offending	−.36	4.76	.03	.70
PICTS: Current Criminal Thinking	.21	13.28	.001	1.23
Constant	5.27	2.86	.09	194.57

A psychosocial model

The sample was categorised into desisters and current offenders according to whether they self-reported offending (a) in the past year and (b) in the past month. Differences between the two groups on measures of age, criminal history, thinking, attitudes and social circumstances were tested in order to establish which factors were associated with primary and secondary desistance. Age, criminal history and cognitive factors played an important role in desistance, while perceived social circumstances did not. Overall, criminal cognitions emerged as the most significant factors in both primary and secondary desistance. As mentioned earlier, dichotomous categorisations can mask subtle changes in criminal activity. In this sample, those classified as offenders had varying levels of criminal involvement, ranging from minor offences, such as buying stolen goods, to more serious offences, such as selling drugs. In spite of this, the analysis identified clear differences between those who were still involved in crime at whatever level, and those who were not.

The role of cognition

Criminal thinking styles, as measured by the PICTS, play a particularly important role during the initial stages of change. It is interesting that research relating to the factor scales in the PICTS shows the three most significant scales in the bivariate analyses (Cut-off, Cognitive Indolence and Discontinuity) load heavily on the first PICTS factor, Problem Avoidance, as does the Current Scale (results reported in Walters 2002a). Problem Avoidance captures offenders' tendency to resort to drugs and crime to avoid dealing with problems. This was evident among the Irish sample. Cillian described how he felt lost and left behind following release from prison. Uncertainty about his future led him to cling to a familiar way of life and he began selling drugs again:

> I just finished 6 year there recently, and when I got out after that, there was nothing out there for me, there wasn't. When I got out, I really wanted to come back to prison, I did ... . All me friends and all had jobs. The people I used to be with and all. And things just were after changing an awful lot and I didn't know which way to go, you know. It's like I was at a dead end ... . So the first thing I done was just went back selling drugs, you know. Instead of going out looking for a job, I just went down looking for old people I knew and all. [KV65]

The following extract encapsulates the tension between taking responsibility for behaviour while maintaining a positive self-image (see also Maruna 2001). Darragh was caught in a moral dilemma. He was aware that the crime he committed was wrong and tried to minimise blame in several ways, including shifting the focus to his girlfriend's drug use. He also tried to highlight his 'core good self' by stressing how he chose to sell drugs in order to avoid harming victims directly.

So me mot [girlfriend] ended up getting into drugs so that's how I got caught in drugs again. Because of her. And that's when I started selling it. We hadn't got the money and she was saying but what if we sold it. And that's what I was saying to you – I knew what I was doing was wrong but we were strung out [suffering withdrawal symptoms] and I could see no other way out of it, you know what I mean. I didn't want to go out and do what other people were doing – robbing people with syringes. So I'd rather turn to drugs than do that to people. So I sold them for about a year or two and I even said it to her – I'm going to get caught and people are going to think we're nothing but scumbags selling this. [KV83]

Pro-criminal attitudes are among the most important predictors of offending (see Andrews and Bonta 2006) and were particularly significant for secondary desisters. People who were still committing crime were more likely to endorse attitudes that were supportive of the criminal lifestyle. In the following extract, Max appears to take pride in his criminal achievements and his skill in evading arrest. His pro-criminal attitudes legitimated his continued offending.

You just can't start selling drugs. Like I was selling for years meself, then I was selling for me brother and then, big drug dealers, they wanted me to sell for them … So you have to know somebody and you have to have a head on your shoulders. You have to know what you're doing. Now all the years I sold I never got caught. Never even got a raid. I was always smart. [KV81]

It is interesting that offenders and desisters in both sets of analysis had similar scores on the CRIME-PICS Victim Hurt Denial Scale, which measures victim empathy, and the PICTS Sentimentality scale, which measures the tendency to use good behaviour to excuse bad. Overall, participants were aware of the effects of their behaviour on their victims and tried to emphasise their core good self in their accounts (see also Maruna 2001). In describing his reaction to hearing his victim's story in court, Carl stresses his unwillingness to harm anyone, claiming it is 'not in his blood'.

The [shop] assistant when she was in court – she put a victim impact report in. She said she was having nightmares, she was having fears. I kind of felt sorry for her. She said she feared for her life. But I tried to put across in my statement that I never hurt anyone. Unfortunately, all I was there for was the money. In any of my crimes, I never hurted anybody. It's not in my blood. But she was upset so I was a bit upset for her. [KV98]

Although social variables were significant at the bivariate level, they did not contribute to the final desistance models, and this was surprising given their prominence in the literature. A number of studies have suggested that offenders are more likely than desisters to report having problems. Burnett (1992), for example, found that although most prisoners anticipated facing a wide range of obstacles prior to release, ex-prisoners who were still involved in crime were more likely than desisters to report problems (primarily financial, vocational and relationships) after release. When difficult social circumstances coincided with poor coping skills, participants reported that they began to entertain thoughts about crime. The following extract illustrates the problems faced by probationers as they moved away from crime. Lee was unemployed and was struggling to find work because of his criminal record. In his view, having money was very important and his lack of it was causing him distress. He explained that, when short of money, he was more likely to think about committing crime.

Yeah, I need to get a better job, you know what I mean, I need to get more money. That's my attitude. Money makes the world go round so people are always surprised when most people's problems are money. And they're like 'why'. Money. Coz money makes everything go round and if you haven't got money you can't do things. You have loads of money, you can do whatever you want and it's true, if you have money you can get away with whatever you want. [KV73]

Zamble and Quinsey (1997) suggested that recidivists may lack the coping mechanisms necessary to avoid or deal successfully with the criminogenic situations that offenders invariably encounter on a regular basis. They found that the problems experienced by reoffenders were not significantly different from those experienced by desisters. Similarly, Maruna (2001) found that persistent offenders tended to have a more negative perception of their lives and future prospects while desisters often displayed high levels of optimism about their futures. Nick, who was in the early stages of change, explained what he found difficult about the process of desistance.

His key problem was dealing with boredom. When he was unable to find activities to keep himself busy, he found himself tempted to commit crime or use drugs.

> It's the way I deal with boredom sometimes. Just the buzz of doing it kind of. What'll I do, crime like. Everything goes through your head from drugs to crime to now going to the pictures. Sometimes you make the wrong decision … . Sometimes you're just so bored and you get so sick, stuck in a rut doing the same thing. Just trying to do something different. Could be drugs or crime or whatever, stealing something. [KV86]

There were no significant differences with regards to neighbourhood deprivation for either secondary ($t = .14$, $p = .89$, ns) or primary ($t = .21$, $p = .83$, ns) desistance, although desisters at both stages tended to live in slightly less deprived areas. Analysis of participants' narratives suggested that poverty may have played a role in the onset of their criminality, if not their decision to desist. Andy, aged 24, grew up in a very deprived area and described how he regularly witnessed drug addicts who had overdosed being abandoned on the street and in stairwells. There was a highly visible criminal culture in his neighbourhood of joyriding and drug dealing. As he explained, his childhood experience of poverty had a significant impact on him and led him into crime.

> My mother had five boys, me father didn't work at the time. And we were bullied terrible because we wore these little shorts, these black pumps that like if you stood on a bean it would puncture the fuckin' things, like … So we were victims for the older kids in the flats, who had the Nike and had the Levis … we didn't have any of them … . Every day we were down the flats it was a torment for us, you know … . The five of us learnt how to fight together coz we had to … When I was younger, growing up, I always said, 'I can't wait till I get bigger' and I remember my brothers telling me that they heard me dreaming, 'I'm going to have 10 pairs of Levis.' [KV22]

As he grew up, he began to commit crime in order to acquire the lifestyle and respect that he craved as a child. He stopped offending when his child was born but could not afford to leave the area. At the time of the interview, he was still experiencing financial difficulties and reported that his former associates were threatening him. In

73

spite of his difficult circumstances, he was not offending when he was interviewed.

The majority of participants, whether they were desisting or still involved in crime, were experiencing high levels of social disadvantage. Those who encounter significant social obstacles will have to exercise more personal agency than those with few problems if they are to desist. Studies confirm that successful desisters often have higher levels of personal agency than people that remain involved in crime, who tend to possess less stoicism in the face of adversity (Maruna 2001). It may not be the individual's objective social circumstances that are important for desistance, but how they respond to the structural obstacles they encounter. It is possible to exercise agency even in structurally constrained circumstances (see Evans 2002).

The salience of psychological factors supports the view that offenders are active participants in desistance and do not simply respond passively to social events, as suggested by the delinquency and drift and social control perspectives. Instead, these findings resonate with Giordano *et al.*'s (2002) theory of cognitive transformation, which portrayed the offender as an active decision-making agent interacting with the social world to create a new identity as a non-offender. They hypothesised that the individual's subjective stance is especially important during the early stages of change when the new identity is at a distance. The results reported here suggest that this might be the case. The relationship between cognitions and crime is a complex one but there is evidence to suggest that psychological states may mediate the experience of social problems (see LeBel *et al.* 2008). It is theoretically possible therefore that participants' past social circumstances may have been involved in generating their current level of criminal cognitions.

Change and continuity

In addition to criminal thinking, age and age at onset of criminality also emerged as important predictors of primary desistance, while age was significant for secondary desistance. Early onset of criminality is considered an indicator of criminal propensity and has been linked to reoffending (Paternoster *et al.* 1997). The relationship between age and crime is also well established (e.g. Gottfredson and Hirschi 1990). Age and criminal history are classed as static factors while criminal cognitions are classed as dynamic factors (see Andrews and Bonta 2006). 'Static' variables cannot be altered through intervention, while dynamic factors can.

It has been argued that there is strong continuity between antisocial behaviour in childhood and criminality in adulthood (e.g. Gottfredson and Hirschi 1990). Others dispute this, proposing that change is possible for even the most persistent offenders (Laub and Sampson 2003). Certain variables may be significant during certain developmental windows but their effects may not endure. For example, employment appears to be significant during emerging adulthood but not earlier in the life course (Morizot and LeBlanc 2007). Similarly, age and criminal history are important during adolescence but their influence fades over time (Laub and Sampson 2003). This analysis suggested that both static and dynamic risk factors are involved in desistance. If this is the case, static factors may increase the probability of offending, but proximal dynamic factors, such as thinking and attitudes, are more influential in determining whether offending is actually occurring (Healy, forthcoming). Despite some overlap, different factors were related to primary and secondary desistance. This raises the possibility that different processes may be involved in the onset and maintenance of desistance, as suggested by Lemert (1972). It may therefore be helpful to conceptualise temporary and permanent desistance as unique, but intertwined, processes.

A tipping point?

This study found that the contrast between offenders and desisters on key desistance-related factors was very striking in the short term. This suggests that the initial stages of change are characterised by dramatic and sudden cognitive change for at least some desisters. Evidence from the psychotherapy literature indicates that change can be abrupt and dramatic and may occur early in the recovery process. In a study of pathways to recovery from depression among individuals who were participating in a cognitive therapy programme, Tang and DeRubeis (1999) found that around half experienced what the authors termed 'sudden gains'. These gains consisted of substantial and rapid improvements in symptom severity. They typically took place early in the treatment process and usually occurred in one between-session interval (that is, in less than a week). Furthermore, sudden gains accounted for half of total symptom improvement over the study period. Similarly, in a study of survivors of sexual assault, Frazier, Conlon and Glaser (2001) found that the interval between 2 weeks and 2 months after the event was associated with the most dramatic change, after which time the rate of change tended to stabilise. Although this literature has not emerged from criminal career research, the findings have relevance for discussions about pathways to desistance and fit the pattern of results found here.

The concept of a 'tipping point' (made famous by Gladwell 2000) offers a useful framework for conceptualising the onset of the desistance process. Gladwell described how massive changes (whether in the social, business, or cultural realm) tend to be abrupt, rather than gradual. He argued that small events can have dramatic consequences, noting that a single event can often have a cumulative effect that is out of proportion to the cause. When the 'critical mass' is reached, the change occurs. At the boundary between two social worlds, regular patterns break down and earlier certainties fade (see Gleick 1987). However, rapid changes in thinking related to modifications in behaviour may be possible, but may not always last. This fits in with the concepts of 'drift' (Matza 1964) and 'ambivalence' (Burnett 2004). The process of change can be fluid, with individuals adapting their thinking and behaviour to current circumstances. This was evident in many of the participants' stories. Even those who expressed a desire to change were still not fully committed to reform. Dan's account of his journey towards change illustrates this point. In spite of his desire to change, he admits that unemployment combined with a tempting criminal opportunity would test his resolve.

> *How likely is it that you might go back to crime in the future?*
> Very slim because I'm only 23 but I've seen a lot and I've done a lot. I've learnt early I think, I'm hoping anyway. I hope I have. Coz I've seen a lot, I've seen a lot worse than me. I've seen where it leads, you know, so …
>
> *And what if you had the opportunity to commit a crime where there was a low chance of getting caught?*
> I don't know. That would always be a temptation. If that opportunity came along while I was working meself, it would be 'no'. [KV78]

Interestingly, Tang and DeRubeis (1999) found that sudden gains were preceded by significant cognitive changes (which they defined as the correction of negative beliefs through therapy). They hypothesised that substantial cognitive changes triggered sudden gains, which improved the therapeutic relationship and induced further cognitive change in a positive feedback loop, which eventually led the patient to sustained recovery. Others have failed to find evidence to support the contention that cognitive changes are involved in the sudden gains phenomenon (e.g. Vittengl, Clark and Jarrett 2005). In fact, no clear antecedents to sudden gains have been identified. The 'sudden gain' phenomenon has been confirmed in subsequent studies but there is a lack of agreement about its long-term effects. Tang and DeRubeis (1999) found that participants who experienced sudden gains had better long-term outcomes, as measured by reductions in symptom severity, than patients who had not experienced these rapid adjustments. In contrast, Vittengl *et al.* (2005) found no difference between relapse rates among those who experienced sudden gains and those who did not, but they used wider intervals to measure changes. Whether the 'sudden gains' experienced by the desisters in the current study endured will be examined in Chapter 8.

The dramatic gains associated with primary desistance may recede over time as ex-offenders concentrate on consolidating the gains they have made during the earlier stages. Mischkowitz (1994) explained how an episode of primary desistance might translate into enduring transformation. Drawing on chaos theory, he proposed that a small change in one aspect of an individual's life could engender dramatic change in other areas. He proposed that these events precipitate a process, called the 'conformative spiral', which gradually leads individuals out of crime (Mischkowitz 1994: 325).

By elucidating the changes that occur in criminal thinking, attitudes and lifestyle as offenders begin their journey away from crime, this chapter represents the first step on the journey towards understanding desistance. The analysis identified the factors associated with desistance but could not explore how or why people change. This task will be tackled in the next two chapters, which use in-depth analysis of participants' narrative accounts to gain further insights into participants' pathways through change.

Chapter 5

Multiple roads to desistance

In recent times, the previously neglected phenomenon of desistance has become a field of investigation in its own right. A consistent account of the contours of desistance is taking shape and researchers have begun to develop theories about how the process might occur. It is useful to view desistance as a two-stage process (see Chapter 4). The first consists of any hiatus in criminal activity (primary desistance); the second comprises a more permanent state of non-offending (secondary desistance). As explained previously, secondary desistance emerges over time, as individuals gradually develop a new sense of identity as a non-offender.

These concepts are borrowed, in modified form, from labelling theory, which holds that the social and official reaction to rule-breaking creates, over time, a deviant identity. According to Lemert (1972), primary deviation can be initiated by a variety of physiological, psychological and social factors, acting alone or in concert. Secondary deviance is engendered by a negative social response to the initial deviant behaviour. The response can come from either formal or informal sources and usually consists of stigmatisation, punishment, segregation and social control. The person then augments the deviant activity as a means of adapting to societal disapproval. While primary deviation has minimal impact on the individuals performing the deviant behaviour, the social responses involved in secondary deviation become 'central facts of existence' to them, affecting their psychological structure, social roles and self-concept (Lemert 1972: 63). When studying pathways out of crime, it is essential to take account of the dynamic processes that occur during the transition to desistance, particularly since there may be different processes involved in primary and secondary desistance (see Lemert 1972). The mechanisms behind the advancement from primary to secondary desistance can be described as the 'black box' of reform. Although some have begun to study the changes in the behaviour of offenders as they attempt to go straight, the early stages of change remain under-investigated. What foments in the psyches of offenders as they make the often turbulent transition from criminality to convention is difficult for researchers to access but it is important to shed further light on these processes.

A comprehensive model of the desistance process must accommodate individuals who have not yet begun to change. Yet, desistance and reoffending are generally considered separately in the literature. Barry (2007) notes that 'much of the literature on desistance is set apart from that on offending and ignores the possibility of offending and desistance as two dimensions of a process of change over time and space.' Prochaska et al.'s (1992) trans-theoretical model of recovery from addiction provides some insights into the cognitive processes that might occur during the early stages of desistance and takes account of the potential for relapse. Their research suggested that the early stages of change are characterised by ambivalence as people weigh up the pros and cons of continuing their current pattern of behaviour or changing it. During this time, perceived self-efficacy is low and the risk of relapse is elevated.

The chapter begins with an outline of the prototypical 'desistance' story, which attempts to chart the key features of the journey from crime to desistance. Drawing on participants' reflections on their efforts at reform, it examines the factors and processes involved in the onset and maintenance of change. It focuses in particular on desisters' perceived reasons for giving up crime, the strategies they used to implement change, and the social and psychological effects of desistance. Next, it turns to an analysis of more crooked pathways to desistance. It examines persisters' explanations for continuing to commit crime and their accounts of previous relapse episodes with a view to providing a more complete picture of pathways to desistance.

Becoming 'normal'

Participants' narratives revealed information about the main stages on the pathway through change. Participants who were not involved in crime for at least a month before being interviewed (n = 45) were asked to describe the events and circumstances that had initiated the move away from a criminal lifestyle and the events that followed.

Primary desistance: deciding to desist

For the majority of ex-offenders, the process of reform was initiated with a rational decision to change. Building on the cumulative effect of negative experiences, and often triggered by a final significant event, they were 'jolted' out of their complacency and began to explore alternative lifestyles (Biernacki 1986). The triggers were both positive (for example, getting married) and negative (for example, receiving a lengthy prison sentence). Drawing on the life-course perspective, these are regarded as turning points, which can divert the offender from the present life trajectory. Change was often precipitated by a constellation of chances, opportunities and motivating events, rather than a single episode. Several key elements appeared to fuel the furnace of change: social bonds, deterrence and external intervention.

Participants' decisions took place in a number of key settings, which engendered desistance by either increasing the salience of the event or by providing a space in which to reconsider current life paths. Important settings included prison, the courtroom, and therapeutic or psychiatric institutions. Ben, a 25-year-old man who had three previous convictions but had never served time in prison, describes his reaction to receiving a suspended prison sentence. The experience of attending court and facing the prospect of a prison sentence shocked him into an awareness of what he potentially could have lost.

> I got a shock like – Jesus man, I should be locked up and I'm not. Like I got a fright that much that I laughed about it. I know it's not a laughing matter but I freaked out and laughed. You know, with a car crash and the car was worth that much. All you can do is laugh – gee I'm still alive. Then me aul fella gave me a lecture about me young fella and all … He said more or less, you can either get locked up or you can try and make your life fuckin' half decent, you know. Then you're walking out of there, you're seeing a few people getting locked up and they're mad and all crying, their birds, their kids. It has a fuckin' mental impact on you, you know. Well, it did on me anyway. [KV77]

Social bonds

The most common reason for change, which was cited by 19 participants, related to social bonds with participants' parents, partners and children. Strong social bonds help ex-offenders to break free from their criminal pasts because they offer emotional support, the prospect of new social roles and models of pro-social behaviour (see Laub and Sampson 2001). Only strong attachments elicit these effects. Participants described how having children affected their outlook on life. They adopted a new positive perspective and learned to consider someone other than themselves. They began to think about the future and make long-term plans. A sentiment frequently expressed by reforming offenders was the desire to live up to their family responsibilities. Luke, a 22-year-old with three previous convictions, stated that the process of change began when his son was born. His son's mother later died, and it was his drive to get custody of his son that motivated him to deal with his addiction.

> I was just looking forward to my visits every two weeks. I was fighting a lot of court cases. Coz [girlfriend] passed away shortly afterwards and I had to go to court and a lot of issues around custody and the visits, how often I should get visits. And I was concentrating on that up till a few weeks ago. That, like I never did anything like that before ... I never fought ... most things that I did I'd just put my hands up and say, 'yeah, I did it', to get it out of the way but after that I fought all the way. [KV89]

Becoming a father can have a transformative effect on a man's life. Fatherhood inculcates strong social bonds, work attachments and generative concerns. Eggebeen and Knoester (2001) found that fathers who lived with their children spent less time socialising with their friends and had more contact with their extended families. These men were more attached to their work and were less likely to experience unemployment. They had higher levels of community participation and were often involved in community organisations. It appears therefore that having children can engender changes in a number of life domains known to foster desistance. Parenthood will only engender desistance if the parent believes that it is incompatible with a continued deviant lifestyle. Giordano et al. (2002) found that having children did not automatically lead to desistance but rather created the potential for change, which was not always actualised. For some, the impact of having a child is delayed. Darragh described how he decided to change as his children grew older and became more aware of his criminality:

> I don't know, the face on the poor things when we did get raided, do you know what I mean? And the way they were going on – 'Are you bold, da?' I didn't really know what to say to them – said, 'Yeah, chicken.' 'What did you do?' – 'I broke something.' 'No, you didn't.' You know what I mean. I just wouldn't do it for me kid's sake. [KV83]

Six participants cited parental relationships as their primary reason for change. Typically, these participants felt close to their families and did not want to cause them further suffering by continued offending. They recounted how their criminality had resulted in exclusion from family life. Several were unable to attend important family occasions, such as funerals and weddings, as a result of being in prison. Charlie was shocked into a re-evaluation of his life by the early death of his father while he was in prison. Feelings of guilt and shame assailed him as he stood at his father's graveside and this triggered a decision to seek help for his addiction.

> I see me father in the coffin and I just feel really guilty that I let him down, you know. I was looking at him in the coffin and I was thinking, 'All the fuckin' misery and pain I put him through as well.' And I never got a chance to say, 'Look, I'm sorry.' So I think around that time I made the decision I'm not hurting my family ever again. I'm going to make it up to them. I'm not going to be around for God knows how long, but I want to try and bring a bit of happiness to their lives and make me family proud of me for once in my life. [KV88]

Connor's comments reveal how strong family relationships can facilitate desistance. Although his family remained supportive even when he was involved in drugs and crime, he preferred the relationship he had with them when he was drug free.

> Me ma and da are always ... wouldn't say anything. The support is always there. Even me brother and one of me sisters were always sort of in me ear, telling me, 'Do this, and do that', give me advice and suggestions, you know. [...] When I'm on drugs, I've no relationship with any of me family except for maybe – all we talk about is what I should be doing. Never,

'What did you do yesterday?' Normal like that. When I'm not, my relationship with everyone is good. [KV57]

The importance of strong family relationships for desistance has received some attention in the literature. Indeed, Farrall (2002) concluded that families constituted a critical source of social capital for would-be desisters. Graham and Bowling (1995) proposed that strong family relationships can ease the transition to a crime-free lifestyle among young adults. They found that young offenders who remained in the parental home were more likely to desist. They had better relationships with their parents and spent less time with criminal peers. However, desisters may be better placed than offenders to form positive relationships and gain employment by virtue of their stronger inner resources (see also LeBel et al. 2008). This illustrates the need to view desistance as a psychosocial process.

The costs of crime
The second most frequently cited trigger for change was developing an awareness of the negative consequences associated with a life of crime ($n = 18$). Shover (1996) argued that the weight placed on the costs and benefits of crime, which he termed 'the criminal calculus', shifts as the individual ages. Over time, offenders realise that crime does not pay and that repeated contact with the criminal justice system increases the likelihood of a lengthy prison sentence. 'For the overwhelming majority of street offenders, then, extended involvement in crime brings only penury interspersed with modest criminal gains that are depleted quickly in sprees of partying and repeated imprisonment' (Shover 1996: 139). As a result, conventional options become more salient as offenders lower their expectations about what life can offer them.

Many within this category believed that they faced a stark choice between either desisting or incurring serious negative consequences if they continued to offend. In particular, they were concerned about spending large portions of their lives in prison. They began to fear dying or seriously injuring someone else through crime. They realised that their current life path was 'going nowhere' and they wanted to try an alternative, positive, route. In a similar vein, Shover and Thompson (1992: 91) found that desistance was related to the ageing process. They argued that, as offenders aged, they realised that 'time-until-death' was a 'finite, diminishing resource' and were reluctant to risk spending their remaining time in custody. Similarly, many of the participants in this study had lengthy criminal histories and had spent many years in prison. This, along with the other negative effects of offending, affected their enthusiasm for the criminal lifestyle. Bill was on a 4-year suspended sentence for a violent offence. This extract highlights how his motivation to engage in crime waned over time as he realised the high costs and low rewards involved:

> It means picking up stuff [drugs] and going into nightclubs and selling it and cutting it. If you were to put 25 euro an hour for the time you spent doing that, OK, and the time you spent worrying about people owing you money that aren't turning up and the money that you owe – it's not worth it. [KV23]

In most of these cases, there was no specific 'trigger' for desistance. It may be that an unremarkable event caused the tipping point. This process is reminiscent of Weber's law in the psychology of perception, known as the 'just noticeable difference'. This is the smallest difference in sensory input that is perceivable by a human being. Perhaps a similar process is in operation in the psyches of offenders. Maybe the differences in their lives became perceptible only after they reached a certain magnitude – the differential threshold. Jack had spent a lot of time in prison and had been involved with the criminal justice system since the age of 13. The cumulative effect of the prison sentences he served, combined with the damage to his personal relationships, brought him to a point where criminality 'beat' him and he resolved to change. His decision to change was not prompted by a single episode but by an accumulation of negative experiences.

> It would have been back in custody. I didn't care, didn't want to know anybody. I was fed up, deteriorating each time, getting lower and lower. Death was the only place left for me to go. I was going to die young. I'd settled for it [...] I'd burnt bridges with my family. The prisons, courts, police – none of them could stop me. It was a form of self-mutilation, reaching a point of complete hopelessness, a real low point. [KV38]

Being institutionalised provides a lot of free time to reflect on past actions and values. Given the space to think, offenders began to weigh up the losses incurred by their involvement in crime and their view of prison changed. Tony decided to desist following his release from a lengthy prison sentence. In the extract below, he describes how this experience affected his attitude towards the criminal justice system.

He distinguishes between the shorter prison sentences he served as a young man and his current sentence, which separated him from his family for a long period of time.

> *And what was it that had changed for you?*
> The glorification of prison. When I was younger ... you'd go in for 6 months, come out healthy, big, you know what I mean. You'd have a break from crime, you'd have a break from the pressure of having to go get your money, get your drugs and everything else. It would be great. Me last sentence I done 4 years straight ... . The glory of it just fell with that. That's when I started making changes. [KV2]

Not all offenders needed to serve a prison sentence in order to re-evaluate their choices. The effect of a court appearance may be particularly strong for younger offenders with few previous convictions (see Jamieson, McIvor and Murray 1999). Bill, who was in his early twenties and had just one prior conviction, described how his life was on hold due to the length of time between his arrest and sentence. The charges were subsequently dropped and he just wanted to return to a normal life.

> I spent the whole time since I was charged with that, the actual murder, I spent two years out on bail, not caring, not giving a fuck, you know. That's how I ended up doing all sorts of crazy things ... I was 2 weeks in St Pat's and after I didn't know what to do. I wasn't allowed go on holidays, I wasn't allowed make plans, I wasn't allowed to leave the country. So I didn't make any plans, and I didn't allow myself to make any plans for after the trial date. Coz I didn't know what was going to happen. And eventually the whole thing got past, and I just ... wanted me job back. [KV23]

Burnett (1992) also found that prisoners considered imprisonment an important deterrent to future offending. This was used by Michael Howard, the then British Home Secretary, in support of his 'prison works' campaign. A follow-up study conducted 10 years later showed that over 80 per cent of the sample had in fact reoffended on release (Burnett 2004). For prison to act as a deterrent, offenders must have something to lose. Research has shown the importance of social capital (such as a good job or relationships) for the process of desistance (Laub and Sampson 2001). In this study, the negative consequences of prison ranged from missed opportunities to spend time with family to the loss of freedom.

External intervention

External intervention also played a role in desistance. Four participants claimed that attending a programme, whether therapeutic or educational, constituted the turning point in their offending behaviour. For many of the participants in this category, their relationships with the practitioners were often more influential than the content of the programme. Maruna (2001) contended that when ex-offenders receive assistance from an outside force who believes in them, it empowers them, enabling them to pursue their life goals. Sam was on probation for theft. He initially began an educational programme as a way of making money but soon found his attitudes changing. In addition to the educational qualifications he attained, he comments on the family atmosphere that prevailed between the staff and clients.

> I first came to the project the first thing I remember is how close everyone was. And it reminded me of an extended family. Everyone was great. Don't get me wrong, it took me a while to settle into the structured way in which [programme] is run. But after a while and a lot of encouragement and guidance, I finally felt part of something. [KV25]

Some were required to attend a programme as a condition of their supervision. Others participated in a programme on a voluntary basis. The impact was not always immediate, however, as the following story demonstrates. Gerry was arrested with over €13,700 worth of Ecstasy and had his prison sentence suspended on condition that he attended a treatment programme. (This case is also a good example of the flexible Irish judicial attitude to sentencing, as such an offence should attract a 10-year term.)

> *What made you decide to attend this programme?*
> Well, I didn't really decide to go … my probation officer said you have to go to this place and sort your head out. That's the only reason … I wouldn't even have thought of going to the place, you know what I mean. Coz like I was offending so much and I was doing this and doing that, the probation said you better go here … the judges want you to do this programme or you're getting locked up, you know the way. [KV9]

He openly admitted to attending the programme mainly to avoid a prison sentence, yet his perspective changed as the programme progressed. He graduated successfully and went on to do an apprenticeship.

> At the start, I thought I'd go to keep me out of prison. After going in every day, I got to like it. I got to meet new friends and that, so it was grand ... by the time I finished it, I was delighted about it.

Some have suggested that different desistance factors become salient at different stages of the life course (see Jamieson *et al.* 1999). To examine this, statistical analyses were performed with age, age at onset and previous convictions in order to explore whether these factors impacted on the reasons given for desistance. Although the numbers involved are small and the results must therefore be interpreted with caution, some interesting patterns emerged. 'Social bonds' explanations appeared to be favoured by desisters with more entrenched offending behaviour. These explanations were cited more often by participants who had more previous convictions ($F = 2.95$, $p = .06$), were older at the time of the interview ($F = 3.162$, $p = .05$), and started offending earlier in life ($F = 2.57$, $p = .09$. In contrast, 'costs of crime' explanations were more common among less criminalised participants. They tended to be younger, had fewer previous convictions and had begun their criminal careers later in life.

Secondary desistance: exploring new horizons

In the previous section, the important role that strong social bonds can play in the onset of desistance was highlighted. The influence of strong personal ties was similarly evident in participants' accounts of long-term change. McNeill (2006) argued that strong social networks link putative desisters to a wider range of resources and opportunities, enabling them to build and sustain a crime-free life. As they desisted, participants developed stronger social bonds within their local networks and also began to branch out to wider networks through work, recreation and help-seeking activities.

Strengthening relationships

Initial involvement in crime and drug use was exciting and seemed liberating, insofar as it provided a welcome escape from the drudgery of lives that were often characterised by social marginalisation, poverty and boredom. The participants' stories of their early involvement in crime reflected a desire to be different. They portrayed an image of themselves as the archetypal outsiders, searching for quick thrills and rejecting society's norms (see Wilson 1956; Becker 1963). This was followed by a downward spiral into addiction, crime and negativity. Following the decision to change, their values came full circle, and their stories of reform were permeated by a desire to lead a 'normal' life. As Calum explained:

> Like I'm no different from anyone else, sometimes I get hurt, sometimes I get mad, sometimes I get sad and there's so many other people like that out there. And to be able to say to myself – I'm normal. I remember, as a young child, always getting into trouble with the police, and my mother said, 'Why can't you be normal?' and having said that repeatedly, eventually I would have believed it. [KV92]

Desisters began to adopt new conventional social roles centred on work and family life. Maruna and Farrall (2004) suggested that secondary desistance takes place once new conventional roles are adopted and internalised. Neil described how being employed affected his lifestyle. Instead of staying out partying all night, he wanted to lead a 'normal' life with his family.

> I just don't want the hassle of it. I just want to be left alone, have a bit of peace and quiet, live a normal life. I want to have a family, I just want to work, like I do want to work, that's how I know I've changed coz I get up at 6.30 in the morning. I used to only go to bed at 8 o'clock in the morning. [KV28]

Participants' social bonds, both immediate and distant, underwent extensive changes during this phase of desistance. In particular, participants described improvements in the quality of their relationships with the important people in their immediate social circles. Conventional social bonds can encourage desistance both by providing structure to ex-offenders' lives and by acting as sources of informal monitoring and emotional support (Laub and Sampson 2003). Participants recounted how they were earning higher levels of trust from family, friends, partners and children. In return, they began to trust people and were learning to open up and engage in their relationships. Gerry experienced difficulties with anger management and, in the following extract, described the changes that occurred in his relationships once he had this problem in hand:

The biggest change would be getting on with my ma and all, getting on with my girlfriend. [...] I don't snap as much anymore, I don't really snap at all. Yeah, I'm having great relationships now with my friends, my girlfriend, me ma without giving out to everybody, you know that way, as if there was a block on my shoulder. [KV9]

Cian described how he gained confidence in his interactions with non-criminal others. He was spending more time in the company of people who were not involved in crime and was beginning to feel comfortable in this new milieu:

Associating with people that are not involved in crime. That's the biggest change – and how I speak to them and deal with them. Very confident like, there's comfort there, here I am like. I've no problem talking to anyone, I'm assertive like. Very clear on what I want. [KV56]

Participants also cited improvements in relations with the wider community. This has particular resonance in the Irish context. During the 1980s and 1990s, as heroin addiction decimated working-class neighbourhoods in Dublin, community activists began an anti-drugs campaign, which involved direct confrontation with local drug dealers (see Lyder 2005). One outcome of this campaign was the stigmatisation of drug dealing and criminality. Many participants in this study described how they had been ostracised in their communities as a result of their criminal activity. As they showed signs of desisting, they began to gain acceptance and to receive recognition for the changes they had made. Nathan, who had a history of chronic heroin addiction, described the impact of receiving support and recognition from people in his community. His comments highlight the important role that communities can play in reintegration.

Things are starting to look a lot better for me now than they were before I went into prison. Before I went into prison, there were an awful lot of people in the area that hated me and what I was doing. Since I got out, I'm trying to make a change in myself and, more or less, they're giving me the benefit of the doubt. I didn't even think that was possible. [KV60]

The process described here calls to mind Braithewaite's (1989) work on reintegrative shaming, which emphasises how community disapproval of a behaviour must be accompanied by attempts to restore the individual to the community, if it is to encourage desistance. Maruna, LeBel, Mitchell and Naples (2004) suggested that social recognition of a desistance attempt may encourage secondary desistance through a de-labelling process in which putative desisters play an active role. They proposed that ex-offenders must feel that their reintegration is earned by their own efforts.

The process of change was not always easy. Participants frequently referred to the difficulties associated with trying to desist while living in communities which were rife with drugs and crime. Some, like Seán, tried to avoid particular people or places so that they would not encounter opportunities to offend.

> It's even, a good bit where I live and all. Over at the bus stop and around by the chapel is where they all stand to sell the heroin, you know, so. If I go out or anything, I always have to … well, I don't have to, but for my own safety, I walk up to the bus stop up the road just to avoid them […]. So they're not asking me, do I want it? Coz I know if someone says, 'Do you want it?', me head will think about it, you know. [KV76]

The process of 'knifing off' often required the dissolution of ties with partners, friends and acquaintances who were still involved in crime. This was more difficult for those who had built up close bonds with their criminal associates. As a result, many reduced the time they spent with friends rather than cutting ties completely. Ben decided to stop offending after narrowly avoiding a prison sentence for a drugs offence. Although he continued to see his old friends, he made it clear to them that he no longer wanted to be involved in criminal activities.

> I severed all the terms with all the boys. They weren't happy but it had to be done. [KV77]

Only three desisters failed to identify any positive changes that occurred after desistance. Interestingly, one of these described how he missed the respect and status he used to have in his area as a result of his criminality. This suggests that, desistance may be more difficult in neighbourhoods that condone criminality.

Developing new social networks

Desisters also began to extend their reach beyond their immediate social networks, by taking up new employment and recreational opportunities. Several participants described how desistance and becoming drug-free broadened their horizons and opened up new opportunities to engage in conventional activities. They began to participate in wider, and more conventional, social networks. Having employment was important, as many felt that they were now capable of earning enough money through legitimate employment and no longer needed to offend. The then flourishing Irish economy may have contributed to this, as research suggests a link between increased prosperity and reduction in property crime (see O'Donnell and O'Sullivan 2001). The transition to new roles was not always smooth. For some, this lifestyle change required a significant adjustment in their attitudes towards money. Gerry described the difficulties he experienced adjusting to his new non-criminal way of life and a lower standard of living. He had to learn to subsist on a vastly reduced income and was beginning to adapt to his new circumstances.

> When I was selling drugs, I wasn't even working, I wasn't even on the Labour and I was making a fucking mint. It took me a while to get used to what I'm getting now. Like I used to go out on a Friday night and I'd spend what I get in a week … like €125 […]. It was really hard. I had to limit myself to going out one night a week. Now, like I've no money and my head's wrecked. [KV9]

Others began to engage in recreational activities, often for the first time. Luke's account shows how he was finding positive ways to enjoy life that did not involve substance use.

> I've done things that I never was into … . I've been to a couple of matches … I'd never been to a match before – didn't know what a football field looks like! Boat trips … done loads of activities, played football … . Just all the variety of things you can do when you're off drink and drugs, when your head is sorted out. [KV89]

The transition to secondary deviance may be influenced by the availability of relevant social roles, the resources available, and the person's motivation to adopt them (Lemert 1972). McNeill and Whyte (2007: 183) note that 'without access to social capital, it may be very difficult indeed to embark upon and sustain a pathway towards desistance.' As shown in Chapter 3, few participants had managed to find employment in spite of the booming economy and, as a result, many had to lower their expectations about what life could offer in order to sustain desistance.

Better emotional well-being

As these strategies were put in place, and showed signs of success, there were corresponding changes in the way offenders viewed themselves and their worlds. Social changes were often accompanied by improvements in the cognitive, emotional and physical domains. Positive emotions have been linked to desistance (see Giordano *et al.* 2007). Participants described feeling more confident, calmer and happier than they had been when they were involved in crime. Ben described the peace of mind he experienced as a result of desistance, as he no longer had to worry about the police or managing his drug trade.

> I'm glad to be away from it you know. Me life is not complicated. I wake up every morning … or I go to bed every night and wake up every morning with no problem. Coz there'd be times, there'd be a million things through me head and I'd wake up and there'd be a million more things going through me head. Overload like a computer but now there's no worries at all. The only worry I have to do is make sure I do a good job at me work in the morning. [KV77]

During this phase, desisters began to distance themselves from their criminal identities. Maruna (2001) found that ex-offenders often attributed responsibility for their criminal pasts to events outside their control in order to preserve a positive self-image. Dylan, who was desisting, rejected the image of himself as an offender, claiming 'that wasn't me in the first place'.

> Well, it didn't happen overnight. It was a graduation of things. Like I got sick of being on drugs, sick of listening to people on about crime. That wasn't me in the first place – I just done it because I wanted drugs. [KV17]

Finally, participants cited improvements to their physical health. Once they had stopped using drugs, they ceased to experience the symptoms associated with drug withdrawal. They began to feel healthier and to look after their physical appearance, as explained by Aidan.

> I sleep at night now and I don't wake up in bits in the morning, you know. And I feel healthy and I'm after putting on loads of weight. I'm after putting on about 4 or 5 stone. I was like a little boy African! I'm still slim but I was really bad. I was skin and bones, yeah. Like a lot has changed for the good, for the better. [KV12]

Curved pathways

It is important to recognise that desistance can take a considerable amount of time to attain (see Prochaska *et al.* 1992). Existing research suggests that the journey to desistance is rarely straightforward and desistance often follows a zigzag rather than a linear pathway (see Glaser 1964). Not all will progress beyond primary desistance and some will revert to a life of crime. According to Lemert (1972), some may remain in a transitory condition and continue to drift between conformity and deviance. Whether desistance is successful will depend on the 'reasoning and resources' of the individual (Pawson and Tilley 1997). A significant number of putative desisters are likely still to be engaged in some forms of offending. Leibrich (1993) introduced the concept of a 'curved' pathway to account for the members of her sample who had ceased serious involvement in crime but continued to commit more minor offences.

This section outlines the curved pathways taken by participants along the route to desistance. It is interesting to analyse cases where desistance is not straightforward, as this provides additional insights into the aetiology of the change process. Twenty-eight participants, all of whom were still involved in crime at some level, could be described as being in the crucible of change. Eighteen of these were still involved in serious or persistent criminality at the time of the interview. In addition to committing less serious crimes such as theft and handling stolen goods, this group committed more serious offences. The most common were dangerous driving ($n = 7$), selling drugs ($n = 6$), fraud/forgery ($n = 5$) and threatening someone with a weapon ($n = 4$). The remaining 10 continued to engage in petty crime but described themselves as desisters. Of these, seven had handled stolen goods (for example, bought counterfeit DVDs) and four had shoplifted.

Nine participants described themselves as desisting, despite having committed several crimes in the past month. This category illustrates what Leibrich (1993) termed the 'curved' pathway of change. She recognised desistance as a dynamic process where offenders are 'going' straight as opposed to having 'gone' straight. Participants viewed desistance as a long-term process of change and considered relapse as an inevitable part. Vincent said he had first begun to change over 5 years ago, mainly because he was sick of the criminal lifestyle. He attributed his recent offences to a drug relapse but regarded himself as a desister:

> Everything doesn't work out the first time. I've bad communication skills. It took me a long time to get here. I don't trust people. It's easy to come off drugs. It's staying off that's hard. The offences I committed was because of the relapse. I needed money. I haven't committed any serious crime in years. [KV62]

Others struggled to see offences like buying stolen goods as 'real' crime, particularly when contrasted with their previous criminal activity. Also, such practices are normal in the working-class communities where these offenders live, where there are usually thriving markets in stolen goods such as tobacco, electronic equipment and clothing. Harry, who was sentenced to probation for armed robbery, discussed his current views about buying stolen goods. He struggled to reconcile his thoughts about buying stolen DVDs with his perception of himself as a desister.

> I never see it as a crime. I rationalise and justify it. Even looking at buying a DVD. That DVD is a counterfeit DVD I'm buying. But I'll be honest and say I think I'll still buy DVDs. I know counterfeit costs the state but that DVD would cost me 50 euros to buy in the shop. [KV66]

The finding that a significant number of people who continue to commit crime are contemplating desistance highlights the continuous nature of the desistance process and the importance of conceptualising crime and desistance as two aspects of a ongoing change process (see also Barry 2007).

No alternatives

The majority of participants attributed their ongoing offending to external circumstances, which they believed constrained their ability to lead a crime-free life. They appeared to lack a sense of personal agency and a belief that they could overcome difficult life circumstances. In particular, they felt trapped by financial problems and addiction, which they believed reduced their alternatives to crime. This belief is characteristic of the narratives of persistent offenders (see Maruna 2001). Six described how they engaged in crime (usually acquisitive) in order to fund their everyday lifestyles. Many found it difficult to manage financially on legitimate sources of income. In such circumstances, the financial rewards associated with crime remain salient. Cillian, who was in prison, believed that he could not survive financially on social welfare and that finding a good job was not a realistic prospect. He planned to return to selling drugs on his release.

> I'm definitely going to go back selling drugs. Like when I get out, like, me friends and all, sell heroin and all, what they'll do is ... they'll all put a bit in a bag for me. It will add up to a couple of hundred pounds. I'd make it into deals, you know. Go out and sell them and that would be all my money then. You put 250 euro off side for your next bit and the rest of your money is yours like. To get you clothes and all. Coz you can't depend on the welfare and all. They only give you 180 pounds or something for clothes. That won't even get you a pair of shoes. [KV65]

In Ireland, approximately one-fifth of the population is estimated to be at risk of poverty (see Whelan *et al.* 2007). Proponents of strain theory (e.g. Merton 1938) argue that criminality occurs as a result of the anomie experienced when goals cannot be achieved through legitimate means. In societies where there is a greater gap between rich and poor, as in Ireland, anomie is enhanced and the risk of crime is higher. In these situations, it may not be the fact of poverty that causes difficulties for people trying to desist but rather their perception that their circumstances preclude any means other than crime to achieve their goals.

Drugs as a trigger were present behind four of the stories. Even where money was identified as the primary concern, it was often required to buy drugs. Although the link between drugs and crime is well established, the nature of the link is still under debate. In this study, the majority of participants began to engage in the use of soft drugs (for example, hash) in early adolescence around the same time as they began to commit petty crime. As they progressed to the use of hard drugs, their criminal activity became more serious and became motivated by a need to fund their growing drug habits. According to the participants, it is difficult, if not impossible, to lead a normal life with an expensive heroin habit. While some initially tried to fund their habit through employment, the costs often spiralled beyond their means and they turned to crime. As Pat explained:

> I still use heroin about once a week so I haven't given it up fully. I enjoy the buzz I get from it. It's hard to give that up. Drugs are the main reason I'm still committing crime. When I give them up, there'll be no need for it. I see other addicts going around in bits and I remember I used to be like that. I don't want to go down that road again. [KV18]

Problematic drug use has been identified as a strong correlate of offending (e.g. May 1999), but the exact nature of this link is unclear. Participants were asked to report whether they had used illegal substances in the past month. Over half (n = 39) stated that they had. Of these, 22 reported that they were continuing to use illegal substances, but that they were not involved in criminal activity. These were counted as desisters in the study but are included here to illustrate the non-linearity of the change process. Table 5.1 shows the main drugs used by these non-offenders. As some participants reported using more than one substance, the totals add up to more than 22.

The most commonly used drug was cannabis, although a significant proportion were using harder drugs, such as heroin and cocaine. While some continued to use heroin at a reduced level, others experienced an occasional lapse into heavy drug use during their

Table 5.1 Drug use in the past month

Cannabis	18
Heroin	7
Cocaine	6
Benzodiazepines	2
Ecstasy	2

supervision order. Keith, who was trying to overcome his addiction to heroin, sometimes relapsed but believed that he was working towards desistance.

> Sometimes I relapse on the drugs the odd time but have the probation here looking at that as well. I have the courts looking at it, my solicitor looking at it, Pearse St. [drug treatment clinic] looking at it. I'm getting help, I have a counsellor as well. I see him on a Saturday and I see [probation officer] here twice a week. [KV46]

If people perceive significant obstacles to change, this may reduce their motivation and render them more vulnerable to temptations to offend. Six participants described situations which gave the impression that they struggled on an ongoing basis with the temptation to commit crime. Lee described how he sometimes acted automatically without thinking, and his account illustrates the tension between shedding the old life and embracing the new.

> It is hard work staying away from it and it won't go away. It's a constant thing, it will always be there but I mean for the impulse. There he's not looking [mimes taking money off the table]. It's not like I come in here to rob the place but 'What can I do with that, I can buy a packet of nappies. 20 bottles of Bud, 20 smokes' ... but literally you have the little devil here saying, 'Ooh' and this little voice here saying, 'Don't, don't, don't, you don't want to get locked up, you don't want to get locked up.' And that's what it is with me so it's always there. But lately, it's not that I haven't been taking any heed of it, I just haven't been doing it. Saying it's there, so what. [KV73]

Owen explained how his continued offending was due to his ongoing association with people who were still involved in crime. The following extract illustrates how a lack of self-control creates a risk that reoffending will occur.

> It's always there in the background. Boredom is a problem for me. I still meet the same friends, live in the same area. [KV31]

Drawing on Kennett (2001), Bottoms (2006) introduced the concepts of synchronic and diachronic self-control to the study of desistance. Synchronic self-control is that which is exercised by individuals at the time of temptation to dissuade them from acting on it. In the case of diachronic self-control, the individual takes evasive action to avoid the temptation (for example, terminating contact with friends who are still involved in crime in order to avoid encountering opportunities to offend). Both of these forms are illustrated by the examples provided above. Self-control is most commonly conceptualised as a personality trait (see Gottfredson and Hirschi 1990). Wikstrom (2006) argued that it is better viewed as a situational factor rather than a personality trait. He pointed out that people only need to exercise self-control in situations where the temptations conflict with internal moral rules.

Going round in circles

Relapse is considered a highly probable initial outcome for individuals who attempt to change their behaviour. Relapse can occur at any stage but individuals are particularly vulnerable during the early stages of change (see Prochaska et al. 1992). In fact, research suggests that even prolific offenders have a low frequency of offending and regularly experience periods of temporary desistance (Piquero 2004). Participants' police records showed significant conviction-free periods in their criminal histories. The average gap was 36.8 months (SD = 27.7) with a range of 2 to 134 months (median = 32; mode = 16). It was not possible to control for exposure time in this study so it is not clear how much of the apparent crime free gaps were due to time spent in custody. Nevertheless, over a third of participants (n = 26) spoke about previous attempts to desist that had subsequently resulted in relapse. Many claimed to have maintained their crime-free status for significant periods of time before returning to crime. Participants' explanations of failed desistance attempts centred on internal factors, namely, low motivation and poor coping skills.

Lack of commitment to change was behind many relapse stories (n = 13). Within this group, some had not made a decision to change but stopped and started offending as and when they needed to (for example, when they had committed a crime that resulted in a big pay-out). Others tried to stop but knew all along that they were not really ready to change. They often initiated their change attempt because family or friends put pressure on them. Colin, a 26-year-old, described how he previously entered a detox programme but admitted that he had no real commitment to change at that time. He resorted to justifications and excuses to sabotage his efforts at reform.

Was it [drug use] something you did constantly during that time, or did you ever try to stop?
Yeah, I did actually. Treatment programmes – it was only like detoxes, like the first few weeks they would work, when they're giving you 40 ml of methadone but then they start cutting you down. It was helping you but you're thinking in your head, 'This is stupid – it's not working, I'm only on so much, blah, blah, blah', and you're going off robbing again when you don't need to, you're only … going round in a circle and you're ending up back here, going round and round, yeah. [KV14]

Following receipt of a suspended sentence, Cormac found a way to pursue his enjoyment of joyriding without stealing cars. He modified rather than changed his criminal lifestyle, and that suggests a lack of commitment. When he was arrested for a road traffic offence, he mistakenly thought this would automatically activate his prison sentence. He immediately returned to his old ways, finally receiving a new charge. He was interviewed in prison.

I wasn't really robbing before I got this sentence anyway. I used to buy Travellers' cars. I kept getting pulled by the guards – I got loads of summonses. I knew my 3-year sentence would be reactivated if I got a new charge so I thought I was going back to prison anyway. I had all these summonses and I thought I would do as much as I could before I got sent back to prison. I got sick of buying cars coz I had no money, so I robbed one. I got these new charges then. [KV75]

Several accounts (*n* = 13) suggested that participants were unable to sustain their desistance attempt because of an inability to cope. In these cases, participants described how they had tried to change but their efforts were incomplete. For example, Dylan stopped offending and managed to find a job but continued to use heroin. He lost his job as a result of his drug problem and returned to crime to fund his habit. He was trying to desist again at the time of the interview. As he explained:

I did try, yeah … I got a job. I didn't like it – whatever money I had I spent in on getting drugs. I tried to go straight – I just couldn't coz of the drug problem. I tried to deal with it myself but it just didn't work out, you know. [KV17]

A number of participants explained how a previous desistance attempt failed because of a change in circumstances, usually in a negative direction and not always of their choosing. These changes included failed relationships, the loss of a job or a move to a new area. Five of them described finding it difficult to maintain desistance in areas with a high prevalence of crime and drugs. Nathan travelled to England to escape this influence and managed to come off heroin but relapsed on his return. He subsequently stopped offending again.

> And then I went over to England and I got off it then, say, 18, 19, I got off it in England for about 2 years. Then I came home and I started again then. Getting away from the area. Then I got away from it again then and then I got back into it again. And when I got back into it again, I got into it too badly. [KV60]

This explanation resembles a category of 'temporary desisters' identified by West (1963, cited in Bottoms *et al.* 2004). He found that crime-free gaps among some offenders tended to occur during sheltered periods in their lives (for example, when they were in a relationship). Zamble and Quinsey (1997) implicated coping skills as a primary precipitator of failure in their theory of recidivism. Poor coping skills reduce the likelihood that a person can deal successfully with high-risk situations.

Overall, it was difficult to isolate a key event or thought pattern that explains why desistance did or did not occur. For many, desistance was prompted by the cumulative effect of a series of life experiences, rather than a single critical event. The correlates of both desistance and recidivism often overlapped. For example, some participants claimed that contact with the criminal justice system induced change. For others, however, it engendered reoffending, as in Bill's case, which was described earlier. Bill was originally charged with murder, aged 18. There was a delay of 2 years between the initial charge and his court appearance. He spent this time on bail. He expected to incur a lengthy prison sentence and continued to offend. The charge was subsequently reduced to violent disorder and he was sentenced to probation.

This illustrates the subjectivity of the reform process and raises a number of questions. Are any of these triggers really unique to desisters? If not, why does this group see them as catalysts for change while others regard the same factors as reasons to keep offending? It may be that it is the offender's interpretation of the event rather than the event itself that is important. A seemingly negative experience, such as serving a long prison sentence, may also be given a positive interpretation (for example, an opportunity to gain an education). Such events do not effect change but rather, constitute windows of opportunity, which have the potential to develop into desistance. This accords with the analysis reported in Chapter 4, which suggested that psychological processes operate at the forefront of change while the social context provides a framework that supports or constrains desistance. The process of desistance is complex, subjective and contingent on the particular experiences, interpretations and abilities of offenders.

Examination of participants' desistance narratives revealed several important themes. In particular, strong social capital appears to play a significant role in successful long-term change. Close relationships with family, partners and children often prompted participants to try to transform their lives and, as desistance became established, these relationships continued to strengthen. Over time, they started to build bridges to wider social networks, as they began to enter the workforce and engage in conventional recreational activities, often for the first time. Their efforts to change earned recognition and forgiveness from their local communities, which further enhanced their desistance experience. These positive developments no doubt contributed to the perceived improvements in their physical and psychological well-being.

In contrast, the review of participants' reasons for relapse and continued offending suggested that they lacked a sense of personal agency. They implicated poor self-control, difficulty coping with problems, feeling trapped by addiction and a perceived lack of alternatives to crime, in their rationales for reoffending. Perhaps these factors thwart their efforts to change. Failure to recognise alternatives to crime may impact on feelings of hope for the future and commitment to desistance. Perceived lack of control may make it more difficult to initiate change. Poor coping skills may decrease their ability to deal with life's obstacles when they arise. The next chapter will examine these themes in more detail through an in-depth exploration of participants' self-narratives.

Chapter 6

Into the crucible

The liminal period is characterised by introspection, ambiguity and withdrawal but it is also a time when personal transformation and growth can occur (see Turner 1970). During this time, individuals must come to terms with their criminal pasts, overcome obstacles and forge new futures. Researchers have begun to recognise the value in studying ex-offenders' accounts of the desistance process but little is known about the narrative identities of individuals who exist in the liminal space 'betwixt and between' crime and convention. This chapter delves more deeply into participants' narratives in order to explore how they integrate their past, present and future selves into a coherent account. It examines their efforts to come to terms with their past selves and to construct plausible future identities, and explores how this process is influenced by the opportunities and obstacles encountered in the present (see Evans 2002).

In doing so, it attempts to describe the lived experiences of individuals on the cusp of change and elucidate their subjective understandings of their life world as revealed by their narratives (see Kvale 1996). Self-narratives have been described as the fundamental scheme that humans use to imbue their experience of the world with meaning. As McAdams (1993: 30) observed, the 'human experience is storied.' Personal narratives serve several purposes (see Murray 2003). They are not simply records of the individual's experience but aim to impose order and meaning on a complex and ever-changing world. The human imagination is mythopoeic, and people actively create personal myths about themselves in order to integrate their otherwise segmented experiences into a meaningful, coherent and purposive account. The fluid nature of the narrative identity means a life story can be modified to incorporate new experiences and information. Different meanings may be assigned to a single life event at different times in a person's life. In narrative psychology, it is the meaning the individual attributes to an event rather than the experience of the event that is most important. As Jung (1963: 18) observed when reminiscing about his life:

> Recollection of the outward events of my life has largely faded or disappeared. But ... my bouts with the unconscious are indelibly engraved on my memory. In that realm, there has always been wealth in abundance, and everything else has lost importance by comparison.

Clear differences emerged between the narratives of participants who were desisting and those who remained involved in crime. Desisters attempted to gain something positive from their criminal pasts, while offenders tried to reject theirs. Both groups had clear ideas about who they would like to become, but offenders were less confident that they could realise their new, non-criminal, identities. Although both groups expected to face significant obstacles to change, desisters were more confident that they could overcome them and were more willing to draw on their social networks to support their efforts at change. Both groups expressed a desire to desist, but desisters were more committed to change than offenders, who remained uncertain and ambivalent. Overall, desisters were using a proactive and agentic approach in their lives. An agentic approach may assist individuals in successfully making the transition to adulthood. It enables 'individuals to explore their potentials, build personal strengths, and sustain some sense of direction and meaning' (see Côté 1997: 577–578). Individuals who adopt an agentic approach are more likely to form a coherent sense of identity and successfully achieve their life goals. They are better equipped to take advantage of life's opportunities and to negotiate any obstacles they encounter (Schwartz, Côté and Arnett 2005). In contrast, individuals whose lives are dictated by circumstance and impulse rather than agency have greater difficulty in creating a coherent adult identity (Côté 1997).

Shame, redemption and the past

The first, and possibly the most difficult, component of the narrative identity relates to the past. As Kafka put it: 'Nothing has come easily to me, not just the present and the future but even the past, that thing that each man receives as his birthright: even that I have to conquer and perhaps that is the hardest task.' In order to maintain a coherent self-narrative, ex-offenders must find ways to accommodate their past criminal selves. They can achieve this either by repudiating their past or by integrating it into their new identity.

In this study, the majority of participants (n = 32; 43 per cent) adopted passive 'rejection' narratives. Their scripts emphasised feelings of shame and disappointment and were characterised by a desire to reject their criminal selves. About a third (n = 23) adopted active 'integration' narratives. Focusing on the positive outcomes that emerged from their past behaviour enabled them to retain a positive self-image. The final category, comprising just 16 per cent of the sample, employed 'stable' narratives. They viewed their criminality as a 'normal' part of growing up, and did not appear to be cognitively restructuring their pasts. This group came closest to casting their criminality in a positive light. Overall, desisters were more likely than offenders to employ an integration narrative, although these differences were not statistically significant. A higher proportion of secondary desisters' scripts were classed as integrative (42 per cent compared to 31 per cent of offenders). The differences were more striking for primary desisters. Forty per cent of primary desisters' accounts were classified as integrative compared to just 26 per cent of offenders.

Rejection narratives: dismissing the past

Participants in this category tended to reject their pasts. They frequently expressed feelings of shame, remorse, anger and disappointment when discussing their past. They regarded it as a dark period in their lives, during which time they caused a lot of suffering to others that could not be repaired. They saw their lives to date as a waste with only negatives to show. Failure to find meaning can increase the feelings of distress incurred by a traumatic event (Frankl 1984; Davis, Nolan-Hoeksema and Larson 1998). These thoughts, illustrated in the following quotes, permeated the scripts of some participants.

> Total regret, not character-building or anything like that. Not putting it down, 'Ah, it's experience.' It's nothing like that. Nothing to be proud of. [KV35]

That's one part of my life I'm not proud of, I've never been proud of being on drugs, robbing. I've never been proud of it, I've always hated it. [KV60]

Some have suggested that shame is linked to desistance (see Leibrich 1993) but there is also evidence to suggest that it may increase the risk of recidivism (e.g. Hosser, Windzio and Greve 2008). Braithewaite's (1989) work provides insight into the mechanisms through which shame might operate to bring about desistance or recidivism. He proposed that, in societies with strong social bonds, shaming can deter people from committing crime. Shaming practices establish a clear set of moral rules for individuals to follow, and people conform to avoid the loss of social approval. If shaming practices are not accompanied by efforts to reintegrate the offender into the community, shame can become stigmatising. Criminality may increase as the individual is drawn deeper into criminal subcultures and further from conventional society. This finds support in a recent longitudinal study, which found that regret for past involvement in crime increased the likelihood of desistance while feelings of stigma reduced it (LeBel et al. 2008). In the same study, however, feelings of shame about past behaviour had no impact on long-term outcomes.

Many within this category dwelt on their wasted talents and missed opportunities that they believed could never be reclaimed. They often contrasted their lives with the lives of friends or neighbours who had taken alternative conventional routes, and described clear visions of who they might have become had they not taken the criminal path. Among the lost possible selves were a footballer, a soldier, an entrepreneur, a worker and a family man. In recounting his thoughts about his past, Connor reflected on what he had lost.

A lot of people told me that I could have made it as a professional soccer player. I could have played for Dublin as well. Me next door neighbour got a shot of playing for Dublin minors a few years ago and I was way better than him. So if he done it, I could have done it. Yeah, I could have done great things. [KV57]

Max explained the personal damage that can be inflicted by drug addiction. He felt that the changes to his personality were permanent and could not be reversed or repaired.

I'm not very proud of it. I always wish I never went on drugs. I was always a very hyper young fella. I was always cracking jokes. I was always the clown of the class, you know what I mean. Like I think I had a good personality, but that's all gone. You can lose your personality when you're on drugs, you lose your friends, you lose your family, you don't care about anybody only but yourself. [KV81]

Their accounts conveyed a sense of fatalism about their pasts and they repeatedly stressed that they had no choice but to commit crime. Being unable to revision their pasts in a positive light, they repeatedly referred to a desire to turn back the clock and start their lives again. This possibly served as a strategy to help them to cope with their feelings of regret about lost life chances. Scott, who was in his early twenties, was adamant that, if given a second chance, he would not make the same mistake twice:

If I could change it, I would. I'd change it back to when I was a baby. I'd start all over again. ... I'd change ... not going on drugs. I'd change ... I'd have a job. I'd probably still have me daughter with me girlfriend. Coz she's not into drugs or anything. I'm with her since I'm 16. So that would be still there. So it would just be that I'd be working and I wouldn't be near drugs. I know I wouldn't. [KV53]

It is possible that a sense of fatalism arises among chronic offenders who face significant obstacles to reintegration. This is illustrated in Alex's narrative. On his release from prison, he was provided with social welfare assistance, and, believing that a decent job was beyond his reach because of his criminal history and health problems, he felt it was not worth seeking employment.

When I got out of prison I got rent allowance you know, for flats and that. Then I was getting a job and I was told you'll lose your rent allowance and again, you pay tax and all – start with an awful lot less than I would when I was collecting me Labour [social welfare payment] and me rent allowance – so why should I work? Then if I do go to work, that means I have to pay for me medications as well, for me phy [physeptone – heroin substitute] and me tablets, that would probably leave me with about 60 euro for meself ... You're trapped. And what's the hope of getting a much better job than that now. [KV54]

Integration narratives: the search for meaning

Although participants in this category also expressed regret about the negative consequences of their criminal pasts, they believed that they had gained valuable wisdom as a result of their experiences. They felt they had learnt from their mistakes and were proud of who they had become. Lee, a man with seven previous convictions, explains how his past mistakes made him the person he is today.

> Well, it's stood me ... coz I'm the type of person I am now because of me experiences, you know what I mean. I've never led a sheltered life, so I've experienced more things, I'm 24 this year, I've experienced more things in my 24 years than people at 50 could say. [KV73]

On an interpersonal level, participants described how they had increased their ability to demonstrate empathy and compassion. Ken, who was desisting, described how he acquired a non-judgemental attitude towards others as a result of his own experiences with addiction. There are also elements of generativity in his account.

> Well, I don't regret it. It was an experience, do you know what I mean. Like if I have kids now, at least I'll be able to tell them coz I went through it, do you understand. It's just like ... you can't help it. It was just the way it turned out so I wouldn't be quick to judge others. Some people wouldn't know anything about that. I'd have more of an understanding coz I've done it. I understand about addictions and all now. You know the way some people walk down and see somebody stoned out of their head. They'd automatically walk across to the other side of the road. So I know the score, yeah. [KV74]

Their relationships with the people closest to them also improved. Sam had attempted to go straight in the past but later relapsed on drugs. He explained how he now understood the impact his behaviour had on those close to him.

> I didn't think what effect it was having on my ma, police kicking in her door. And I used to just think, 'Ah, will you snap out of it. Stop crying.' But really it was hurting her and now I can see this. [KV25]

They also gained a new appreciation for life as they realised how lucky they had been to escape the negative fates that befell friends and associates who had died, been imprisoned, suffered addiction, or been forced to emigrate to avoid police capture. Ben confessed his relief at managing to avoid serious consequences of crime.

> In a way I'm laughing, well, I got away with it and I still have all my money! So some of me friends weren't as fortunate, you know. That's the way it goes like. You're either lucky or you're not. Well, when it comes down to the crunch, I was lucky, you know. A few of the others weren't, a few of the others had to leg it with their birds [girlfriends]. Well, that didn't matter, anything to get out of this bleedin' horrible country, but the ones who are caught now and locked up, I'm sure they're not bleedin' smiling! [KV77]

They began to view the criminal lifestyle in a more negative way and often characterised their offending as childish and immature – the folly of youth. In some cases, they felt they had changed so much that their past no longer had any relevance in their present. Gerry was on probation for possession with intent to supply. He described the thoughts that occurred to him as he drove past a prison where he had previously been incarcerated. He felt little empathy with the person he was then.

> I was just remembering back the way I was and that but I definitely wouldn't think about doing it again. It would just come back on me, thinking about ... saying, 'You bleedin' eejit, you were off your head.' [KV9]

Looking back over his life, Brendan, a 34-year-old man who was released after serving a 9-year prison sentence for robbery, explained that crime was not worth the price he paid.

> The prison time, it wasn't worth it. Like I lost an awful lot of time with me son. That's mostly what really hurts me, you know. [KV39]

He realised that his son was becoming increasingly upset by his constant absences. As a result, he made significant changes to his life. In his view, the most important of these was spending more time with his son and improving their relationship.

I've got a better relationship with me son. We do a lot of things together. Every Sunday is for me and him. It's either Saturday or Sunday ... We go out for walks, things like that. For a meal, you know.

Positive changes in the face of adversity have been documented by others. In their review of the literature on post-traumatic growth, Tedeschi, Park and Calhoun (1998) identified a range of positive outcomes that can emerge following adverse events. Some of the personal outcomes that may occur include improved self-perception, increased sense of self-efficacy, a greater appreciation of life, spiritual development and wisdom acquisition. Interpersonal improvements, related to increased compassion, empathy and altruism, may also occur. These reflect the changes reported by participants in this study. Some changes, such as increased empathy, may occur early in the process of recovery, while others, such as recognising personal strengths and finding a sense of purpose in life, may take longer to manifest (Frazier *et al.* 2001). People who report positive changes after a traumatic event often experience lower levels of distress than individuals who do not report positive outcomes (Frazier *et al.* 2001). The ability to find meaning in negative experiences may also assist people in converting a negative life experience into a positive guide for future behaviour (Maruna 2001).

Stability narrative: growing out of crime

The final category consisted of a small group (*n* = 12) who described their past in mostly positive terms. They reminisced wistfully about the 'buzz' they got from committing crime and about the stress-free lifestyle they enjoyed. In general, this group regarded criminality as a normal part of growing up. They gave it up primarily because of the negative consequences they had experienced or believed they would incur if they continued along this path. Calum missed the criminal lifestyle but could not countenance the risks associated with continuing to offend:

I wouldn't say I regret it because it was such a great buzz at the time. The consequences of living that now is maybe a bit dodgy but at the time it was great. Coz everyone loved me. I was everyone's best friend, all the girls in the estate, everything. So I was a real cool kid so I was doing what I was doing and it was socially acceptable in that circle. [KV92]

Rather than knifing off from their criminal pasts, successful desisters are more likely to attempt to reconstruct their pasts into a positive narrative (see also Maruna and Roy 2007). Psychoanalysts agree that negative life experiences and undesired characteristics must be integrated into the life story in order to achieve a unified identity (see Jung 1968). Nevertheless, although desisters were more likely than offenders to endorse a search for meaning, it is important to remember that only a third of the sample was attempting to re-envision their pasts in this way. Instead, the majority rejected their criminal pasts. This may reflect the fact that the many of the participants were in the early stages of desistance. It is possible that, as their criminal pasts become increasingly distant, the negative emotions will fade and be replaced over time by more positive feelings.

The search for a meaningful new identity has been identified as a core task for desisters. Farrall (2005) suggested that, by reflecting on their past and future selves, desisters gain greater insight into who they are and who they would like to become. In the short term, this process may elicit feelings of shame about past behaviour and anxiety about potential new roles. In time, these emotions may give way to positive feelings about the future. Farrall and Calverley (2006) discovered that, on the journey towards desistance, ex-offenders first experience shame and regret about their past lives but later report increasing levels of pride in their non-criminal achievements.

Creating a new self

The exploration of future possibilities constitutes the second component in the narrative identity. As individuals reject or reframe their past selves, they must begin to create new identities. Several theories claim that, to maintain change, desisters must develop new pro-social identities (see Maruna 2001). Possible selves theory (Markus and Nurius 1986) offers a useful starting point for examining desistance identities. An individual's possible selves consist of personalised representations of their goals and fears. They include the selves the individual would like to become as well as the selves they would like to avoid. In this way, they provide incentives and guides for future behaviour. Narrative identity is inextricably linked to life goals. As Maruna (1999: 7) stated: 'life goals give us a direction in which to act, our self-narratives provide the shape and coherence to our lives.' The process of creating a new identity may take a long time as individuals must select, explore and then commit to a new self (Farrall 2005).

Participants' desired selves were explored through the goals they would like to achieve within the next 6 months. All but three were able to describe clear goals and their plans for achieving them. A striking feature of the Irish interviews was the ordinariness of their aspirations. Participants were primarily concerned with 'becoming normal' and the vast majority aspired to having conventional 'adult' roles in work and family (see also Laub and Sampson 2003). The process of creating a new self can be reinforced by the new social roles and opportunities that ex-offenders encounter through their involvement in pro-social work and relationships (Farrall 2005). Particpants' most common goals, in descending order of importance, were to find a good job or further their education ($n = 49$), to stop using drugs or come off methadone ($n = 23$), and to get their own homes ($n = 17$). A further nine stated that they wanted to improve the quality of their interpersonal relationships, particularly with girlfriends or partners. Only six mentioned that they would like to become good fathers. Neil described how his acquisition of conventional adult bonds affected his criminal activity. Drawing a clear contrast with the negative aspects his criminal past, he explained how his desire for a 'normal' family life provided him with the incentive to stay away from crime.

> I think of what I have today – that I don't want to lose it, jeopardise my relationships, my baby, me health, job, I have a value for life. I really don't want to go back to prison, wake up sick on drugs … I just want to be left alone, have a bit of peace and quiet, live a normal life. [KV28]

There was little evidence of generativity in the sample (see Healy and O'Donnell 2008). This contrasts with Maruna's (2001) finding that desisters tended to seek fulfilment and a higher purpose through working with others. A number of Maruna's participants were already engaged, or seeking employment, in generative areas like counselling, while few members of the Irish sample were working in this field or expressed a desire to do so. This brings to mind Maslow's (1954) hierarchy of needs, which postulates that basic human requirements such as food and shelter must be satisfied before higher goals, such as self-actualisation and the search for meaning, become salient. Perhaps generative goals were not as prevalent among Irish probationers because they were still pursuing more fundamental needs. Aaron was focused on acquiring the trappings of a normal life, such as a home and a job.

> I don't know what it is when you get older, no one trusts you in your home ... . It's horrible. So you just want to be like everyone else – a job, a house, go out and work all day and come back. But you can never have anything like that if you're on drugs. [KV7]

The average number of generative themes was quite low at 0.67 themes per 1,000 words (see Healy and O'Donnell 2008). Nine participants had no generative themes at all in their narratives, and in only half a dozen cases were there more than five. When generative themes did occur, most (n = 18) related to children, with participants reporting a desire to take on responsibility for their upbringing. Gerry, a 25-year-old father, revealed how the birth of a child can contribute to desistance:

> My girlfriend had a baby. That had a big effect on me – coz it wasn't just myself. Like even when I was with the girlfriend, it's mostly yourself, like the girlfriend is there but she's after having a baby now and it's your responsibility as well, you know. It makes you look up to things, you know that way – a positive future. [KV9]

The absence of generative themes may be partly explained by the use of different sampling procedures. Maruna (2001: 45) deliberately sampled individuals at 'the two ends of a spectrum between unequivocal success and failures,' while the participants in this study were drawn from the general probation population. Perhaps generativity is not as prevalent in the middle of the spectrum. In addition, the Irish sample was younger than Maruna's and, unlike his, did not include women. Generativity typically emerges during middle adulthood and may not yet have manifested in the lives of the younger Irish sample. Generative pursuits may also be more common among women, particularly in relation to child rearing. Further research is required to explore the role played by generativity in the desistance process.

Overall, there was uniformity in the aspirations expressed by participants, irrespective of whether they were offending or desisting. The fact that both offenders and desisters aspired to conventional identities suggests that they can be constructed at any stage. It is conceivable, for example, that an individual could be both an 'offender' and a 'family man' at the same time. Contemporary reviews suggest that identity is fluid and adaptive, particularly during early adulthood (see Dunkel and Anthis 2001). During this time, people actively struggle with their goals and beliefs and have not yet made a commitment to the new identity (Marcia 1966). This was evident in the following account. Stan described the ongoing conflict he was engaged in between the pull of his criminal lifestyle and his desire to look after his son. He described the impact his son's birth had on him.

> When I saw my little son, I just thought, 'Oh shit, responsibility.' I'm responsible for that little life. [KV41]

Despite his good intentions, he relapsed but always made sure he was drug-free when he visited his son. He began to commit crime again and was arrested for selling drugs. When he was interviewed, he was on remand awaiting sentence. Expecting a long sentence, he expressed regret about the time he would miss with his child.

> It's too late to do anything now though. I've missed my son's first tooth and I can't get that back. I wanted to be the one who would bring him to school on his first day. I won't be able to now.

Desisters were more confident than offenders in their ability to achieve their goals. When asked to rate the likelihood that they would achieve their goals, secondary desisters were significantly more likely than active offenders to feel confident that they would achieve their goals ($t = 2.22$, $p < .05$). There were no differences with regards to primary desistance ($t = 1.36$, $p = .18$), suggesting that confidence may grow over time. This finding accords with existing research, which suggests that self-efficacy tends to increase over time (see Prochaska et al. 1992).

Agency, ambiguity and ambivalence

The fact that desisters were more likely to regard their possible selves as achievable implies that they had higher levels of self-efficacy and feelings of control over their lives. Strong motivation and perceived self-efficacy are vital for successful reform (Burnett 2004). Maruna (2001) suggested that ex-offenders are more optimistic than offenders about their futures. To explore this, the narratives of the Irish sample were examined for the presence of 'agency', using a coding manual pioneered by McAdams (1995) and utilised by Maruna (2001). Using this definition, a 'language of agency' appeared to be absent from participants' narrative accounts (see Healy and O'Donnell 2008). In total, the scripts of 35 participants had evidence of agentic themes; the remaining 14 had none. The average number of agentic themes per script was low (M = 1.08, SD = 0.89) and there were no significant differences between offenders and desisters. This suggests that ex-offenders do not experience high levels of agency, at least in the early stages of change.

McAdams (1993) classified agency into four components linked to themes of self-mastery, victory, achievement and empowerment. In other words, only individuals who had experienced personal success were classed as having agency. It is perhaps unsurprising that this form of 'agency as achievement' was not present among the Irish sample, given that the majority had yet to experience many life successes. Only a minority of the sample had successfully achieved conventional 'adult' identities. Just 10 participants were engaged in full-time employment, and social welfare payments constituted the primary source of income for many (37 per cent). Some found it difficult to support themselves or their families, with 38 per cent (n = 28) reporting that they found it difficult to pay for basic necessities sometimes or often. Another marker of adulthood involves leaving parents' home, establishing a long-term relationship and starting a family. At the time of the interview, 37 participants still lived in the family home. Their achievements in relation to children were more substantial. Of the 38 who had children 26 reported that they had regular contact and a good relationship with them.

If adult identities are difficult to achieve, as is suggested by these findings, ex-offenders may need to exercise more agency in order to remain committed to their goals and to achieve desistance. This, in conjunction with higher levels of self-efficacy, should eventually lead them to a more successful adult identity. Desisters' accounts suggested that they were more likely than offenders to adopt an agentic approach to life. This contrast can be seen from the following two examples. The first was desisting and the second was still involved in crime. Ian's probation officer told him about job opportunities in drugs counselling. On discovering that his employment prospects need not be limited to low-skilled jobs, he decided he wanted to train as a drugs counsellor. He grasped the opportunity that was offered and maintained an ongoing commitment to his goal. At the time of the interview, he was working as an unpaid volunteer in a drug rehabilitation programme in order to gain the necessary work experience. He had been crime free for over a year.

I just got a bit of information [...] that maybe I could do a bit better than doing security. Like there were opportunities, places out there that would take people with experience of using drugs and they needed these people with the experience to come in and show other people and to work with people like that. So that started to open me up a bit to whole new possibilities. [KV50]

In contrast, Max professed a strong desire to change but tended to drift with circumstances rather than take active control of his life. In his account, he identified several incentives which strengthened his desire to become crime-free. His family, with whom he was very close, were upset by his offending and he wanted to avoid any further damage to his relations with them. He was also concerned about having his prison sentence reactivated if he was caught. He was enjoying his work and felt it could lead to a good career but did not use it as a pathway out of crime and continued to offend. His narrative suggested that he did not deliberate extensively on the choices he made in life, preferring instead to make decisions in the moment. Although he wanted to stop offending, he was continually drawn back into crime through his ongoing association with criminal associates. This is highlighted in the following extract:

I've done a few robberies since. Now I wish I didn't do them. I've got a lot of money out of it but afterwards – 'Jeez, what the hell did I do that for? Will I be caught?'
How did they come about?
Just no money, really, you know what I mean. Out with me mates and just go doing things. It was just the friend that I was with [...]. He does a lot of robberies. From hanging around with him ... if I hadn't been with him, I probably wouldn't have been doing them ... . But because I was with him a lot of times, I was doing robberies, stuff like that. And just making a lot of money for Christmas at the time and after Christmas, for holidays and stuff like that. [KV8]

Max encountered several opportunities for desistance but did not avail himself of these chances. Nor did he alter his behaviour to avoid temptation. He also appeared to be evading personal responsibility by blaming his friend for his offending. Unlike Ian, he focused on short-term problems, such as finding money to buy Christmas presents, rather than long-term solutions, such as learning the skills he would need to find a decent job. Like the desisters in the sample, Max wanted to lead a 'normal' life but he doubted that he could achieve this through conventional means. Individuals are socialised to aspire to conventional identities and, if they lack legitimate avenues to realise these dreams, they may turn to crime to achieve their goals (Merton 1938). In such circumstances, some people exercise their agency by choosing a life of crime. Others, like Max, want to stop offending but have little faith in their ability to achieve a meaningful alternative future. Such individuals have trouble resisting temptation and find it difficult to develop strategies to avoid high-risk situations (see Chapter 5).

Participants' intentions in relation to crime were examined, using a modified version of a scale, devised by Burnett (1992) and adapted by Farrall (2002). The majority of participants wanted to go straight (94.5 per cent) and believed they were capable of change (84.9 per cent). Compared to desisters, however, offenders expressed more ambivalent attitudes to their commitment to change. Although both groups had reservations about desistance, offenders were more likely to state that they might reoffend, than primary ($\chi^2 = 18.9$, $p < .001$) and secondary ($\chi^2 = 4.74$, $p < .05$) desisters. They were also more likely to state that they would be tempted by a low risk opportunity than primary ($\chi^2 = 18.08$, $p < .001$) or secondary ($\chi^2 = 9.99$, $p < .005$) desisters.

A lack of certainty regarding future behaviour was evident in their responses. They perceived a lack of control over their behaviour and their decisions appeared to be contingent on external circumstances rather than personal agency. During this time, their resolve was vulnerable to environmental influences that simultaneously swayed them away from, and towards, crime. For example, some claimed that they would not reoffend if they received appropriate treatment, had enough money or avoided provocation from others. Seán, professed a desire to change, yet he used words like 'hopefully' throughout his explanations, suggesting that he did not feel he was in charge of his future – he 'can't say' what would happen. Again, this reflects a lack of preparation for the inevitable risky situations he may encounter in the future.

> I suppose, I can't say that I'll never. Hopefully, I never, you know, but I can't say that. Hopefully – I have it in my head to never. I don't want to anymore.

> *Would you be tempted if it was a low-risk opportunity?*
> I suppose I would. The temptation would be always there.

And do you think it's possible you might go ahead with it?
I could. Hopefully not but I could. I can't say, to be honest with
you. I have it in me all intentions of not. But I can't say what
would happen. [KV76]

In the early stages of change, ex-offenders may be ambivalent about
desistance (see also Burnett 1992). When individuals first begin to
think about changing their behaviour, they are torn between a
positive evaluation of the behaviour and their negative feelings
about the amount of effort required to modify it. During this time,
individuals may oscillate between crime and conformity, and their
behaviour may be guided by prevailing circumstances (Horney *et al.*
1995). Until this tension is resolved, the struggle can induce profound
ambivalence (see Prochaska *et al.* 1992).

Barriers, coping and social support

In order to sustain desistance, individuals must be capable of
maintaining their new identities in the face of life's stresses and
obstacles. A critical step along the journey involves identifying barriers
to change and successfully overcoming them. The 'chances available
in the current moment' constitute the final element in the narrative
identity (Evans 2002: 262). Structural opportunities and constraints
shape the life story and, in turn, it mediates the individual's social
interaction (Maruna 1999). It is widely accepted that offenders often
experience substantial social and personal problems that may thwart
their efforts to change. Studies have catalogued a range of difficulties,
encompassing vocation, addiction, health, housing and attitudinal
issues (Social Exclusion Unit 2002). Participants in this study were no
exception and many anticipated facing significant barriers to change.
The vast majority, whether desisting or offending, identified potential
obstacles, with less than one-fifth (n = 16) claiming that they faced
no obstacles to change. Similar proportions of desisters and offenders
expected to face obstacles at both the primary (χ^2 = .005, p = .95) and
secondary (χ^2 = .012, p = .91) desistance stages.

Many participants anticipated facing problems with obtaining work,
qualifications, and accommodation. These problems were often interlinked as was the case for Aaron, who had attempted to desist but
was returned to prison following a breach of his probation order:

Like you need to make a living, a stable place, but it's very
hard to get that ... they put me into hostels and when you go

> in there they're all bleedin' stoned and using drugs and it's just horrible. You'll never get nowhere in life like that. But if you had your own place, your own key of your own flat, whatever, then you could go out and get a job. At least you'd have somewhere … you can't get a job with nowhere to live. [KV7]

The following extract illustrates how these kinds of difficulties can adversely affect motivation to desist. Lee felt that his problems were insurmountable.

> Because I had no money, I got locked up and now I'm being victimised, you can call it victimised because now I'm trying to change and no one's willing to listen. So therefore which is easier, keep on banging your head against a brick wall or go with the flow and rob whatever you can? [KV73]

Almost all of the participants in this study had histories of addiction and many expected this to be a significant obstacle. Examination of participants' drug use revealed that they were at different stages in dealing with their addiction. Almost half (n = 36) were on methadone at the time of the interview and many within this category wanted to reduce their dependence on it. A further 15 per cent described themselves as regular drug users. Even those who were no longer using drugs (n = 21) were conscious that, no matter how long they remained drug-free, relapse was always a possibility. This is illustrated in the following extract from Adam, who felt that being complacent about his addiction could heighten the risk of relapse:

> You can never say you're not going to relapse so 'never say never' coz I don't know. I know people who, ah, someone dies in their family, they use that as an excuse. People look down on people that, when they stop heroin, they look down on you and they wouldn't say hello to you. But then probably 2 years down the line, they're back on heroin. [KV95]

Others believed the biggest obstacle they faced to desistance was psychological or internal. This category contained two subgroups. The first believed that they had not fully rescinded the thinking patterns and attitudes that led them to crime and felt that they needed to complete this work before they could consider themselves fully away from crime. However, the majority within this category were struggling to cope with day-to-day life. They found it difficult to lead a 'normal' life, particularly in relation to managing on limited finances or filling their time during the day. Neil, a 26-year-old man, had succeeded in moving away from crime and building a new life for himself. Although he had a job, it was low skilled and he believed he was capable of doing more with his life.

> I have plans and dreams but I can't achieve them. I'd like to work for myself eventually. I'm very sensitive and I let things get to me. If I'm stressed, I don't eat and I find it difficult to cope. [KV28]

Friends who were still involved in drugs and crime also posed a problem for some. Participants believed that, if they continued these associations, they would leave themselves vulnerable to pressure from their friends to commit crime. Although many succeeded in breaking old ties, others felt they could not give up the friends they had known all their lives. Sam decided to cut ties with his partner and his closest friends. His statement highlights the social and psychological turmoil associated 'knifing off' the past:

> The thing that I found made it most difficult was – I know that they weren't my friends, they were associates. I found it very lonely and like, bored. I got very bored so I was saying, 'Holy shit.' Like not being involved in that, it was so boring, how does everyone get on with it. [...] Because I had to finish with the girlfriend I was going out with because she was still involved in drugs and stuff like that. [...] And when I left that behind I was devastated, you know what I mean. I had no one. No confidence. My self-esteem was right down. Like it's only coming back now. [KV25]

Participants faced a range of structural, personal and interpersonal barriers to desistance. When faced with significant barriers and poor employment prospects, it is easy to become discouraged, as can be seen from the following statement. Ben's primary motivation for offending was to make money. Although he was desisting, he noted that even his 'intelligent' peers did not try to earn money through legitimate employment because they knew they could make more money through crime in a shorter period. He explained:

> Coz everybody knows you're not going to win the Lotto or ... get a great job or anything like that. Like even intelligent

people, my mate – he's very intelligent, computer whizz, and fuck it, he just went into hacking then! There's no point working in a government bleedin' building or anything like that. Sitting there, getting paid … or sitting there from 8 to 5 getting paid, what – a poxy 700 a week – you'd make that in two nights, you would. [KV77]

Yet, many succeeded in becoming crime free in spite of these problems. This suggests that additional factors may be at play. In one of the few theories to address the phenomenon of recidivism, Zamble and Quinsey (1997) discovered that desisters do not experience fewer problems than reoffenders. They proposed that poor coping skills were responsible for recidivism. They compared a sample of recidivist prisoners to a sample who did not reoffend on a range of indicators and found that the most significant factor differentiating the groups was their coping skills. Would-be desisters with poor coping skills are more vulnerable to what are known in the literature as 'high-risk situations'. Successful desistance requires cognitive resources, such as determination and problem-solving abilities, in addition to strong social support networks (Rumgay 2004). Many offenders live in areas where crime is considered a normal fact of life. It is not always practical to remove oneself from family and friends, so an important aspect of relapse prevention is to learn to deal effectively with problem situations.

Coping and social support

Research suggests that the majority of offenders want to desist but many lack confidence in their ability to translate this desire into action. Poor coping skills, coupled with the very real obstacles faced by offenders who try to change their lives, make it harder for them to desist. Without strong personal and social resources, some may return to a life of crime. Ken was a primary desister who decided to change during his last prison sentence. He felt lost and did not know where to turn for help when he was released and was trying to change without any assistance.

> *And what was the first thing you did to make that change?*
> To be honest with you, I didn't know what I was going to do till I got out that [prison] gate. It was all right saying I was going to do this and that when I was locked up in a cell, you know what I mean. Just took it day by day when I got out, that was it. [KV74]

Access to and willingness to use social supports increases the likelihood that an individual will desist. In a study of people with alcohol-related disorders, participants who did not seek help for their addiction were more likely to relapse (Moos and Moos 2006). Given its potential importance, willingness to seek help was examined in relation to self-reported offending, and some interesting patterns emerged. A significant number of participants (n = 32 or 44 per cent) claimed that they would try to solve their problems themselves before seeking outside assistance. While many of these claimed that they would then seek help from others if they could not solve the problem, over half (n = 18 or 24.6 per cent of the total sample) said that they would not access any additional source of support. In other words, a significant proportion of participants preferred to solve their problems themselves rather than enlist additional sources of help. However, any delay in obtaining help could lead someone to reoffend. Sam's account revealed the importance of getting immediate assistance with problems.

> It could be the making or breaking of you, like. If you need to talk to your probation officer about why you're not doing certain things right. If he's not there, it could easily just lead you back into reoffending or taking drugs. Without even thinking. And then you're digging yourself deeper into a hole. That's what I find anyway from personal experience. [KV25]

Secondary desisters were significantly more likely than offenders to report that they would avail themselves of social supports to help them to cope with problems (χ^2 = 4.48, p <.05). Participants who were still involved in crime preferred to deal with their problems alone. This is particularly interesting given that both groups were equally likely to expect to face problems, and indicates that desisters may adopt different strategies to deal with their problems. There were no differences between primary desisters and offenders (χ^2 = .25, p = .62, ns), suggesting that access to, or willingness to use, supports may increase over time.

While this may indicate that offenders had higher levels of self-efficacy or better coping skills and therefore did not need outside assistance, this explanation is unlikely. Research suggests that people who have been involved in crime or addiction are less willing to seek assistance when they encounter problems. In fact, many only seek help when the problem becomes so serious that it results in social, financial, legal and other difficulties (see Tucker, Vuchinich and

Rippens 2004). Personal attitudes, such as denial that the problem exists, the belief that the problem can be resolved without assistance, and poor motivation to change, may act as barriers to helpseeking (Evans and Delfabbro 2005). Traditional masculine values, such as competition and restrictions on emotional expression, may also engender negative attitudes towards helpseeking among offenders and reduce the likelihood that they will seek help (see Fischer and Farina 1995). Jake described how he waited until his life had reached crisis point before approaching a counsellor for help. By then, his situation was critical:

> I was really fed up at that time. I told him I was suicidal and all, you know, I was on the streets, it was coming up to Christmas and all. It was just a terrible time and he got me on then to a GP within 2 weeks so I've been on it since then. [...] I didn't care about anything. Once you have that [heroin], that's your friend like you know. [...] That's how lonely and sad my life was. [KV61]

Participants were given a list of possible sources of support and asked to name the people or organisations that they would go to for help if they had a problem. As can be seen from Table 6.1, participants had access to a wide range of supports, both formal and informal.

Table 6.1 Sources of support

	Number	Percentage
Family/partner	25	34.2
Friend	23	31.5
Probation officer	10	13.7
Organisation/programme	5	6.8
Counsellor	4	5.5

It is interesting to note that the vast majority of participants did not regard professional agencies as potential sources of support. Probation officers were mentioned by just under 14 per cent of the sample, while organisations (such as employment agencies and Narcotics Anonymous) were cited by only 6.8 per cent and counsellors by 5.5 per cent. (The role of probation in desistance will be explored in more detail in Chapter 7.) Kyle experienced a range of problems on release from prison, including addiction, homelessness, and health concerns.

He addressed his addiction while he was in prison, as he believed this was the primary cause of his offending. After his release, he received further assistance from his probation officer with his remaining problems and was crime free at the time of the interview.

> Started coming down off me methadone, giving clean urines and all, not taking drugs. Knocked that on the head, I knew that was where me problem was so I knocked that on the head and everything else just falls into place. [KV44]

This does not mean that participants were passive in dealing with their problems. The majority were prepared to seek help but were more likely to draw on support from informal social networks, such as family and friends. Cian explained why he did not feel the need to approach a professional agency for help:

> I don't necessarily need someone to talk to. I've plenty of friends around me. I'm not the type of person that keeps things bottled in. I've very good friends that are much older than me that I do keep in with. I've taken advice from them for years and years. And when they told me not to do something and I went and did it – this is where I am, you know. [KV50]

Studies of help-seeking confirm that people are more likely to approach informal social networks for assistance than access help through professional agencies (e.g. Kaukinen 2002). Family and friends can provide invaluable social support, but strong investment in local networks may mean that ex-offenders are less likely to try to develop ties with outside networks that may provide access to additional sources of social capital (see MacDonald and Marsh 2005). In these circumstances, high levels of bonding capital may potentially have negative effects on life chances. Unless individuals succeed in forging links with new sources of social capital, it is difficult for them to escape limiting life conditions.

Another component of successful coping involves learning how to deal with thoughts about crime. While the majority of desisters claimed that they no longer even thought about offending, over a third ($n = 16$) admitted that they thought about it either sometimes or often. This proportion is similar to the number of participants in Zamble and Quinsey's (1997) study. This highlights the fact that desistance is a gradual process. Even when individuals have stopped committing crime, they may continue to experience thoughts about offending. Desisters were asked to describe the strategies they used to neutralise these thoughts. The most common response ($n = 9$) was that they thought about the negative consequences that reoffending would entail. They reminded themselves about why they had decided to stop, concentrating in particular on wanting to stay out of prison and avoid causing further distress to their families. Others focused on the positive developments they had experienced in their lives since they stopped offending. As Dylan explained:

> Say, walking by a place, you look in, there's a bank. Jaysus, I wonder would you get anything out of there. Things like that. But then you have to stop and think of jail. I think of the next time. I missed me son's communion, I missed his birth, I missed his communion and I missed his confirmation. I don't want to miss his twenty-first and his wedding. I want to be there for those. [KV17]

In conclusion, several important themes characterised the narratives of individuals in the liminal state and some important differences between offenders and desisters emerged. Ex-offenders were more likely to adopt an agentic self-narrative. They were more likely to seek meaning in their criminal pasts and try to derive wisdom from their negative experiences. They were forward-looking and their aspirational identities centred primarily on conventional adult pursuits, which they felt confident they could achieve. They did not endorse generative concerns or demonstrate evidence of agency as measured by self-mastery, victory, achievement or empowerment but were committed to desistance and developed clear strategies to address any barriers they expected to encounter. For the most part, these themes characterised the narratives of both primary and secondary desisters. However, having self-belief in relation to future goals and access to social support networks was associated with secondary, but not primary, desistance, suggesting that these elements may emerge over time. If we look at these groups in isolation, secondary desisters were significantly more likely than primary desisters to report that they would avail themselves of social supports ($\chi^2 = 6.45$, $p = .01$). In all, 90 per cent of secondary desisters and 54 per cent of primary desisters would access sources of social support for help. There were no significant differences between primary and secondary desisters in relation to their level of goal confidence ($t = 1.35$, $p = .19$, ns).

In contrast, offenders adopted a passive self-narrative. When speaking of their criminal pasts, feelings of shame, remorse and regret were common. They also aspired to conventional identities but were less confident they could achieve them. Although motivation to change was high, the majority expressed ambivalent attitudes towards desistance. They expected to face significant barriers to change but were less willing to utilise external supports to deal with them.

Chapter 7

A catalyst for change?

Knowledge about desistance from crime has advanced rapidly over the past decade yet, to date, its findings have had limited impact on rehabilitation practice. Maruna, Immarigeon and LeBel (2004) queried why this might be the case. They concluded that practitioners may feel uncomfortable with desistance research because of its focus on the processes of self-change, which, on the surface, appears to conflict with the goal of rehabilitation, which is to encourage desistance through formal interventions. Official interventions comprise only a small part of an individual's life and many additional factors, such as family, employment or level of motivation, impinge on the process of change. By providing insight into the wider social and personal contexts of change, desistance research can add an extra dimension to research into the effectiveness of offender rehabilitation. Research on the 'natural' process of desistance therefore offers a potentially fruitful avenue that could assist formal efforts to promote desistance. Maruna, Immarigeon and LeBel (2004: 12) proposed a 'truce and a marriage proposal' between the rehabilitation and desistance literatures, claiming that they could benefit from each other. With this in mind, the focus of the book, which so far has been trained on the process of natural desistance, will now turn to the final element that will be considered – the role played by probation.

A key challenge for desistance researchers is to render their findings accessible to practitioners. Work has begun on developing a model of 'desistance-focused practice' that translates these findings into practical guidance for practitioners. Proponents of desistance-focused practice argue that practitioners should aim to build social as well as human capital. McNeill (2006) explained that, in order for change to occur, the offender needs the motivation and the capacity to change (human capital). Unless the offender is also provided with opportunities to exercise his or her new-found skills (social capital), these resources are insufficient to bring about lasting change. Without rejecting the risk factor paradigm outright, he proposed that practitioners should aim to enhance natural protective factors and should focus their work on building existing strengths as well as reducing risk and need. Drawing on Maruna (2001), he advocated using formal intervention to open up avenues for probationers to engage in generative activities, thus enabling them to integrate back into their local communities. All of this, he argued should take place in an atmosphere which fosters relationship building between the practitioner and their client.

Because Irish probation practice contains some of the key elements that constitute the desistance practice paradigm, its relevance for desistance can be examined empirically. In Ireland, probation officers continue to operate within an explicitly social work framework, which values high-quality supervisory relationships and offers practical assistance with social problems. This provides an opportunity to learn more about whether this approach can promote desistance. Much of the following analysis will come from the participants' personal observations about probation and its role in desistance. To date, few researchers have asked probationers directly what they think and, as a result, little is known about probationers' opinions about probation. This chapter provides a rare glimpse into the impact of probation as seen through the eyes of probationers themselves. Given the importance of wider social and personal contexts in change, the impact of probation is examined within the broader perspective of participants' own efforts at desistance. First, an overview of the development of the Probation Service, and its functions, aims and ethos is provided.

Advising, assisting and befriending

The Irish Probation Service has attracted little critical attention or empirical scrutiny. It still functions under the legislative framework of the Probation of Offenders Act 1907, which the Probation Service itself describes as 'outdated' (Probation and Welfare Service, nd: 18). Although its guiding legislation dates back to the turn of the twentieth century, probation was not used widely as a sanction until the 1960s.

After being restructured in 1979, the Probation and Aftercare Service (as it was then known) took on a new incarnation as the Probation and Welfare Service. In 2008, it became The Probation Service. It began producing annual reports on its work in 1980. Like many areas of criminal justice in Ireland, very little information has been collected regarding the Probation Service. This section will attempt to piece together what is known about the Probation Service, its work, and the people who come into contact with it.

The Probation Service does not function as a distinct corporate agency within the criminal justice system, but comes under the aegis of the Department of Justice, Equality and Law Reform. The Department ultimately makes decisions on its levels of funding, staffing and the resources allocated. Although the budgetary allowance for the Department of Justice has increased dramatically over the past 10 years, the budget of the Probation Service is approximately 10 per cent of the prison budget. The goals of the Probation Service have evolved through a religious ideal of the saving of sinners, through a medical approach, which aimed to 'treat' the offender, to the current social work model (O'Dea 2002). All probation officers train as social workers and this is evident in their focus on the welfare aspects of their work with offenders. The primary technique used is the individual casework approach, with an emphasis on rehabilitation. The Probation of Offenders Act 1907 requires officers 'to advise, assist and befriend' their clients and ensure that they fulfil the conditions of their order.

The Probation Service has a wide range of functions, which include the provision of assistance to offenders in prisons and other places of detention, the preparation of court reports and victim impact statements, and work with juvenile offenders. The Probation Service also plays a role in various other arenas, including a small number of probation hostels and several training workshops. In addition to these tasks, the Probation Service carries out three main activities – the Probation Order (established by the Probation of Offenders Act 1907), the Community Service Order (established by the Criminal Justice (Community Service) Act 1983), and Adjourned Supervision (no legislative basis). Table 7.1 shows the number under supervision for each sanction between 1998 and 2007. Adjourned supervision has become the most frequently used of the three options (in 2007, 3,402 cases compared to 2,756 on probation orders and 1,519 on community service).

A probation order is intended to be rehabilitative in nature. The 1914 amendment to the 1907 Act strengthened this focus by allowing

Table 7.1 Numbers under supervision 1998–2007

	1998	1999	2000	2001	2002	2003	2004	2005	2006	2007
Probation	1,836	1,568	1,345	1,228	1,265	1,21,7	1,878	1,274	1,779	2,756
Community Service Order	1,269	1,342	998	756	916	893	843	1,167	1,158	1,519
Adjourned Supervision	2,417	2,403	2,625	2,373	2,334	3,048	5,623	5,230	5,714	3,402
Total	5,522	5,313	4,968	4,357	4,515	5,158	8,344	7,671	8,651	7,677

Taken from National Crime Council (www.crimecouncil.gov.ie)

conditions to be attached to the order (for example, in recent times this would allow participation in drug treatment to be mandated). Community service, on the other hand, is regarded as a punishment and the judge must specify a default period of detention at the time of sentencing. These orders operate as a direct alternative to custody and require the offender to perform between 40 and 240 hours of unpaid work in the community. Failure to comply with a community service order is punishable by either a fine or a revocation of the order.

Adjourned supervision superficially resembles a probation order in terms of the activities undertaken. It is used when the judge is unsure whether the offender can fulfil the conditions of a probation order and defers the penalty until a later date. In the meantime, the offender is placed under probation supervision and, after a specified period, a progress report is submitted to the court for consideration. Because this penalty has no legal basis, there is no official limit on the length of supervision or on the penalty that can be imposed if the supervisory conditions are not met. The Expert Group on the PWS (1999) recommended that this type of supervision be placed on a statutory footing.

Probation officers also supervise released prisoners. Offenders may be ordered to serve a portion of the custodial sentence, and then come back to court for a review. If the review is favourable, the remainder of the sentence may be suspended. This practice was discontinued in 2000 when the Supreme Court ruled in the case of Finn that it interfered with the power of the executive to commute sentences (cited in Kilcommins et al. 2004: 148). Probation officers also supervise prisoners serving suspended sentences in the community.

Although widely used for many years, suspended sentences were not given a statutory basis until the Criminal Justice Act 2006 (section 99). If an offender breaches the conditions of his suspended sentence, the judge may activate the custodial sentence and the offender may be obliged to serve the full prison term.

The 2008–2010 Strategy Statement emphasises the role of research in supporting the work of the Service. However, accountability is still limited and only basic statistical information about the numbers of offenders receiving each sanction is made public. The most recent statistical information about the demographic or criminal histories of people under supervision relate to 2003. These statistics show that clients are broadly comparable to other criminal justice populations, being young, male, and predominantly from urban areas. The most common offences committed were property and motoring offences. An unpublished survey showed a high incidence of drug use among probationers in Dublin (cited in O'Donovan 2000). There is no published information on reconviction rates. There is a paucity of information on probation in general, with practically no research or evaluation having been carried out and published. One exception is a national study of community service orders, which found that 81 per cent were successfully completed (Walsh and Sexton 1999). The study also found that older and first-time offenders were more likely to successfully complete their orders. Higher revocation rates were found for offenders from urban areas and for those found guilty of public order offences. Unfortunately this study was not accompanied by a study of reconviction rates following completion of the order, when the threat of prison was removed.

Recent developments

During the 1990s, probation services in the Western world witnessed a shift towards more punitive community penalties. In England and Wales, for example, the National Probation Service experienced a 'wholesale conversion' to managerial practices (Raynor 2003). The new ideology emphasises control over care and the realignment of values away from traditional social work concepts towards the more punitive goals of other criminal justice bodies. Programmes that aimed to address offenders' cognitive deficits have increasingly begun to replace efforts to address their personal and social problems. This trend reflects the wider 'culture of control' that Garland (2001) saw permeating criminal justice in the Western world. These international developments did not have the same impact in Ireland, where the risk discourse is still in its infancy (see Healy and O'Donnell 2005). Probation practice in Ireland is beginning to show signs of moving towards this model of probation supervision and some of these practices have begun to influence its work.

The Probation and Welfare Service underwent a 'rebranding' exercise in 2008. It was renamed the Probation Service, symbolically removing the word 'Welfare' from its title. The rhetoric of managerialism has also made its way into recent Probation Service publications. The 2001–3 Strategy Statement described pre-sanction reports as outlining 'lifestyle, criminal history and risk of reoffending', while probation supervision aims to 'address patterns and criminogenic factors and motivate them to change' (Probation and Welfare Service n.d.: 12). In the 2008–2010 Strategy Statement (2008), the purpose of the Probation Service was 'to increase community safety and prevent victimisation by motivating, challenging and supporting offenders in leading a crime free life' (Probation Service 2008). This reflects strong interest in the victim and community safety, although it maintains its traditional welfare concerns with 'supporting' offenders.

The Probation Service also introduced structured risk assessment. The LSI-R (Andrews and Bonta 1995), a risk assessment instrument first pioneered in Canada, was piloted by the Service in 2003. Two 'what works'-style intensive probation programmes are now operating in Cork and Dublin, and target persistent offenders with a history of drug use. These have been evaluated, but only on a small scale, so the findings must be interpreted with caution. Results have indicated that approximately 70 per cent of persistent offenders receiving these sanctions go on to receive a further conviction within 3 years (Phillips 2002). Although the prospects for persistent offenders appear relatively bleak, outcomes may not be as negative as they first appear. Phillips (2002) found that although 77 per cent of his sample reoffended, they also demonstrated significant reductions in reoffending rates compared to a matched group of prisoners. Their average prison sentence length after completion of the programme was also significantly reduced relative to sentences received before participation. Day-to-day practice remains largely unaffected by these developments. Whether the changes are merely cosmetic or will become as influential as they have abroad will be revealed in the coming years.

Support or surveillance?

Internationally, there is debate about whether the surveillance or welfare-oriented functions of probation should be prioritised. There has been little research on which elements of probation practice increase its effectiveness, but what evidence does exist favours the social welfare model. In Rex's (1999) study, only three participants, all of whom were first-time offenders, saw the 'surveillance' function of probation as keeping them out of trouble. Instead, probationers tended to value the welfare features of probation, such as their relationship with their supervisory officer and assistance with practical problems, rather than the surveillance elements. The managerial approach has been subject to extensive criticism in the literature. In particular, researchers have emphasised its failure to address the wider social and structural circumstances that constrain offenders' ability to change their lives (see Kemshall 2008).

Surveillance alone may be insufficient to engender true commitment to change and appears to be more effective when combined with some form of treatment. The RAND Corporation sponsored the evaluation of 14 intensive probation supervision (IPS) programmes (Petersilia and Turner 1993). One year later, the IPS group had reconviction rates (defined as arrests and technical violations) of 65 per cent compared to only 38 per cent for controls. Despite the apparent ineffectiveness of IPS, there was evidence that it had been effective for a subgroup of participants. IPS participants who were also enrolled in a treatment programme showed significant reductions in arrests compared to the control group.

Community penalties rely on offender cooperation in order for them to be effective. Compliance with community penalties, as measured by completion rates, appears to have fallen sharply in England and Wales since the introduction of the managerial model. Robinson and McNeill (2008) distinguished between formal compliance, which denotes behaviour that technically meets the requirements of the order (for example, attending appointments), and substantive compliance, which requires active engagement and cooperation with the requirements and which leads to long-term compliance with the law. They suggested that the work undertaken by individual probation officers as well as the organisational ethos of correctional agencies can influence the motivational posture adopted by offenders. They argued that the current emphasis on formal compliance portrays 'an image of community supervision as a superficial exercise which principally involves "turning up" and "signing in", rather than a meaningful piece of work undertaken in the context of a relationship between offender and supervising officer' (Robinson and McNeill 2008: 442). In addition to enabling offenders who have no desire to change to complete their order with minimum effort, it may also undermine the efforts of individuals who are genuinely committed to desistance but find it difficult to fulfil the technical requirements of their orders. The authors conclude that, if probation officers are to encourage substantive compliance, they should address offenders' beliefs and attitudes and aim to generate positive social bonds. The perceived legitimacy of the order and the wider criminal justice system is also important. If offenders believe that they have been treated harshly or unfairly by the system, they are less likely to comply.

Collectively, this evidence indicates that the social welfare model may offer a better alternative to a managerial approach. Since the welfare model remains central to Irish probation practice, this offers an opportunity to examine whether this is the case. First, confirmation that the welfare model is dominant was sought by analysing probation officer reports of the work they undertook with participants and probationers' perceptions of probation supervision.

Probation officers were asked to describe the work they planned to undertake with their clients during the supervision period. Just under 10 per cent stated that they did not have a formal supervision plan and simply required participants to attend regular appointments. Among probation officers who had formulated a plan, the vast majority intended to work on what have been described in the literature as desistance-related factors (see McNeill 2006). For example, around two-thirds of supervision plans aimed to address addiction-related issues. A third mentioned help with employment or education problems. It is also particularly interesting that, in 17 per cent of the plans, probation officers stated that they intended to work with offenders' families. Desistance research suggests this might be an appropriate target (see Farrall 2002). In contrast, only a third of supervision plans contained elements that specifically aimed to address offending or 'cognitive' factors. Looking at supervision plans therefore, it is clear that the primary focus of probation work is on the social problems experienced by probationers. In general, the areas selected for intervention by probation officers reflected the social obstacles identified by participants (see Chapter 6), suggesting there was good agreement between officers and their clients about appropriate intervention targets.

Probation officers were also more likely to use a casework approach to address these issues. The vast majority (n = 61) used 'talking' techniques. In addition, over 50 per cent of participants were referred to external agencies for assistance ($n = 39$) or received direct practical assistance from their probation officers ($n = 40$). Role play and written activities were used with 21 per cent ($n = 15$) of participants. In around a third of cases ($n = 23$), probation officers reported having direct engagement with the offender's family. It is important to have adequate time during probation sessions to build a rapport and to identify and address social problems. Probation appointments lasted more than half an hour in 45 cases (62 per cent), but the frequency of sessions was relatively low. In 31 cases, meetings were held at least once every 2 weeks and 21 took place on a monthly basis. This means that 29 per cent of the sample saw their probation officer less than once a month. Probation officers explained that they often reduced the frequency of meetings when they believed their clients were progressing well.

Participants were asked about their perceptions of probation. Their responses were coded according to whether they viewed probation as 'support only', 'surveillance only', or 'both'. The majority of participants saw the work of the Probation Service as welfare oriented (see Table 7.2). Just under half of the sample cited the supportive aspects of probation, suggesting that probation is seen as predominantly rehabilitative by participants. Responses were also examined in relation to current level of offending. Overall, offenders were more likely than desisters to identify a surveillance aspect to probation (29 per cent of those who provided a response, compared to 11 per cent of primary desisters; 21 per cent, compared to 11 per cent of secondary desisters).

Overall, these findings suggest that, despite current rhetoric, the work of the Probation Service remains entrenched in the welfare model.

Table 7.2 Participants' perceptions of the role of probation

	Primary desistance		Secondary desistance	
	desisters	offenders	desisters	offenders
Support only	21	13	10	24
Surveillance only	4	7	2	9
Both	13	4	7	10
Total	38	24	19	43

Experiences of probation

Participants were asked a series of questions about their experiences on probation – if it was having any impact, what they had found helpful, and what they would like to see done differently. Their responses were coded according to whether they made positive statements only, made negative statements only, or held mixed views. In total, 65 probationers expressed an opinion about their experience on probation that could be coded. Some interviewees did not enunciate any opinion regarding probation (in some cases, for example, participants had just begun their order and felt it was too early to judge). Probation officers were also asked to rate their clients according to their attitudes towards supervision, their attendance, and their level of engagement during sessions.

Overall, the majority of participants (n = 38) referred to positive features of probation only, indicating that they held favourable attitudes towards supervision (see Table 7.3). Only five individuals expressed purely negative views, although a substantial proportion (n = 22) expressed mixed views. Differences between participants who were desisting and participants who were still involved in crime showed, not surprisingly, that current offenders were less likely to express positive views about probation than primary desisters (52 per cent compared to 63 per cent). The proportion expressing mixed or negative opinions about probation was slightly lower for offenders than desisters (for example, 48 per cent compared to 38 per cent of primary desisters).

T-tests were conducted to establish whether age and criminal history differentiated attitudes towards supervision. Probationers were categorised into two groups – those with exclusively positive

Table 7.3 Participants' attitudes towards probation

	Primary desistance		Secondary desistance	
	desisters	offenders	desisters	offenders
Positive	25	13	13	25
Mixed	14	8	6	16
Negative	1	4	1	4
Total	40	25	20	45

views and those who held negative/mixed views. Although those holding positive views about probation (M = 25.9, SD = 4.4) were slightly older than those expressing negative/mixed views (M = 24.9, SD = 4.3), the difference was not statistically significant (t = .92, p = .36). The 'positive only' group had a slightly higher average number of previous convictions (M = 7.4, SD = 6.1) compared to the negative/mixed group (M = 7.1, SD = 6.8), but this difference was not statistically significant (t = .15, p = .88). These results suggest that age and criminal history were not related to attitudes towards probation.

Corroboration of these findings was sought through assessments provided by the participants' probation officers, who were asked to rate participants' attitudes towards supervision. Research has found that probationers described by their supervising officers as having a positive response to supervision tend to have lower rates of reconviction than those rated as having negative attitudes (McIvor and Barry 2000). The results were in line with the self-reported attitudes of probationers. Again, most participants' attitudes were rated as good or very good by the officers (83 per cent of the total). Only 10 were described as having an average or poor attitude towards probation. Disaggregating the figures, offenders were more likely than primary desisters to be rated as having average/poor attitudes (26 per cent compared to 12 per cent) and less likely to be rated as having very positive attitudes (5 per cent compared to 38 per cent). The sample was divided into two groups ('good/very good' and 'average or less') in order to conduct a chi-square analysis. This showed no significant differences between the groups (χ^2 = .87, ns), suggesting that there is no difference in attitudes between those currently involved in crime and those who are currently desisting.

Further confirmation was sought through questions relating to participants' behaviour. Probation officers were asked to rate participants on their level of attendance. Ratings on the whole were positive, with 78.6 per cent described as having 'good' or 'very good' attendance. Although the numbers in this analysis were small, the results indicate that active offenders were more likely than primary desisters to receive ratings of 'average/poor' (44 per cent compared to 12 per cent). Similarly, 56 per cent of primary desisters were rated as having 'very good' attendance compared to 22 per cent of active offenders. The cell counts were too low to allow a chi-square analysis. This suggests that primary desisters had better attendance at their probation appointments. The results also show that a significant proportion of those still actively engaged in criminal activity were attending their appointments regularly.

Finally, officers were asked to rate their clients according to their perceived level of engagement during the sessions they had attended. Again, the majority received positive assessments, with 80.3 per cent described as having 'good' or 'very good' levels of engagement. Nevertheless, active offenders were more likely to receive a rating of average or poor (42.2 per cent compared to 9 per cent of primary desisters). Current offenders were also less likely than primary desisters to receive ratings of 'very good' (11 per cent compared to 52 per cent of primary desisters). Cell counts were too low to conduct a chi-square analysis.

In sum, probationers had a positive attitude towards probation, showed good attendance at appointments, and engaged well during sessions. In general, surveys of probationers find that the majority have a positive perception of supervision (e.g. Mair and May 1997). Active offenders, however, scored lower than primary desisters on all three indicators. Given the predominantly positive view of participants regarding probation supervision, it is useful to explore what participants found useful and how these aspects of probation supervision impacted on their behaviour.

Facilitators and constraints

When investigating the impact of an intervention, it is important to understand not only *whether* it effects change, but also *how* it does so (see Pawson and Tilley 1997). Probationers were asked to describe the most helpful features of probation. Table 7.4 lists their responses. The two central themes that emerged were the provision of practical help and having someone to talk to about problems. These and other key features of probation supervision are examined in more detail next.

Table 7.4 Positive features of probation

Practical assistance	15
Therapeutic alliance	14
Threat of custody	13
Insight into offending and related issues	9
Gives you a chance to change	7

Practical assistance

Fifteen participants appreciated receiving practical assistance, particularly in relation to employment, education and addiction. Officers played two roles, both keeping them motivated and seeking out suitable programmes on their behalf. Nathan described how being on probation helped him to overcome his drug addiction. His statement highlights the need for probation officers to use a flexible approach and adopt a long-term perspective on recovery (see also Maruna, Immarigeon and LeBel 2004). When he relapsed on drugs, his probation officer did not immediately re-enter his case (although this was a breach of his conditions). He recovered and was crime and drug free when interviewed.

> It helped me to deal with my drug problem. When I started with [Programme name], I was off drugs and all. But I still had the cravings there. I did have a slip, I did go back to the drugs for a while and I went to my probation officer and said it to him. So I worked on getting onto a phy [methadone] course then. It stopped the cravings so I'll do the phy course for 12 months and then come off the phy. Only for that now I would have been straight back to square one by now. [KV60]

Farrall (2002), among others, recognised the importance of building human capital for desistance but stressed that ex-offenders must also be provided with opportunities to exercise that capital. This is illustrated in the following case. Lee became very frustrated because, despite strong interview and employment skills, he found it extremely difficult to find employment. He attributed this failure to his criminal record, which he was obliged to disclose during interviews. Having a criminal record is particularly problematic in Ireland, where an adult record is never expunged.

> I'm very articulate, I can speak and I'm confident in speaking and stuff like that, like I've great interview skills. And the job would more or less be mine but as soon as I mention, 'Yeah, well, I do have a criminal record' – OK, we'll get back to you. And you never hear from them. I'm up against the wall already. … So it's always going to be held against you – unless you get an employer that knows you personally and knows the reasons why you've been locked up and is still willing to give you a

chance. And I don't mean help as in … employment skills, it's more links with employers that are willing to give people a second chance. It's not the help like going to FAS [Ireland's National Training and Employment Authority] and getting courses and stuff like that. [KV73]

He eventually found a job through informal networks.

The only reason I'm hired at the moment is because the chap that knows me, knows I was locked up. […] Like I buzzed him for about 6 months, I used to go and talk to him at the door and I was saying, can you get me a bit of work?

The therapeutic alliance

Fourteen people cited their relationship with their probation officer as a key feature of probation. They appreciated having someone to talk to, as this helped them to cope with problems that arose. Having a probation officer who seemed genuinely interested in helping them strengthened their resolve and encouraged them to maintain their positive behaviours. Dermot's experience highlights the impact a positive relationship with a probation officer can have on offending behaviour.

It's kinda helping me to keep it together, make sure there's no trouble, so I'm not going to be out drinking on the streets, giving police hassle, getting bad reports back from the local police station to [probation officer]. I want to keep him happy as much as keep myself happy – everyone's happy then. I don't want to be pissing him off, getting backlash and feedback from that. I don't see him as authority. He's on the level, a straight kind of guy.

You said it's helping you stay out of trouble. How's it helping you to do that?
It's not as in fear, more as in respect. He's a nice kind of guy and I wouldn't want to let him down. I'd feel bad coz he wouldn't give out really, he'd just say, 'Ah, what have you done?' or 'This is not good', you know. But he would be strict enough as well. He'd put his foot down, do his job. I wouldn't want to let him down out of respect. [KV35]

Although they were not asked specifically to list positive characteristics of their supervising officers, many probationers volunteered this information. Key themes included being treated with respect and feeling the probation officer was approachable. Other characteristics mentioned were being genuine, caring, and straightforward. There is a growing awareness regarding the importance of the therapeutic relationship in reducing offending (e.g. Trotter 1995). Rex (1999) found that probationers who described probation as active and participatory were more likely to attribute changes in their offending to supervision. With such an approach, the probationer felt engaged in the process, not just monitored. In Rex's study, encouragement from their officers was a key feature, particularly for younger offenders and those with longer criminal histories. Similarly, McIvor and Barry (2000) found that the most important characteristics of a probation officer were showing understanding, listening and giving helpful advice. According to a recent meta-analysis, successful approaches tend to contain most or all of the following elements: a strong working alliance, based on empathy, warmth and respect, and a person-centred approach (Dowden and Andrews 2004).

Threat of custody

As shown earlier, a significant number of participants ascribed a surveillance function to probation. Thirteen participants stated that the threat of imprisonment helped them to desist. This is interesting given that the stated aim of the Probation Service is to 'advise, assist and befriend'. Participants believed that they would be sent to prison if they breached the conditions of their orders. This knowledge deterred them from committing crime. This is an inaccurate perception. Legally, if an offender does not comply with the conditions of his or her order, the probation officer is required to notify the court (Expert Group 1999). The local garda station is then notified and will issue a warrant. The offender must then appear in court. There is a very real possibility at this stage of returning to prison to serve a custodial sentence, but it is not set in stone. Nevertheless, these participants, who wanted to stay away from crime, viewed the threat of imprisonment as an incentive. As Max explained:

It's turned me life around. Since I got caught with the drugs. I'm always in court. I have to see my probation officer all the time. I've to give clean urines twice a week. So if I fuck up at all, I'm going to be locked up so like … you know what I mean. It's something on me head all the time. I got pissed off going to court and stuff like that. But me ma does say but to keep an eye on me, which it is. Always in the back of my mind I'm saying, 'If I do that, I'll be locked up.'… Where if I wasn't in court and I hadn't got probation, I'd just go ahead and do it. Or I'd go ahead and take drugs, you know what I mean. But I can't – there's a lot I can't do. So it is good then. [KV81]

Max had reduced but not stopped offending. In his view, his sentence contributed to this reduction but he was not sure how he would feel when his period of supervision ended.

The way the court case is, yeah, I want to stay away – I have to stay away! Or I'm going down for 5 year. But after that, I don't know how I'll feel. I won't have that pressure on me if I get caught.

Seán's statement below further confirms that the experience of probation as a deterrent is somewhat superficial. It is an external imposition rather than an internal change.

But I do come into [probation officer] to prove that I'm trying to get my life together and trying to stay off drugs and all. And if I hadn't got anyone like that, you know, what's stopping me then? I'd be just out using drugs, and robbing and doing anything I could. [KV76]

Insight into offending-related issues

Nine participants commented on the work probation officers undertook in relation to the cognitive aspects of crime. In general, cognitive-behavioural approaches aim to help participants to understand the motivation for their actions and the consequences of their behaviour and to teach them new ways to manage their behaviour (see McGuire 2002). Ian, who got out of prison early on review, described his experience when he had to talk about his offence in a group-based cognitive-behavioural programme for the first time. For him, it was not just a matter of dealing with his feelings about the offence, but also the acceptance he received from both staff and fellow participants after revealing his crime.

> I had a lot of shame and a lot of guilt over the crime that I committed and I got to address some of it – it was dragged out of me! I know from experience, addicts and drug users – very secretive people. And the only way someone could get them to admit and to look at things is the direct approach. Upon the spot approach. So when I went through the offending and I went through my part in it and what I did. And I remember the day it came out about the crime, I went, 'Fuck, I'm not going back there', coz I felt it – it's over now. And the thing that got me when I walked in the next morning, the same people said 'Howya.' I wasn't being judged for it even though it was horrendous. [KV50]

The final seven appreciated being given an opportunity to change but did not cite any specific probation work that was particularly helpful. In general, they were relieved that they had avoided a prison sentence.

Unhelpful aspects of probation

Not everyone felt that probation was having a positive impact on their lives. A number of participants had relapsed into crime by the time they were interviewed. Their stories were described in more detail in Chapter 5. They were asked to explain why probation did not work for them. For some, events in their lives interfered with its ability to work. Three participants, who relapsed while on probation, described their experiences. Although they had a positive perception of the Probation Service, life events (for example, the death of a child, drug relapses) interfered with its ability to help them. Cillian, who had been released from prison onto supervision, explained that his relapse was due to the gap between release and being seen by an officer and accepted onto a treatment programme.

> I think they got in touch with me when I was out for about a month or two. It was too late, it was. It was well too late. So I think that when people get released, they should have interviews and all for the next day and all, you know. Keep them busy in the first week. [KV65]

Table 7.5 lists the negative features of probation described by the participants. Three participants felt that being on probation actually made things worse for them. All were still involved in crime. One

Table 7.5 Negative features of probation

	No.
Inconvenience of appointments	6
Too much control	6
Too much interference with life	4
Not enough practical help	4
Supervision period too long	3
Intensive sessions difficult	3

of the main difficulties was the need to travel to appointments. This was especially problematic for people who worked at a distance from their probation office and had to take time off to attend appointments. Ben's experience suggested how this problem might be overcome.

> Well, the first couple of times when I was coming in every bleedin' second week, just really pointless like, and I was taking time off work and I was getting shit at work and all, you know. And then I had to bleedin' say to him and then [probation officer] there coming out to me house, you know. It could have worked both ways, you do get compromised here and there. [KV77]

Many of the complaints related to the surveillance function of probation. Some, for example, felt the supervision period was too long and intruded into their lives. They felt that their probation officers had too much control. While this was regarded as a negative feature, it could also be argued that such views showed probation supervision was successfully keeping tabs on offenders under supervision. Nick's comments reveal his disdain for the intrusion into his personal life.

> Basically, the probation officer came out to me house, asking me questions, I thought it was a little bit of a burden, a bit of an intrusion. And I don't know ... it's a nosy kind of job. [KV86]

These participants emphasised the negative experiences of having something 'hanging over your head' constantly and the dislike of people interfering in their lives. Leonard, a 21-year-old male, did not have a good relationship with his probation officer. He claimed that being on probation interfered with family, work and friends. Although he acknowledged that probation could be helpful for those who wanted it, he did not like being on an extended period of supervision.

> I think probation actually made me worse. I never went to appointments so my probation officer kept bringing me back to court and getting me locked up over it. [...] It used to annoy me, the way they keep interfering. I'd tell me ma I was doing well, and she'd come up to the house and tell her I wasn't and get me into trouble with me ma. It would wreck your head. I've always had something hanging over my head since I was 13. [KV63]

Others felt they did not receive enough practical support. Dan, aged 23, described how his probation order was only beginning to have an impact on him. He believed that it could not have been effective until his underlying problems (homelessness and drug use) were dealt with.

> I wasn't homeless any more. I got somewhere to live. I got a bit of support around me in the place I live ... . I'm on methadone at the moment, on a clinic, on supervision and I'm doing well at the moment. But since then, well probation hasn't really helped me, I've helped meself like, you know. [KV78]

The final question that remains to be answered relates to whether probation supervision had an impact on desistance. Existing research has shown that community sanctions are at least as effective as prison (e.g. Kershaw *et al.* 1999), but less is known about how the imposition of probation impacts on reoffending. As described earlier, the majority of participants in this study held favourable views towards supervision and many claimed that it was helping them to stay away from crime. Almost all of the probation officers surveyed (14 out of 15 respondents) also believed probation could reduce reoffending (three qualified their answers, claiming that probation could reduce reoffending, but its effectiveness depended on the motivation, skills and capacities of the offender).

In spite of their positive response to probation, only one participant cited it as a key factor in his decision to desist. This conclusion is supported by existing research. Among a sample of New Zealand offenders who had been officially crime free for 3 years, only half claimed to have found probation useful in helping them stay away from crime (Leibrich 1993). Layton-MacKenzie *et al.* (1999) also found that the number of probationers involved in crime and drug/alcohol use declined during the supervision period, as did their rate of offending. However, the work done by probation officers or their knowledge of breaches and how they dealt with them, did not have any appreciable effect on offending behaviour. Similarly, Farrall (2002) found that the actual work done by probation officers was not associated with changes in offending behaviour. McNeill *et al.*'s (2005) review of evidence from the psychotherapy literature showed that that the nature of an intervention or the therapeutic techniques used are rarely the most crucial variables in determining the success of an intervention. Instead, chance occurrences, external events and client factors play more important roles. Drawing on Asay and Lambert (1999), they reported that the amount of change that is attributable to each of these factors was 40 per cent to client and extra-therapeutic factors, such as ego strength and levels of social support; 30 per cent to the therapeutic relationship; 15 per cent to placebo effects; and just 15 per cent to the therapeutic technique.

This does not mean that probation had no role to play in desistance. Many of the participants felt that being on probation assisted them in staying away from crime and believed that probation supervision played an indirect role by acting as a catalyst for changes that had already been initiated. The success of probation supervision appeared to be dependent on the provision of personal and social assistance and the therapeutic relationship, which participants claimed supported their efforts to change their behaviour. Participants frequently emphasised how they had already resolved to change before receiving their current supervision order and stressed that desistance occurred as a result of their own efforts rather than any intervention they received. In their view, probation gave them the incentive and the resources to implement the decision to change. Ken explained:

And how is it helping you stay away from crime?
It's not helping me, it's pointing me in the right direction if I want to go that way. […] It's up to me, no one can change me, it's up to meself to change at the end of the day. They could say anything they want to me, but, jayz, I could go out the door and do different, you know. So it has to be you to do it, like. [KV74]

Participants were keen to stress their own involvement in desistance and ascribed a secondary role to probation. In many cases, participants recounted extensive and sustained efforts on the part of family, friends and treatment providers to intervene in their behaviour in the past, which met with little success. As in the following example, these participants typically stressed how *they* had to make the decision to stop. This reiterates the importance of the individual's subjective response to objective events in their lives, such as being on probation.

> Me old man tried everything … . And no matter what he tried, I always got around it. I suppose he tried in his way – give me a hiding, keep me in. He gave me a hiding. I went out and did more. He'd keep me in, I'd get out the window, and I'd go missing for weeks, and the whole family would be out looking for me. [KV39]

People who are currently involved in crime may respond differently to the work undertaken during probation supervision. While desisters viewed the monitoring function of probation as an incentive to change, offenders often found it stressful and, in some cases, it prompted relapse. Frank described unsuccessful probation orders he had experienced in the past. When asked to describe what had changed between this sentence and the last, he cited a change in his perspective rather than the order itself:

> Well, this probation that I've been on for the past 12 months, I had an interest in it this time that I didn't have in previous. You know, like, my probation officer before, I didn't pay any attention to him, like they were good to me but I didn't care. But I got probation this time and I knew it would help. [KV37]

When asked whether anything could have been done to help them stop offending earlier, almost half of the sample ($n = 33$ or 45 per cent) said no. Their readiness to change played a critical role in determining whether probation could impact on their behaviour, as illustrated by the following statements:

> *And was there anything that could have stopped you earlier?*
> I had to stop myself, nothing else would have stopped me. [KV43]

> It's all about choices. It was my choice. [KV2]

Farrall's (2002) research also suggested that probation had an indirect impact on offending. He found that its influence was mediated by wider social circumstances related to employment and family, and by individual motivation. In his sample, rates of desistance were highest among groups that faced no obstacles and lowest among those who faced obstacles and did not resolve them. He suggested that probation worked indirectly and in conjunction with changes in life circumstances and levels of motivation to bring about change. In this way, probation may act as a 'hook' for change which, if deemed meaningful and accessible by the probationer, can engender desistance (see Giordano *et al.* 2002). Probation officers in England and Wales have been urged to focus on offending-related factors, such as criminal cognitions, rather than the wider social contexts of crime. As Farrall (2002) noted, this may draw them away from what might otherwise be helpful activities. This is not the case in Ireland, where probation officers strive to build their clients' social, as well as human, capital. This wider remit enables them to better assist probationers in their efforts to desist.

Chapter 8

Looking forward

A central debate in contemporary criminology is whether offenders, particularly those with a history of serious or persistent offending, are capable of change. Some have suggested that there is substantial continuity between antisocial behaviour in childhood and adulthood (e.g. Farrington 1997) but others disagree. Although early life experiences influence the path of life course to some extent, adult life events can exert an equally powerful influence on behaviour. On completion of what is arguably the most significant longitudinal study of pathways through crime, Laub and Sampson (2003: 272) concluded, 'it would appear that child and adult factors are continually and interactively at play in a complex process that winds through time along a number of pathways.' Ezell and Cohen (2005) observed that a stable relationship existed between age and crime from early- to mid-adolescence but discovered that this relationship broke down during adulthood. They suggested that both continuity and change must be taken into account in desistance theory. Morizot and LeBlanc (2007) suggested that there were two possible ways to model the effects of various factors on the desistance process. The 'launch effect' model refers to predictors that are present either before or during the early stages of desistance and have a long-term impact on behaviour. The 'contemporaneous' model refers to factors assessed at the same time as the offending behaviour, which have either a short-term or time-varying effect on behaviour. Distal predictors rarely predict long-term outcomes while factors measured close in time to offending behaviour often show a stronger effect.

The statistical analyses reported in Chapter 4 examined whether static factors, such as criminal history, or dynamic factors, such as social problems and criminal cognitions, best accounted for desistance. The results suggested that both static and dynamic factors contributed to desistance but indicated that dynamic factors, particularly criminal cognitions, were more important. This suggested that contemporaneous factors, such as criminal cognitions and social circumstances are very influential for desistance, while distal predictors, such as age and criminal history, play a lesser role. In other words, the findings supported a 'dual process' model (see Ezell and Cohen 2005). This chapter extends that analysis by examining whether the same factors predict long-term outcomes. Because all of the participants were on probation when they were interviewed, this chapter also adds to an extra dimension to knowledge about the long-term impact of probation supervision for repeat offenders.

Desistance: a long-term perspective

In Chapter 1, several important issues related to the measurement of desistance were introduced. A key issue relates to determining how long an individual must remain crime free before he or she is considered a *bona fide* desister. In reconviction research, a 2-year follow-up period is considered an acceptable standard (see Colledge, Collier and Brand 1999). However, some offenders remain crime free for years before they reoffend. This has led some, including Farrington (1997), to conclude that it is not possible to be certain that someone has desisted until after their death. If the follow-up period is too short, a period of temporary desistance may be mistaken for true desistance. Shorter measurement periods can give a false impression of stability in offending behaviour and it is important to use long follow-up periods to capture the true extent of change in criminal careers (see Ezell and Cohen 2005). For this reason, a follow-up of over 4 years was used in this study.

Kazemian (2007) drew attention to the distinction between behavioural and official desistance. Behavioural desistance refers to the termination of offending behaviour and is usually measured by asking people directly about the offences they have committed. In contrast, official desistance occurs when individuals have no further convictions recorded against them and is usually measured by official records held by the police or other criminal justice agencies. Self-report measures are generally favoured in desistance research because they are closest to the behaviour in question and are capable of accounting for antisocial behaviour that is not necessarily criminal but may be criminogenic (e.g. excessive drinking). However, significant resources are required to collect this type of information, particularly over a long period. As a result, many researchers settle for official desistance as a proxy for behavioural desistance. Renewed contact with the criminal justice system (e.g. rearrest, reconviction and reimprisonment) is one of the most commonly used indicators of reoffending. There are several limitations associated with using official records to measure reoffending.

Official data represents 'only the tip of the iceberg' of actual offending (Farrington 2002: 7). Conviction takes place at the end of a long, funnelling process by the criminal justice system. In order to be registered officially, the crime must first be reported and recorded; then the offender must be caught, convicted, and sentenced or cautioned. What lies beneath the surface is commonly known as the 'dark figure of crime'. It is this domain that is tapped through surveys of reported victimisation and delinquency among the general population. Outcomes may be influenced by the biases of decision makers within the criminal justice system. For example, an offender who is employed may be considered low risk and shown more leniency as a result. Official data may be subject to further biases as a result of local variation in police and sentencing practices. As a result, studies using self-reports may produce different information about causes and correlates of desistance from studies using official records. It is important to bear this in mind when comparing the findings from this phase of the study, which looks at official desistance, to the findings from the first phase of the research, which focused on self-reported desistance. Despite the limitations of official police records, most researchers would agree that, once their shortcomings are recognised, they can provide a useful indicator of criminal behaviour. They are readily available, objective measures of outcomes and are not subject to problems of attrition, memory loss or obfuscation. They are also highly correlated with self-reported offending (see Chapter 3).

Pseudo-reconvictions occur when delays between the commission of an offence and a conviction in court mean that offences committed prior to the sentence are sometimes falsely counted as new convictions. Conversely, new offences occurring during the study period may not reach the courts until after the follow-up period, so are not counted. Pseudo-reconvictions are particularly problematic in the case of non-custodial sanctions. Lloyd et al. (1994), for example, found that 22 per cent of the first reconvictions recorded for their sample of probationers and 28 per cent of the community service group were actually pseudo-reconvictions (compared to 7 per cent for prisoners). To counteract this problem of pseudo-reconvictions in this study, dates of arrest for all reconvictions were obtained and any convictions where the arrest had occurred prior to the interview were removed from the analysis.

Nature and extent of reoffending

Data on all convictions received by the participants since their interview were obtained from the Criminal Records Office up to December 2008. These data included information about arrest dates, conviction dates, the offences for which the convictions were received and the sanctions imposed. The average length of the follow-up period was 1,763.7 days (SD = 121.8) with a range of 1,579 to 2,105 days. This translates to approximately 4.8 years, which exceeds the 2 years recommended by evaluation researchers. The long measurement period combined with the detailed information that was collected about subsequent criminality should provide a reasonably accurate account of actual reoffending.

When estimating the rate of offending across the criminal career, it is important to control for 'street time'; that is, time at liberty in the community. Piquero *et al.* (2001) examined the frequency of offending among a sample of 272 serious juvenile parolees and found that only 7.2 per cent of the sample was still involved in crime by the end of the follow-up period. When they adjusted for street time, this rose to 27.8 per cent. (Of course, it must be noted that offenders can and often do offend while incarcerated; see Edgar, O'Donnell and Martin 2002). In the current analysis it was not possible to take account of time spent in custody. Garda records do not contain details of early release from prison or periods of remand in custody, making it very difficult to establish exactly when participants were at liberty in the community. As very few were reimprisoned during the follow-up period (see below), the results were unlikely to be affected by periods of incarceration, but this possibility should be borne in mind when interpreting the results.

Overall, 48 participants were reconvicted within the study period. This corresponds to 65.8 per cent or almost two-thirds of the sample. The time to first reconviction is illustrated in Figure 8.1. The sharpest rise occurred between the first and second year after the interview and continued to increase steadily throughout the study period. Only

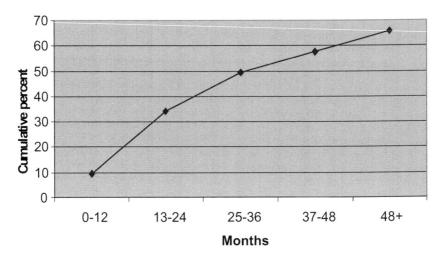

Figure 8.1 Time to first reconviction

a small number received their first new conviction within the first year (n = 7 or 9.6 per cent). By the end of the second year, around a third had been reconvicted (n = 25, 34.2 per cent). Almost half of the sample had been convicted of at least one new offence by the end of the third year (n = 36, 49.3 percent). The percentages that were reconvicted reached 57.5 per cent (n = 42) after 4 years and culminated in 65.8 per cent (n = 48) by the end of the follow-up period.

One of the most striking findings in this analysis was the length of time it took for participants to acquire their first reconviction. On average, the sample as a whole remained crime free for 1,112.99 days (SD = 574.99), or over 3 years following their interview. If we look only at participants who reoffended during the follow-up period, the average time to reconviction was 795.17 days (SD = 407.344). At just over 2 years, this is indicative of a substantial gap in their criminal careers. This pattern is at odds with what is known about reconviction rates elsewhere. Most studies show that those who reoffend tend to do so within the first 2 years after sentencing. McIvor and Barry (2000) found that the highest level of recidivism occurred within the first 6 months following receipt of a probation order, after which the rates began to taper off (47 per cent of their sample were reconvicted within the first 6 months, 74 per cent after 2 years, and 79 per cent by the end of the follow-up period).

There are a number of possible methodological explanations for this gap in participants' criminal careers. It may be explained by the fact that police records were used as the key indicator for reoffending. It is well known that official records only record information about offences that have been reported, prosecuted, and convicted and therefore cannot provide information about the dark figure of crime. It is possible that participants were continuing to offend and their offences simply did not come to the attention of the police. Looking at the 2006 Irish crime statistics (Central Statistics Office 2007b), it appears that only a minority of crimes are proceeded against (for example, 38 per cent of assaults, 13 per cent of burglaries and 21 per cent of thefts). However, the length of the follow-up period provides comfort. Although people tend to get away with crime more often than they get caught, it is unlikely that participants in this study would be lucky enough to evade notice for over 4 years, particularly since they are 'well known' to the police.

A second possible explanation is that the gap was due to delays between the commission of an offence and the conviction for that offence. In 2007, the average waiting time for criminal cases in the Dublin Circuit Court was 15 months. In the Dublin District Court, the delay was much lower at just 2.5 months (Irish Courts Service 2008). It is possible that participants were arrested and then had to wait for their case to come to court and this may explain the lengthy crime-free periods. In order to eliminate this possibility, time to first rearrest was also calculated. The average number of days until first arrest was 960.52 (SD = 680.34), meaning that participants were not arrested for over 2½ years after their interview. (The mode was 1,628 days and the median was 896.00 days.) Looking at reoffenders only, the average time to their first arrest was 569.65 days (SD = 446.834; median = 474.50 days). Although this interval is shorter than time to reconviction, it still represents a significant lull in offending behaviour. In all, this suggests that the observed gaps in participants' reconviction records are likely to be genuine and cannot be explained by low police detection rates or delays in the processing of cases through the criminal justice system.

This is not the first time that crime-free gaps, or periods of intermittency, in criminal careers have been documented (see Piquero 2004). Little is known about what precipitates these periods of temporary desistance or what prompts offenders to revert to crime. In Chapter 5, participants' accounts of their relapse episodes provided three main explanations for their return to crime. They typically attributed relapse to an absence of genuine commitment to change, an unfavourable change in their life circumstances, such as the end of a romantic relationship, or an inability to cope with life's demands. It is possible that similar factors may be involved in the relapse episodes recorded here.

It is also likely that the changing socio-economic context in Ireland played a role. From the mid-1990s, Ireland experienced unprecedented economic growth, which resulted in almost full employment (see Chapter 3). However, from 2006 onwards, economic growth slowed and there was a significant decline in employment levels. The decline was particularly steep in deprived neighbourhoods and in low-skilled employment sectors, such as construction and the service industry. When one compares levels of deprivation in participants' neighbourhoods between 2002 and 2006 (see Haase and Pratschke 2008), there was a significant increase in levels of deprivation in their areas. The average deprivation score in 2002 was –5.58 and this dropped to –9.98 in 2006. This difference was statistically significant ($t = 9.27$, $p < .001$). It is possible that the participants, most of whom lived in deprived areas and were either unemployed or worked in low-skilled sectors of the economy, were particularly vulnerable during the economic downturn. Under such disadvantageous circumstances, their coping skills and commitment to desistance are likely to be tested to their limits.

The lull in offending may also reflect a deceleration in participants' criminal activity (although rates after the interview were not compared with rates before). Recent sophisticated statistical analyses have discovered that offenders tend to reduce the seriousness and frequency of their offending before stopping completely (Bushway *et al.* 2001). Pathways to desistance are often curved and many putative desisters continue to engage in minor offending as they move away from crime (see Leibrich 1993). A focus on reoffending alone provides an incomplete picture of change. Critics argue that defining 'success' as the absence of reoffending is too narrow to capture the less tangible and subtler changes that may accompany successful reform (see Mair 1997). Raw reconviction rates, which have formed the basis of the analysis so far, obscure individual variation and reveal little about the nature of reoffending. They fail to capture nuanced changes in offending behaviour, such as reductions in seriousness or frequency.

Table 8.1 shows a breakdown of offence types for the first new convictions received by the sample. The most common was motoring offences, which accounted for almost a third of new convictions. This category mainly included offences like driving without tax and

Table 8.1 Offences at first reconviction

	Number	Percentage
Motoring	15	31.3
Property	11	22.9
Public order	8	16.7
Drugs	7	14.6
Violence	5	10.4
Other	2	4.2

Table 8.2 Disposals on first reconviction

	Number	Percentage
Imprisonment	9	18.8
Suspended sentence	5	10.4
Community Service		
Order	4	8.3
Fine	18	37.5
Probation	10	20.8
Other	2	4.2
Total	48	100

insurance and driving without a licence. Around a quarter were reconvicted of property offences, which consisted primarily of thefts and some burglaries. Public order offences were also common and were responsible for 16.7 per cent of reconvictions. It is clear that the majority of new offences were relatively minor, particularly when they are compared to the offences for which participants received their original probation order. At that time, their main offences were robbery, drugs offences and theft. This suggests that participants may have reduced the severity of their crimes.

A further indicator of the severity of offending can be adjudged from the sentences participants received. Reimprisonment is often used as an indicator of offence seriousness. Table 8.2 lists the first new sanction received by those who were reconvicted during the study period, in descending order of seriousness. (If there was more than one, the most serious sanction was selected.) Over a third (37.5 per cent) received a fine, making it the most common new sanction dealt to probationers. This is generally regarded as one of the least serious sanctions. A substantial minority of participants received prison sentences (n = 14), although almost half of these were suspended and the majority were of a short duration. Ten were for 6 months or less and only two exceeded 2 years. Probation was the next most common sanction and was received by a fifth of participants (n = 10), followed by community service orders, which were received by four participants.

The frequency of new convictions received was also calculated. Of those who were reconvicted, the majority (n = 19 or 39.5 per cent) received only one new conviction, while 16 (33.3 per cent) received two to three new convictions. Seven (14.5 per cent) participants acquired four to five new convictions, while six (12.5 per cent) received six or more. The average number of reconvictions among the sample was 1.8 (sd = 2.06).

At first glance, the finding that almost two-thirds of the participants reoffended appears to be a negative one, although it is not unexpected given their criminal histories. On a more positive note, the offences for which they were reconvicted were relatively minor and this was reflected in the disposals they received. Overall, these findings imply a de-escalation in seriousness and frequency of offending and suggest that, at the very least, participants were building a momentum towards change. This highlights the non-linear nature of pathways to desistance and draws attention to the fact that, in spite of their best intentions, many of those who attempt to desist do not succeed. Relapse must be viewed as an integral part of the desistance process.

In Ireland, there has been no national study of reconviction rates among probationers. This means there is no base rate against which to compare the progress of this sample, making it more difficult to assess the implications of these results for the probation practice. Baumer *et al.* (2002) encountered similar difficulties when researching recidivism among prisoners in Iceland. Their approach was to compile a list of studies from around the world that measured prisoner recidivism and compare their rates of reimprisonment with those in Maltese and Icelandic samples. They found a remarkably uniform pattern across jurisdictions with around half of all prisoners reimprisoned within 2 years of release. In the absence of a strong Irish research tradition, a similar approach was used here.

The first and only national study of recidivism among Irish offenders concerned prisoners and revealed that almost half were reimprisoned within 4 years (O'Donnell *et al.* 2008). Those most at risk of reimprisonment were male and young, had less formal education, were unemployed, were illiterate and had a prior prison committal.

Higher reimprisonment rates were found for property offenders and fine defaulters. The reconviction rates within this study are much higher than those found in the national prisoner sample. This is unsurprising since the prisoner sample comprised a representative sample of all prisoners, while the current study deliberately focused on repeat offenders, who are known to have higher reconviction rates. Reconviction rates among the Irish sample also compare well to those found internationally. The review shows that around half of those sentenced to community sanctions reoffend (this is similar to the percentages reported by Baumer *et al.* (2002) for reimprisonment rates among prisoners). A perusal of reconviction studies for offenders serving community sentences reveals rates of 13 per cent in Sweden (Berman 2002), 34 per cent in Australia (Smith and Jones 2008), 54 per cent in New Zealand (Nadesu 2008), 32 per cent in the USA (Langan and Cunniff 1992), and 56 per cent in England and Wales (Home Office 2002). (These differences may be partly attributable to differences in the length of follow-up.)

It was important to establish whether the participants who were identified as 'primary desisters' during the first phase of the research maintained their crime-free status throughout the follow-up period or at least for longer than participants who were categorised as 'currently offending' at the time of the interview. This would establish whether the study had captured a temporary lull in offending or the early stages of true desistance. If the desisters were genuinely trying to desist, they should experience a longer time to reconviction or involvement in less serious crime.

Comparison of the two samples showed that participants classed as 'currently offending' at the time of the interview were more likely to be reconvicted and were reconvicted at a higher rate than primary desisters (see Figure 8.2). Although both groups started from a relatively low base, primary desisters demonstrated a lower overall rate of reconviction compared to the 'currently offending' group. By the end of the follow-up period, 57.8 per cent of primary desisters had acquired a new conviction in comparison with 78.6 per cent of participants who were involved in crime. This difference approached significance ($\chi^2 = 2.92$, $p = .09$).

As explained earlier, raw reconviction rates may conceal important information about the nature of the criminal activity in which participants were engaged. It is useful to know whether desisters were committing less serious crime than offenders. This was tested by comparing the number of primary desisters and the numbers in the 'currently offending' group who received a prison sentence

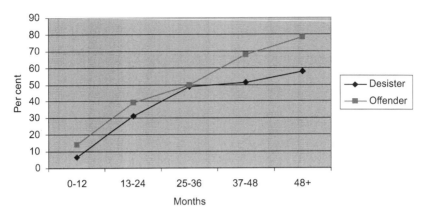

Figure 8.2 Time to reconviction for primary desisters

during the follow-up period (sentences that were suspended were also included in this analysis as it indicates more serious offences). Just over a quarter of primary desisters ($n = 12$) received a new prison sentence compared to over half of the 'currently offending' group ($n = 15$). This difference was significant ($\chi^2 = 5.049$, $p <. 03$). In all, these findings suggest that participants who were categorised as primary desisters at the time of the interview represented individuals at the early stages of change rather than a group of individuals experiencing a temporary lull in their criminal careers. This lends further validity to the findings reported in Chapter 4. (The same analysis was conducted with the secondary desistance groups and similar patterns were observed, although the differences were not as striking. This is not surprising since some of the participants who were involved in crime in the previous year were beginning to desist by the time of the interview.) Nevertheless, it is important to note that, although the majority of primary desisters were moving towards long term change, at least according to their police records, about a quarter of them were reconvicted and some for quite serious offences.

Who desists?

The potential for change in human behaviour and the complexity of the social world render it extremely difficult to make accurate long-term predictions about criminal behaviour. As a result, the impact of various subjective and social variables on the process of change remains a matter of debate. Social factors appear to have a long-term effect on behaviour. Research suggests that their effects are not immediate but are amplified slowly over time (see Laub *et al.* 1998). Several subjective factors, including motivation (Burnett 2004), self-identification as a family man (LeBel *et al.* 2008), and certain personality traits (Caspi et al. 1994), have also shown a lasting effect on behaviour. In contrast, more dynamic cognitive factors, such as attitudes and thinking styles, rarely cast a lengthy shadow over the life course. Overall, it is very difficult to make accurate long-term predictions about offending behaviour using either dynamic or static variables (e.g. Lewis 1998).

The same three psychometric scales that were used in the primary and secondary desistance analyses were employed in this analysis (these variables and the justification for their selection were described in detail in Chapter 4). Two outcome measures were used. The first outcome measure was a dichotomous variable, which measured whether a participant was reconvicted during the total follow-up period. The second measure, number of days to reconviction, was continuous and was defined as the length of time between the interview and the first new conviction. Bivariate tests were used to determine whether there was any relationship between each of these outcome measures and the demographic, criminal history, psychological and social variables.

First, the relationship between the static factors (that is, age and criminal history) and reconviction was examined. Age was not related to reconviction during the follow-up interval nor to time to reconviction. The relationship between the four criminal history variables and the reconviction outcomes also showed no relationship to either of the reconviction measures. The finding that static factors were not significant predictors of long-term desistance is noteworthy, given that they emerged as quite important during the early stages of change. Age at time of interview was important for both primary and secondary desistance and age at onset of offending was important for primary desistance (see Chapter 4). During the early stages of desistance, ex-offenders are just beginning to come to terms with their criminal pasts and to explore positive new identities. During this time, they often face substantial obstacles to change and feel uncertain about their ability to create a new future. Under such circumstances, it is not surprising that their past selves retain a strong hold over their behaviour.

Since static factors were not important for long-term desistance, it seems that the influence of background factors may recede as individuals move further away from crime. As they make the transition into enduring desistance, desisters separate from their criminal identities and start to break free from the determining influence of their pasts (see Chapter 6). Over time, they develop their new conventional identities and begin to participate more fully in pro-social roles. This process may create a positive feedback loop, which can cause the past to lose its hold. This point reaches to the heart of the criminological debate about change and continuity in offending behaviour. Although research shows a stable and consistent relationship between age and criminal behaviour over time (see Gottfredson and Hirschi 1990), there is growing evidence, stemming mainly from longitudinal research on criminal careers, that static factors do not play a determining role in adult behaviour. Their influence may be superseded by that of events occurring in adulthood, such as marriage or employment (see Laub and Sampson 2003).

Although criminal cognitions were particularly important during the early stages of change, the striking relationship between criminal cognitions and offending behaviour did not endure. Pro-criminal attitudes, measured by the CRIME-PICS General Attitude to Crime, were not significantly related to either outcome measure, suggesting that they were not important for long-term desistance. Similarly, engaging in criminal thinking did not affect the likelihood of reconviction. Participants who scored higher on the PICTS Current and Historic Criminal Thinking scales were no more likely than low-scoring participants to be reconvicted. Nevertheless, three of the PICTS subscales were significantly related to reconviction, suggesting that the role of criminal thinking was circumscribed. It is particular styles of criminal thinking, rather than the fact of engaging in criminal thinking, that are implicated in long-term desistance.

Participants who scored higher on the PICTS Mollification scale had a significantly longer time to reconviction ($r = .203$, $p < .04$). Desisters were therefore more likely to try to externalise blame for their criminality and tended to avoid taking responsibility for their actions. In contrast, participants who were reconvicted were less likely to use justifications and rationalisations to excuse their criminal behaviour and to blame external factors, such as difficult personal circumstances, societal injustice or the victim, for their actions. It is of note that desisters achieved higher scores on the Mollification scale, as this has some support in the literature. Maruna (2001) compared the narratives of persistent offenders to those of desisters and found that desisters often attempted to avoid responsibility for their actions by placing the blame for their behaviour on circumstances that they believed were beyond their control to change (similar to Mollification). This enabled them to maintain a positive self-image and continue to identify with conventional mores. Desisters, however, tended to attribute their subsequent reform to their own internal resources rather than external events.

The PICTS Power Orientation scale was also positively related to time to reconviction ($r = .196$, $p < .05$). Power Orientation refers to a need to have control over the environment and other people. People who score high on this scale feel powerless and attempt to regain control by demonstrating their superiority over others primarily through violent acts or conspicuous consumption. Desisters scored lower on the PICTS Cognitive Indolence scale than participants who were reconvicted during the follow-up period ($t = 1.96$, $p = .05$). This means that participants who were reconvicted were more easily bored, tried to avoid personal responsibility, and tended to take the path of least resistance in life (Walters 1990). Individuals who score high on Cognitive Indolence are unable to critically evaluate their thinking and often miss important learning opportunities in their environments. All of these factors conspire to drive them further from attaining their goals. As a result, cognitive indolence is considered to be 'a major impediment to long-term change' (Walters 1990: 148). Conversely, it implies that desisters tended to have good problem-solving skills, accept personal responsibility, and embrace life's challenges. This is reminiscent of the desistance narratives that were described in Chapter 6, which suggested that desisters were more likely to adopt an agentic pathway through life.

Taken together, these findings indicate that criminal thinking plays a minor but important role in long-term outcomes. Evidence regarding the links between criminal thinking and long-term outcomes shows mixed results. Walters (1996) found that prisoners who engaged in criminal thinking were significantly more likely to commit disciplinary infractions. Others have linked certain thinking styles to desistance, including Cut-off and Entitlement (Walters 2005) and Super-optimism (Palmer and Hollin 2004) to reconviction. Overall, it has to be concluded that the role of criminal thinking in long-term desistance has not yet been fully clarified.

Although not significant for primary and secondary desistance, the level of perceived social problems was important for maintaining desistance over time. The only CRIME-PICS scale to show a significant relationship with reconviction was the CRIME-PICS Problem scale, which is a cumulative measure of the obstacles participants believed they faced to desistance. Surprisingly, participants who expected to face fewer problems tended to take less time to be reconvicted (r = .312, p <. 004). Given the apparently important role played by participants' perceived social problems in desistance, further analysis was conducted with each item on the problem scale and time to reconviction. A number of key problem domains were significantly correlated with time to reconviction (using a one-tailed test, p <. 03). These included a mix of social and personal problem areas, namely family (r = .23), relationships (r = .26), boredom (r = .23), and depression (r = .23). For each variable, individuals with higher problem scores experienced a longer time to reconviction. Conversely, this means that individuals who had better relationships with their families and partners were less likely to desist.

At first glance, the findings seem counter-intuitive but there are several possible explanations. First, it is important to remember that the CRIME-PICS Problem Inventory is a subjective measure, which records participants' perceived, rather than their actual, problems. In this regard, it is of note that the LSI-R risk score, which records probation officers' ratings of the problems participants faced, was not significantly related to reconviction. The LSI-R measures 10 criminogenic needs and high scores on just two of these subscales significantly increased the likelihood of reconviction. Participants who were reconvicted during the follow-up period had significantly higher scores on the Finance (t = 2.09, p < .05) and the Peer Relations (t = 2.81, p <.01) subcomponents. That is, participants who were experiencing financial problems and those who were continuing to associate with criminal peers were at a higher risk of reoffending. It is possible, therefore, that high scores on the Problem Inventory reflected participants' assessments of their problems rather than actual difficulties.

People who have poor coping skills and a sense of fatalism about the future may perceive social circumstances to be more problematic than they actually are, compared to individuals with high levels of self-efficacy and good coping skills. This possibility is reinforced by the finding that strong problem-solving and reasoning skills (represented by Cognitive Indolence) are critical for successful desistance. It is possible that desisters are more adept at recognising potential problems and accurately appraising them. Individuals' mindset can influence whether they will reoffend and also whether they will experience social problems. LeBel *et al.* (2008) found that high levels of social problems on re-entry were strongly associated with recidivism among released prisoners. Subjective factors, such as regret about past criminal behaviour and feelings of being stigmatised, play a direct role in desistance and reoffending but also contribute indirectly to desistance by mediating the experience of social problems. LeBel *et al.* (2008: 155) placed agency at the centre of change and posited that a positive mindset enabled the individual 'to triumph over problems and make the best of situations, while a negative frame of mind leads to drift and defeatism in response to the same events'.

This is in line with existing research, which increasingly recognises the importance of emotions for behaviour. Giordano *et al.* (2007) found that adolescents with higher levels of negative affective states, such as anger and depression, had higher adult crime rates. Marital happiness, which was mediated by depression, reduced the likelihood of reoffending. They suggested that people's emotional state could augment or diminish their motivation to change and influence their capacity to take advantage of desistance opportunities. They proposed a central role for emotions in desistance, theorising that they operate alongside cognitive and social processes to generate change. Zamble and Quinsey (1997) also found that ex-prisoners who reoffended after release experienced significantly higher levels of emotional distress than those who did not reoffend. When asked what caused their negative emotional states, they related it to problems in their lives, particularly in the interpersonal domain.

It is possible that participants' social circumstances may have altered in the 4 years between the interview and the reconviction analysis. The deterioration in the Irish economic situation, which led to substantial increases in unemployment, might have left some of the previously low-risk participants more vulnerable to relapse. Unemployment can have a knock-on effect in other areas of people's lives. Losing a job can put a strain on personal relationships, increase negative emotionality, and reduce people's confidence in their ability to continue with a crime-free lifestyle. Poor coping skills would inevitably exacerbate these difficulties. This could also partially explain why the majority of participants who reoffended took such a long time to be reconvicted. Perhaps the period of temporary desistance that they enjoyed was not a genuine desistance attempt based on a considered re-evaluation of lifestyle choices but was instead incumbent on favourable circumstances, such as a high availability of employment opportunities. Their lack of commitment or poor coping skills could have been masked by the favourable economic situation and the supportive criminal justice environment provided by the Probation Service. When these favourable circumstances were removed, the likelihood that they would return to crime increased.

It is interesting that, although they operated in the reverse direction, the key problem domains correspond to the themes identified as components of secondary desistance in participants' narratives. In their accounts, desisters claimed that strong social bonds and emotional well-being were the long-term outcomes of desistance. They described how, over time, they began to develop closer relationships with the important people in their lives and noticed improvements in their psychological health. Many described how they had to 'knife off' from important relationships that were affiliated with their criminal lives and develop new (or rebuild earlier) relationships that were consistent with a conventional lifestyle. It is possible that participants who had difficult personal relationships were better placed to create new identities, as it would be easier for them to break with their past. Relationships with family, friends and partners clearly constitute an important component of long-term desistance, but their role needs to be teased out further. The 'wrong' type of social capital may impede, rather than facilitate, desistance (see also MacDonald and Marsh 2005).

The influence of social factors may be gradual and cumulative and this may also explain why they were not significant in these analyses. According to current thinking, merely having a job or being in a relationship is not enough to elicit change. A would-be desister must also construct a new identity around his or her new roles and this inevitably takes time. Perhaps, as Mischkowitz (1994) suggested, positive relationships may provoke a conformative spiral, where the effects of the initial event becomes amplified over time. Laub *et al.* (1998: 225) expounded further on this idea, stating:

> The emergence of social bonds can be likened to an investment process in that social bonds do not arise intact and full-grown but develop over time like a pension plan funded by regular instalments. As the investment in social bonds grows, the incentive for avoiding crime increases because more is at stake. Thus, while seminal events can dramatically alter long-standing patterns of behaviour, we expect that desistance from crime will be gradual and will accompany the accumulation of social bonds.

Generativity did not play a central role in primary or secondary desistance (see Chapter 6). It was hypothesised that the redemption script may be a later development in, or an outcome of, the desistance process and would therefore not be evident in the early stages of change. In order to test whether generativity was associated with long-term outcomes, the relationship between generativity and reconviction rates was explored. The results supported the idea that generativity may play a role in sustaining desistance. Dichotomous ratings were assigned to narratives if they contained any evidence of generative themes. Chi-square analysis was conducted with this variable and whether the participant received a new prison sentence. There was a strong trend supporting the influence of generativity in long-term outcomes and the result approached significance ($\chi^2 = 3.53$, $p < .06$). Of 38 participants with at least one example of a generative theme, only nine were reconvicted. Because of the small numbers involved in this analysis, this conclusion must remain tentative.

Returning to the question introduced at the beginning of the chapter, the answer to whether persistent offenders can change their lives is a qualified 'yes'. While the majority of participants received further convictions after the interview, these were mainly for minor offences. It is significant that few returned to prison, particularly since many of them had been imprisoned in the past. It can be concluded therefore that the participants were either desisting or had significantly reduced their offending. Individuals who are 'well known' to the police are often watched more closely by them. As a result, they are more likely than other citizens to have their infractions detected and to be convicted (see McAra and McVie 2007). In this regard, it is worth mentioning that among the convictions recorded against participants were failure to display learner plates, having no lights on a bicycle, and possession of small amounts of drugs. Some policing practices may delegitimatise police authority among ex-offenders, who could feel they are being targeted unfairly. Failure to recognise and reward a desistance attempt may also discourage them from changing (Maruna and Roy 2007).

If we bear in mind the issues associated with using reconviction rates to measure reoffending, it is possible to draw some conclusions about the roles played by static, subjective and social factors in long-term desistance from these analyses. Static background factors were not related to long-term outcomes, lending further support to the idea that it is possible for people with entrenched criminal behaviour to move away from crime. The dynamic social and cognitive factors proved to be more important in the long term. Unexpectedly, high levels of social capital seemed to increase, rather than decrease, the likelihood of reoffending. The reasons behind this are not clear but it is likely that the changing economic conditions in Ireland may have contributed. Participants who had strong social capital when interviewed may have been particularly vulnerable as they watched their future plans slip away. Poor coping skills may have exacerbated their social difficulties. These findings highlight the need for practitioners to focus in their work on imparting flexible cognitive, social and employment skills that can be transferred to new roles if and when necessary.

Chapter 9

Betwixt and between

This book examines the dynamics of desistance among repeat adult offenders. One of its primary aims is to provide a phenomenological account of the psychosocial factors associated with desistance. Drawing on a variety of data sources, including in-depth interviews, police records and psychometric instruments, the study reported in these pages aimed to produce a detailed account of the shifts that occurred in participants' offending, cognitions and social circumstances as they negotiated the transition away from crime. This chapter synthesises and interprets the findings and assesses them against the backdrop of existing research and theory on desistance. Its purpose is to outline an empirically based model of the desistance process and to offer guidance to practitioners in the field of criminal justice.

Turning points, transitions and transformations

> In science as in life, it is well known that a chain of events can have a point of crisis that could magnify small changes. But chaos meant that such points were everywhere. They were pervasive. (Gleick 1987: 23).

The model provided in Figure 9.1 illustrates the fluid nature of the interaction between individual factors, cognitive processes and the wider social context. These elements are not separate but are in constant motion in a complex and dynamic system. Adopting a holistic perspective on criminal careers, Ulmer and Spencer (1999:

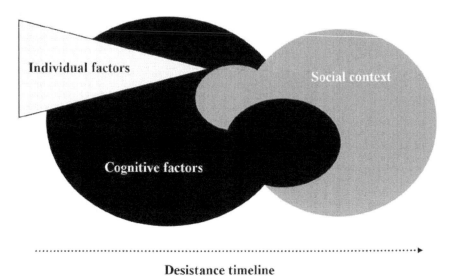

Desistance timeline

Figure 9.1 The dialectic of desistance

105) proposed that continuity and discontinuity 'are inseparable and mutually constituting phases of a dialectical process'. Whether someone acts in a particular way is contingent both on past experience and current opportunities (representing continuity and constraints) and choice (representing discontinuity). In their view, biology, social circumstances and broader structural factors influence, but never determine, decisions to offend or desist. As with chaos theory, there is always the potential for novel and unpredictable choices.

As can be seen, criminal cognitions are at the forefront during the early stages of change and remain relevant throughout the desistance process. Criminal thinking was strongly implicated in the analysis of primary desistance, while pro-criminal attitudes were involved in secondary desistance. Four years later, criminal thinking and pro-criminal attitudes were not as important. This diminution in influence is to be expected since dynamic factors, such as thinking and attitudes, do not generally predict long-term behaviour (Lewis 1998). Instead, three particular styles of criminal thinking, reflecting the desire to externalise blame, to gain control over others, and the presence of cognitive indolence, were significant.

Individual, or static, factors were influential during both primary and secondary desistance but were not related to reconviction. Age was significantly associated with both primary and secondary desistance, while age at onset of offending was important only in relation to primary desistance. This is unsurprising given the consistent finding in the literature that age and criminal history are among the most important predictors of recidivism (Gendreau, Little and Goggin 1996). Bottoms *et al.* (2004: 372) suggested that static factors, such as age and criminal history, provide what they termed the 'programmed potential' for offending. That these characteristics were not related to long-term outcomes suggests that ex-offenders can escape the determining influence of their criminal pasts after a certain amount of time has elapsed. Perhaps as new identities, centred on the successful adoption of conventional ties, become stronger and more developed, the pall cast by the past may diminish.

Social factors played only a minor role in primary and secondary desistance but became increasingly salient over time. Though not significant during the earlier stages, participants who successfully maintained desistance over time had more problems. In particular, they had weaker social bonds, particularly with family, partners and friends. This finding is unexpected since social capital features strongly in many desistance theories and was named by participants as an important factor for change. Several explanations were suggested. Participants' social bonds, while strong, may not have had the qualities to facilitate desistance (for example, they may not have increased access to other forms of social capital). Alternatively, desisters' social circumstances may have changed during the 4-year-period. Whatever the explanation, it seems that desisters were desisting even though they had high levels of social problems, came from socially deprived areas, and had acquired little additional social capital since they decided to stop offending.

It is possible that initial involvement in crime precipitated a downward spiral, cutting off opportunities to access conventional sources of social capital. Growing up in deprived areas, they were starting from a low base. The typical participant's biography was characterised by early school leaving, few qualifications and little work experience. Involvement in crime led them towards people who had similar life histories and away from individuals who might have increased their social resources. In their narratives, participants typically emphasised their own role in separating themselves from sources of social capital. The same inner resources would later be used to assist them as they moved away from crime. It may be that they needed to exercise high levels of agency if they were to desist under such circumstances, and this may explain why cognitive factors were so important. Desistance theories present an ideal situation where desisters acquire social capital either before or during the desistance process. In reality, ex-offenders must work very hard to make any gains and the results take time to manifest in their lives. On a positive note, many eventually attain reasonable levels of life success (see Farrington *et al.* 2006).

While the social context provides a framework for action, individual choices and capacities, otherwise known as agency, then come into play. Offenders do not simply react passively to social events but, instead take an active role in bringing about change in their lives (see Chapter 6). Giordano *et al.* (2002) claimed that agency was the primary factor in desistance. While acknowledging that choices are socially embedded and are always made within specific social contexts, Giordano *et al.* assigned a secondary role to social and structural factors. In their theory, the offender must encounter an opportunity for reform, called a 'hook for change'. For desistance to occur, the offender must already be motivated to change and recognise the hook as an opportunity for change. Giordano *et al.* proposed that the eventual outcome of this process is a transformation from a criminal to a non-criminal identity. At the point of change, these new lifestyles will be at a distance, and the individual's subjective stance is especially important during the early stages of change.

The findings of two separate studies were used to reconstruct this composite picture of the desistance process. The studies used different methodologies and different units of measurement and the findings may be partly attributable to this rather than genuine differences. Kazemian (2007), among others, suggested that predictors identified by self-report studies may differ from those identified by studies using official measures. Given the strong relationship between self-reported and official offending observed in this study (see Chapter 8) and others (see Chapter 3), it can be argued that this is unlikely.

The transition to desistance

The study also contributed to knowledge about the early stages of desistance. Short-term changes in behaviour were accompanied by immediate and dramatic changes in participants' cognitions and, to a lesser extent, their social circumstances (see Chapter 4). Participants who were actively involved in crime at the time of interview (at whatever level of seriousness) displayed significantly stronger criminal cognitions, attitudes and problems than those who were not. This indicates that the early stages of desistance may, for some, be characterised by rapid and dramatic cognitive reorientations away from crime. It is striking that such significant differences were evident after a relatively short interval of time. A similarly strong pattern was not repeated when psychometric scores were examined in relation to whether participants had committed crime in the past year or in the subsequent 4 years. In the long term, the difference between those who had not offended and those who had was smaller and less consistent. It is possible that the strength of changes in attitudes and beliefs dissipates or stabilises over time.

Chaos theory serves as a useful metaphor for conceptualising what happens at the boundary between criminality and convention because it is concerned with 'phase transitions'; that is, the shift from one state to another (see Walters 2002b; more generally, see Gleick 1987). Although originally developed in the physical sciences, it has been applied in criminology to explain, among others, rural, property and white-collar crime (see Milovanovic 1997). Walters (1998), for example, found non-linear mathematics did a significantly better job of modelling the curve for inmate-initiated assaults in prisons. Chaos theorists agree that change can occur rapidly and is often abrupt, rather than gradual. At a critical point, the linear patterns of the current system (in this case criminality) are disrupted and a new, novel pattern of behaviour (for example, conformity) emerges. According to Byrne (1998: 15), new behaviours 'appear' rather than emerge and often display new properties which cannot be explained by their antecedents.

As suggested by Crooke *et al.*'s (1992: 5; cited in Byrne 1998) concept of 'phase-shift processes', the transition to desistance may resemble a quantum leap, that fundamentally reconfigures an individual's behaviour. Studies show that important life events can induce dramatic, significant and enduring change. Miller and C'deBaca (1994) discovered that transformative life experiences frequently induce powerful, sudden and pervasive changes in all areas of the person's life. These 'quantum changes' appear to be permanent and durable (see C'deBaca and Wilbourne 2004). Individuals who are in crisis or who have suffered prolonged adversity are more likely to experience quantum change (Tennen and Affleck 1998), suggesting that this phenomenon may be relevant for many offenders. Although a single transformative experience is capable of inducing change, most form part of an ongoing process of personal growth (see also Farrall 2005).

Existing research suggests that cognitive processes may be fluid and individuals may adjust their thinking, self-perception and behaviour to suit prevailing circumstances. Reconsideration of an attitude has been shown to occur when confidence in the existing attitude is low; for example, when people are faced with contradictory information (Chaiken 1987). This re-evaluation has a knock-on effect on other areas of their thinking. Some researchers hold that attitudes exist as part an interlinked network, which incorporates all related views and experiences. When one attitude is altered, this will affect the nature of the overall evaluation (McGuire 1981). If this is the case, a negative experience related to the criminal lifestyle might trigger an overall re-evaluation of criminality among putative desisters. Walters (2003) found that the criminal identities and cognitions of first-time prisoners are fluid and adaptive. They increased during the first 6 months of their sentence, compared to those of veteran prisoners, which remained stable. He argued that the development of a criminal identity was a survival strategy for novice prisoners.

Social factors are also closely related to short-term behavioural changes. Research indicates that criminal activity (and its associated belief systems) is sensitive to changes in the immediate social environment. Horney, Osgood and Marshall (1995) asked 658 recently convicted offenders to recall their life circumstances prior to their most recent arrest. They found that changes in offending behaviour were related to changes in proximal life circumstances. Offenders were more likely to engage in criminal activity when they were involved in drug use or heavy drinking; offending was less likely when they were living with their wives. The current study extended Horney et al.'s (1995) research by examining the impact of psychological as well as social variables on recent offending behaviour. These results suggested that psychological factors may play a more important role than social factors.

If the transition to desistance occurs abruptly, as is suggested by these findings, shorter measurement periods are required to capture the dynamic processes that occur during the onset of change. Because attitudes are stable but mutable, their correlation with behaviour should be tested close in time to the behaviour of interest (see Mills, Kroner and Hemmati 2004). Indeed, Maruna's (2001) work suggests that significant cognitive changes may be recognisable after one crime-free year. Much of the desistance research to date has focused on studying change retrospectively (although see Farrall 2002; Bottoms et al. 2004; Burnett 2004), but it is also useful to document the process of reform as it happens. Further research is needed to explore the subjective changes that occur as individuals progress towards desistance.

Ever-decreasing circles

It is important to examine desistance in the context of the criminal career as a whole. There is growing evidence that even the most persistent offenders do not constantly offend but cycle in and out of criminal activity throughout their lives, and criminal careers often contain significant crime-free periods. In their study of American prisoners, Greenwood *et al.* (1978) found that even high-frequency offenders only averaged about one crime per month over their entire careers. Qualitative research also suggests that offending tends to follow a zigzag, rather than a linear, pathway (Glaser 1964). Piquero (2004: 108) defined such periods of intermittency as 'a temporary abstinence from criminal activity during a particular period of time only to be followed by a resumption of criminal activity'. This has led some to observe that desistance happens all the time (Maruna 2001). Analysis of police records revealed similar periods of intermittency in the criminal careers of Irish offenders.

The phenomenon of intermittency raises an important question: why do offenders periodically cease their involvement in crime? One perspective that influenced this study was Matza's (1964) concept of delinquency and drift. He introduced the concept of 'drift' to describe how the majority of juvenile delinquents do not consciously choose to engage in crime or conventional behaviour, but drift from one state to the other as prevailing circumstances dictate. Burnett and Maruna (2004: 168) described a more active concept of drift. They argued that ambivalence results from an interaction between 'opposing drives and desires in relation to crime' and is 'a state in which one is pulled in two mutually exclusive directions or toward two opposite goals'. This is in line with what is known about human decision-making. Decisions are more often based on cognitive shortcuts and past experience than extensive evaluation and consideration of future goals (Kahneman, Slovic and Tversky 1982). People do not make well-thought-out decisions but rather plan from moment to moment.

According to reversal theory (Apter 2003), people constantly switch back and forth between opposite states (such as seriousness and playfulness). They avoid moderate levels of arousal, seeking instead high and low levels. Similarly, rather than engaging in moderate but continuous criminal activity, offenders may switch back and forth between convention and crime. Apter (2003: 474) described his dynamic view of the personality:

There is an ever-changing internal context to our actions as well as external environmental forces. We want different things at different times and, partly as a consequence, we see things differently. In this respect, our personalities are shifting and unconstant.

The reversal process is involuntary and is triggered in three situations – by environmental events (particularly negative occurrences), frustration (for example, when an individual is unable to achieve aims on the current course of behaviour), and satiation (where the force for change builds up over time irrespective of events and frustration). In this study, three of the major factors that prompted the decision to change conform to Apter's descriptions of the triggers of a reversal – a negative experience with the criminal justice system, the incompatibility of parenthood with the criminal lifestyle, and becoming tired of the criminal lifestyle.

If people continuously drift in and out of crime, how can we account for the finding that almost all offenders eventually desist completely? The idea of a dialectical process is helpful as it views change moving in spirals, not circles. It is possible that, as each discrete episode of primary desistance occurs, it contributes to the generation of a momentum towards enduring change. Prochaska, DiClemente and Norcross (1992) also modelled change as a spiral process. Their research into drug addiction revealed that the majority of people relapse many times before finally abstaining completely. With each relapse, people regress to an earlier stage of the cycle but rarely return to the first stage.

Short-term changes in behaviour are influenced by changes in immediate life circumstances but these changes have a multiplicative effect, which can impact forcefully on the overall pattern of desistance. Each episode may have a gradual amplification effect, inducing a conformative spiral that draws the individual further towards a conventional lifestyle (see Mischkowitz 1994). Considered individually, each may be a necessary element of desistance, but none is sufficient. The power is in the interaction. As Horney *et al.* (1995: 671) observed:

The combined effects of several crime inhibiting local life circumstances may lead to the accumulation of enough social capital to motivate an individual to work at maintaining the social bonds. The maintenance of the bonds may, in turn, provide additional social capital and even reduce offending. If such a process continues to spiral, it could produce the kind of incremental change that results in a major alteration of a life trajectory.

As participants took their first tentative steps on the journey towards permanent desistance, they were experiencing significant cognitive change. Their scripts were characterised by uncertainty and ambiguity but evidenced an emerging commitment to change. This is in accord with liminality theory (see Chapter 2).

Going straight?

The path to personal transformation is best described as a zigzag process, which is characterised by tenuous motivation, instability and uncertainty. Those who are not currently committing crime are always vulnerable to relapse, even when their behaviour has been stable for a long time. In one study, Barnett, Blumenstein and Farrington (1989) found that a subgroup of 16 frequent offenders were reconvicted after 7 to 10 crime-free years. This highlights the need to consider relapse as part of the desistance process. Exploration of periods of temporary desistance, even if it does not result in permanent change, is worthwhile, as better knowledge about the processes behind the transition could be used to develop interventions that would encourage or prolong periods of temporary desistance.

From a dialectical perspective, the process of change is driven by a struggle between two opposing forces. As the opposing side becomes dominant, a critical mass is reached and a massive shift or landslide occurs. Perhaps a similar process is in operation in the psyches of offenders. Offenders and early-stage desisters are known to be highly ambivalent about crime. They experience inner conflict as they oscillate between the attractions of the criminal and the conventional lifestyle (see Prochaska *et al.* 1992; Burnett 2004). As the pull of the conventional lifestyle intensifies, the balance may be tipped in favour of conformity and sudden and dramatic changes occur. At the same time, the fluid nature of cognition indicates that desisters could reignite their criminal cognitions if they were to revert to crime.

Participants' accounts revealed that poor coping, lack of commitment and negative changes in social circumstances were the main factors that precipitated their relapse episodes. Those who were involved in crime similarly appeared to lack coping skills, problem-solving abilities, self-efficacy and commitment to change. Compared to desisters, they seemed to be led by external circumstances rather than feeling in control of their lives. The reconviction study also suggested that people with these characteristics were likely to be reconvicted. Desistance is not a process that unfolds uniformly over time (see Glaser 1969). Desistance theorists must leave scope for lapses, reversals and temporary cessations along the journey towards desistance (e.g. Prochaska *et al.* 1992).

Whether the balance in favour of convention is maintained depends on the 'choices and capacities' of the individual (Pawson and Tilley 1997: 216). To engineer an enduring change in an attitude requires the motivation to rethink the current position as well as the cognitive resources to do so (see Petty and Cacioppo 1986). Rumgay (2004) catalogued the qualities needed to maintain reform, particularly in the face of obstacles. These included access to a repertoire of coping strategies and a strong social support system, which appeared to be lacking among those who were committing crime.

The majority of offenders in this study wanted to stop offending and had clear ideas about who they would like to become. Their life goals were centred largely on conventional pursuits related to family life and employment. The process of creating the self is an 'ongoing project' (Farrall 2005: 369) that extends over the life course. It is likely that many of these identity templates will be tested, modified and occasionally rejected before a suitable one is found. Vaughan (2007: 393) argued that putative desisters engage in 'moral conversations' with themselves, where they assess available courses of action to decide whether to commit to a new non-criminal identity. Even when offenders have nominally dedicated themselves to a new non-criminal identity, they may still experience setbacks as they negotiate their way from a criminal lifestyle with its associated benefits and demands to a completely new way of being. In the chaotic, uncertain times of primary desistance, their long-term goals may become temporarily sidelined, particularly among those with low levels of agency.

Re-constructing reality: the role of personal myths

Maruna (2001) proposed that ex-offenders lived by what he termed a redemption script. On the one hand, they professed a sense of helplessness and lack of control when reminiscing about their past involvement in crime. Typically, ex-offenders perceived themselves to have a 'core good self' that was always present but sometimes obscured. They attributed their negative behaviours to environmental causes rather than personal responsibility, yet insisted that change only came about as a result of their own efforts. (A Jungian analyst might propose that this is evidence of the conflict between a guiding hero myth, and its opposite, the demon, being played out in the psyche of the offender. The end result of this struggle would, ideally, be an integrated self.) Maruna, Porter and Carvalho (2004) claimed that these personal stories, with their focus on strengths, empowerment and generativity, represent powerful instruments for change and argued that practitioners should adopt these narratives in their work with offenders.

Participants' desistance narratives showed some evidence of agency, albeit not of the kind observed by Maruna (2001). In general, desisters had higher levels of self-efficacy, better coping skills, and better developed support mechanisms (see Chapter 6). Compared to offenders, they were more committed to change and sought to learn from, rather than reject, their criminal pasts. They had constructed clear conventional identities and felt confident that they could attain them. They were willing to seek help with this task and had strong support networks that they could draw on when necessary. This is reminiscent of Côté's (1997) conceptualisation of agency, which defined agentic individuals as those who take an active role in determining the direction of their lives. According to him, people with high levels of agency typically experience high self-esteem, perceive a purpose, feel they are in control of their lives and successfully achieve their goals. When they were interviewed, Irish desisters were taking their first steps on this journey away from crime. They had many of the raw ingredients needed to succeed in this task and were making some headway but had not yet attained significant levels of conventional success.

The ambivalence about reform which was evident among this group and the very real obstacles they faced would probably preclude a strong sense of agency. Perhaps as their successes in the non-criminal world increase, they will become more confident in their ability to change. Until then, they hedge their bets and do not fully commit to reform. According to McAdams (1993), agency is present when individuals discover new goals, gain insight into themselves, successfully meet a challenge or are empowered through association with something larger than themselves. The scripts of Irish desisters showed little evidence of this. It is possible that individuals who are at an earlier stage in the desistance process would not yet have experienced these forms of agency. These findings suggest that, at least in the early stages of change, ex-offenders do not possess the strong sense of agency that is sometimes ascribed to them.

In contrast with ex-convicts in Liverpool (Maruna 2001), the aspirations of the current sample were modest and their life stories were seldom characterised by generative concern. Instead, the narratives of Irish offenders revealed a preoccupation with achieving 'normal' identities, focused on relationships and work. Similar concerns have been reported by ex-offenders elsewhere (e.g. Laub and Sampson 2003). This raises an interesting question; namely, how might ex-offenders progress from a concern with accumulating the trappings of a 'normal' life to a preoccupation with generativity? It is possible that the former are intermediate goals, which lead indirectly to desistance, as proposed by Laub and Sampson (2001). Achieving these goals forges new commitments and results in a new identity as a good father, domestic provider and so forth (Farrall and Calverley 2006). Once their basic needs are resolved, offenders are free to focus on a different, and possibly more altruistic, set of goals (Maslow 1956; Healy and O'Donnell 2008).

Irish desisters were at an earlier stage of the reform process than Maruna's, and it is possible that the redemption script may not be the precursor to desistance but rather the end product or a corollary of the process. These findings have implications for the measurement of desistance, which is usually done retrospectively; for example, by asking ex-offenders to describe the process of going straight. By this time, interviewees have had time to rework their experiences to fit their new identity as a non-offender into their existing personal myth. If people's desistance stories reflect their personal myths rather than the actual process of reform, different results may emerge when the termination of criminal careers is measured prospectively. For example, when Hall, Havassy and Wasserman (1990) asked alcoholics to retrospectively describe relapse episodes, they associated relapse with stressful situations. However, stress measurements made before and after the relapse episodes showed no changes in stress level. It would be interesting to study the emergence of desistance identities prospectively in order to chart the changes as they occur.

Desistance in practice: a new agenda?

The past decade has witnessed significant changes in criminal justice practices in the Western world. There has been a shift towards evidence-based practice and more punitive community penalties have been introduced. Many probation services have witnessed moves away from traditional welfare-oriented approaches towards a new managerialist approach, which is concerned with risk management and control. Programmes that aim to address offenders' cognitive deficits have increasingly begun to replace efforts to deal with their personal and social problems (see McNeill 2006). This has met with resistance from both practitioners and academics. According to Barry (2007), the current focus on surveillance, punishment and blame undermines efforts to address the social exclusion of marginalised young people, thereby reducing the overall effectiveness of the criminal justice system. These international developments have not had the same impact in Ireland, where the risk discourse is still in its infancy and the social welfare approach remains dominant (see Healy and O'Donnell 2005).

An exploration of the views of probationers regarding the work of the Probation Service and its perceived impact on their behaviour was therefore both timely and useful. Using data obtained from the Criminal Records Office, the patterns of reconviction among the 73 probationers were examined. Overall, two-thirds of participants were reconvicted during the 4-year follow-up period but this was mostly for minor offences. In Ireland, there has been no national study of reconviction rates among probationers, making it more difficult to assess the implications of these results for the Probation Service but this rate is largely in line with what is known about reconviction among persistent offenders (see Chapter 8). This study also offered an opportunity to examine the role played by probation supervision in desistance and to identify a number of key components that should be included in a model of desistance-focused practice (Figure 9.2)

First, at the individual level, criminal cognitions offer promising targets for change and may be particularly important for early-stage desisters. In this study, recent offending behaviour was strongly associated with pro-criminal attitudes and criminal thinking. Although their influence receded over time, cognitive factors remained significant throughout the desistance process. Given their importance, practitioners should continue to address them. A number of cognitive-behavioural programmes have been developed in recent years and they are widely used in criminal justice practice. Typically, they include components that aim to increase competence in areas such as problem solving, critical reasoning, empathy, interpersonal relationships and anger management. Research suggests that these programmes can have a highly significant short-term effect on

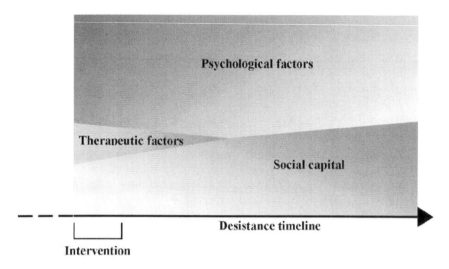

Figure 9.2   Desistance-focused practice

recidivism but do not reduce reoffending in the long-term (see Merrington and Stanley 2004). This suggests that other factors must be involved in maintaining desistance over time.

Commentators have expressed concern that cognitive-behavioural programmes do not address the wider social and structural circumstances that may constrain offenders' ability to change their lives (see Kemshall 2008). There is strong evidence to suggest that the resolution of social difficulties is critical to the successful negotiation of change (Farrall 2002). Although this study found that social factors were not strongly related to offending behaviour in the short term, they appeared to be more influential for long-term desistance (although not in the expected direction). When social capital was present, particularly in relation to personal relationships and employment, it seemed to aid and reinforce individual efforts to desist. Furthermore, if putative ex-offenders had access to strong social resources, they would not need to rely as heavily on high levels of agency to escape a life of crime. In reality, many have low social capital and have to work hard to achieve a successful conventional life.

If favourable social circumstances can ease the transition to a crime-free life, it may be short-sighted to focus only on the psychological aspects of desistance. Even if pro-social cognitions are important during the early stages of desistance, ex-offenders need strong social supports to sustain and reinforce their efforts at change over time. Although the cognitive-behavioural approach has been subject to much criticism from desistance researchers, they have not dismissed it out of hand. Instead they suggest that it should form part of a holistic approach, which recognises that informal sources of support and personal resources play a role in desistance alongside professional treatment (see Maruna, Immarigeon and LeBel 2004). They caution against an overemphasis on offence-focused factors, arguing that probation officers should also target 'desistance-related factors', such as employment status and family ties (see Farrall 2002).

Participants in this study were principally concerned with finding employment, housing and drug treatment and expected to face significant obstacles to attaining these goals. They believed that they benefited from the practical assistance they received from probation officers, especially in relation to addiction and employment issues. This supports the notion that it would be worthwhile for probation officers to offer practical assistance to those under their supervision in an effort to increase their levels of social capital. If practitioners laid the groundwork during the supervision period (for example, by helping probationers to find education or training programmes), probationers could continue to build on this foundation even after the programme is complete (for example, by using their newly acquired skills to find meaningful work). Efforts to reduce risk and need should be supplemented with attempts to increase social and human capital and develop individual strengths (McNeill 2006). Such activities can have a very real impact on crime. In an Irish context, significant reductions in drug-related crime between 1997 and 2001 have been attributed to improved drug treatment provision and low unemployment (O'Donnell and O'Sullivan 2001).

With regards to social problems, participants' relationships emerged as being particularly important for long-term desistance, although they seemed to increase rather than reduce reoffending. Farrall (2002) argued that offenders' families constitute a largely untapped resource and suggested that probation officers should address family problems during their work with offenders. When families have links to wider social networks, they can connect the probationer to other sources of social capital. They can also provide social support to ex-offenders as they work towards desistance. On the other hand, if the probationers' relationships are criminogenic or cannot facilitate an escape from socially constrained circumstances, strong social bonds could make it more difficult for people to desist. Either way, relationships should be a core focus in a desistance focused model.

Practitioners should therefore focus on building social capital as well as cognitive skills in their work with ex-offenders. To some extent at least, Irish probation practice already aims to fulfil these tasks as probation officers continue to operate within an explicitly social work framework and the correctionalist discourse that has come to characterise probation practice in England and Wales is present but not ingrained (see Healy and O'Donnell 2005). The role of the Irish probation officer is to 'advise, assist and befriend' their clients, and key elements of their work involve providing practical assistance to offenders, including working with their families. This is a legacy of the Probation of Offenders Act 1907, which became law when Ireland was a British colony and remains in force.

At the therapeutic level, the relationship between probation officers and their clients is important. As shown in Figure 9.2, it is hypothesised that the influence of this positive relationship on the desistance process extends beyond completion of the programme. A strong therapeutic alliance between practitioners and their clients can play a critical, if circumscribed, role in desistance (see McNeill *et al.* 2005). Probationers felt one of the most important functions of probation was to provide access to someone to talk to about their problems. They were also concerned about what their probation officers thought of them and, as a result, did not want to disappoint them by reoffending. This and other studies have demonstrated the fragility of motivation, particularly in the early stages of reform. Burnett (2004) suggested that ambivalence about change may best be addressed through one-to-one casework, with its emphasis on the therapeutic relationship, the social context of reform, and strengthening probationers' motivation. McNeill (2006) concurred that effective probationer–officer relationships could help probationers to increase their feelings of agency, which is necessary to overcome structural disadvantages. A recent meta-analysis showed that five 'core correctional practices' contributed to increased effectiveness in offender treatment (Dowden and Andrews 2004). The study suggested that practitioners should endeavour to model and reinforce pro-social attitudes and behaviour, teach effective problem-solving skills, develop a strong therapeutic alliance, employ a firm but fair approach, and use community resources.

When considering the resources that can be mobilised to encourage desistance, it is important to broaden the scope beyond the immediate environs of a rehabilitation programme or a probation office. There are a number of wider societal factors that make it harder for someone to desist. In a survey of Irish employers, only half said they would be willing to employ ex-offenders and even then, would only consider them for low-level positions (Lawlor and MacDonald 2001).

This finding is particularly noteworthy given that the survey was conducted at a time when the booming Irish economy had produced widespread labour shortages. In addition, adult convictions never expire in Ireland, meaning that a criminal record is attached to ex-offenders for the rest of their lives, making it even more difficult to find a good job. Providing offenders with opportunities to increase their human capital (such as job interview skills or educational qualifications) will be of little benefit if they do not have the means to use their newly acquired abilities to improve their life chances. These difficulties were reflected in the fact that most of the participants in this study had low levels of social capital and few had achieved the identities to which they aspired. High unemployment rates, low educational attainment and family problems are issues that tend to affect many of the communities in which the participants resided. For this reason, it is important for ex-offenders have access to support after they finish their sentence. As seen in Chapter 8, some desisters can re-offend after a lengthy period of desistance. In general, ex-offenders are reluctant to engage with formal support services so creative solutions are required. Community-based support services staffed by community members, including ex-offenders, may offer a way forward.

There are a number of possible ways to improve the situation. Farrall (2004) suggested that local communities could provide sheltered employment opportunities for ex-offenders. The Linkage Programme, which is funded by the Probation Service and supported by the business community, and which provides job training and work placements to ex-offenders, is a good example of such a programme. Better support for employers, in the form of advice and contact with a probation officer, may encourage employers to employ ex-offenders. In MacDonald and Lawlor's survey, 63 per cent of respondents said they would consider employing ex-offenders if they were given such support. Furthermore, communities are often reluctant to welcome ex-offenders back into their midst, and it is necessary to work with them to assist them in (re-)integrating ex-offenders. It is also important to help ex-offenders to re-engage in a meaningful way with their local communities and enable them to fully participate in community life. McNeill (2006) suggested that interventions should provide opportunities for participants to engage in generative activities, as this would enable them to achieve redemption and 'make good'. Similarly, Barry (2007) suggested that practitioners should try to increase probationers' participation in constructive activities in the community. It would also be helpful if structured activities were available to minimise the time spent with criminal peers and help build pro-social networks.

The ring of Gyges: compliance or genuine change?

> No man is just of his own free will, but only under compulsion, and no man thinks justice pays him personally, since he will always do wrong when he gets the chance. (Plato, *The Republic* 1955: 47).

In Book II of *The Republic*, Plato related the tale of Gyges, the Lydian shepherd, who found a ring that had the power to render the wearer invisible. Plato used this story to explore the nature of justice, arguing that 'goodness' was not intrinsic to human nature but was only pursued for the benefits it can endow, such as a good reputation. In the fable, invisibility freed Gyges from normal social and judicial constraints. Consequently, he committed regicide in order to obtain the throne for himself. The question posed is whether he would have committed these actions under the public gaze. This ancient fable and its moral have relevance for the current discussion. It draws attention to the difference between enforced compliance and genuine change.

Genuine change is more powerful than enforced compliance, although it may follow from it. When a new attitude is internalised, people will generally choose to engage in consistent behaviour later on (Kelman 1958). The imposition of sanctions is essentially an official attempt to constrain criminal behaviour. A well-known adage claims that it is not sufficient to win control over the bodies of the conquered, but their 'hearts and minds' must also be captured. Robinson and McNeill (2008) concluded that the best way for practitioners to encourage this kind of compliance is to work on offenders' beliefs and attitudes and help them to develop positive social attachments. If people change their behaviour as a result of coercion, it is more likely that they will revert to their previous behaviour when the threat is removed. Empirical research suggests that surveillance alone is insufficient to encourage lasting behavioural change when it is not accompanied by a treatment component (Petersilia and Turner 1993).

Ex-offenders in this and other studies of desistance place great emphasis on their own role in the change process. Typically, they attribute changes in their behaviour to their own actions and feel that formal interventions are merely an added incentive to remain crime free (or an additional deterrent to further criminal activity). As a result, it has been argued here that formal interventions should aim to support, rather than direct, probationers' efforts to change (McNeill 2006). There are a number of existing sentencing options that might be used to enhance individual efforts at desistance. One option is the suspended sentence. Osborough (1982: 222) aptly described the suspended sentence, which evolved in Irish common law, as a sword of Damocles, observing, 'what alone causes the sword to descend ... is the offender's own later misconduct. Here, in the legal, as much as in the literal sense, he remains the master of his fate.' Many of the participants in this study, whether or not currently involved in crime, stated that their desire to commit crime was suppressed to some extent by knowing that a prison sentence was hanging over their heads.

In the absence of a modern legislative framework, Irish judges have tended to innovate, as in the case of adjourned supervision, which has no statutory basis. In such cases the judge defers sentence until the offender has had an opportunity to demonstrate a willingness to respond to a specified intervention. Again, this option places responsibility for change in the hands of the individual and also provides motivation to maintain these changes.

Farrall (2002) argued that interventions should become 'desistance-focused' (that is, should aim to increase the social capital of offenders through work with families and employment) as well as focus on reducing risk of reoffending. Despite the well-documented shortcomings of the 'what works' approach, it would be ill-advised to discard this model completely, particularly since criminal cognitions are so important for desistance. Scotland, which has its own probation traditions backed by an indigenous research culture, may offer a good model to follow. It has adopted a mixed model, which contains some elements of evidence-based practice such as a focus on high-risk offenders and the introduction of National Standards, without losing features of the social welfare model, such as an individualised approach and an awareness of the importance of social factors (McIvor 2004).

Maruna, Immarigeon and LeBel (2004: 15) argued that success should not be defined as the outcome of a single programme, favouring the view that 'recovery is a long-term cyclical process involving a series of different interventions' over the life course. They advocated a blurring of the distinction between official intervention and spontaneous self-change, proposing that programmes should work to enhance and complement natural processes of recovery. Tied to this is a need to adopt a more flexible approach to deal with people who experience difficulty in complying with the conditions of their order, such as missing appointments or experiencing drug relapse. This study suggested that some participants, particularly those who are still involved in crime and therefore most in need of assistance, found it more difficult to cope with the requirements of supervision and with the challenges of desistance.

The accounts chronicled in this book illustrate the multi-faceted nature of desistance. Participants described criminal careers that were frequently punctuated by temporary cessations and relapses, which eventually culminated in desistance. Most participants expressed a desire to change but those who were still involved in crime found it hard to move away completely. In the words of Nick:

> Well, I've always tried but I hadn't got the willpower. I just want to make a go of things, put it all behind me, you know. I'm sick of going back to prison. It's stupid. It never ends. Things aren't getting any easier, doing what I was doing. I had to grow out of it sometime or I'd just keep going back to prison. Seeing other people getting on with their lives while I'm still stuck at square one on the game of snakes and ladders, you know. It's what it's like, get caught – back down the snake. When you get the money – back up the ladder. It's crazy. It's just up and down. [KV86]

It is hoped that this book has provided useful insights into the process of personal change among persistent adult offenders and that its findings will provide guidance to practitioners and policymakers on how best to use their resources to assist putative ex-offenders on their journey towards desistance. Significant life events constitute opportunities for change that can be exploited. But desistance does not automatically follow and offenders must be assisted along the journey. In addition to social support, successful change also requires strong reserves of personal agency. This book closes with an extract from Neil, who offered the following advice to other putative desisters:

> Stop using, be open-minded, look for a bit of inner strength or inner wisdom coz everybody has it. Just find a few good friends, decent people that can actually help you and cling onto them. That's what I done. I asked myself, 'What do I fuckin'

want?' Even though it's going to be hard but you only feel that if you have fear – 'I can't do that.' Put your mind down to it, nothing's impossible. [KV28]

Appendix

Table A1 Mean psychometric scores

CRIME-PICS	M	SD
General attitude towards offending	42.34	8.57
Anticipation of future offending	13.53	3.57
Victim empathy	5.85	2.46
Evaluation of crime as worthwhile	11.90	3.02
Problem inventory	30.78	10.15
PICTS		
Confusion	14.53	4.93
Defensiveness	15.92	4.07
Mollification	16.46	4.58
Cut-off	20.24	6.15
Entitlement	16.46	4.70
Power Orientation	15.85	5.59
Sentimentality	19.38	4.68
Super-optimism	18.65	4.86
Cognitive indolence	20.92	5.86
Discontinuity	20.47	5.89
LSI-R		
Risk of reconviction	24.97	8.82
History	5.97	2.15
Employment	5.56	2.83
Finance	1.13	.74
Family	1.54	1.32
Accommodation	1.10	.85
Leisure	1.02	.83
Peer	2.07	1.42
Substance use	4.77	1.80
Emotional	1.20	1.53

Table A2 Psychometric scores and secondary desistance

	Persist		Desist		
CRIME-PICS II	M	SD	M	SD	t score
G scale	44.94	8.31	37.04	6.50	4.08**
A scale	14.35	3.41	11.88	3.38	2.92**
V scale	5.51	1.95	6.54	3.20	1.45
E scale	12.61	3.09	10.46	2.28	3.03**
P scale	32.14	10.16	28.00	9.77	1.66
PICTS					
Confusion	15.31	5.07	12.87	4.26	1.99*
Defensiveness	15.63	4.03	16.52	4.16	.86
Mollification	16.35	4.69	16.70	4.41	.30
Cut-off	21.24	6.14	18.09	5.70	2.08*
Entitlement	17.14	4.38	15.00	5.11	1.83
Power Orientation	16.06	5.69	15.39	5.46	.47
Sentimentality	19.27	4.60	19.61	4.92	.29
Super-optimism	19.16	4.86	17.57	4.78	1.31
Cognitive Indolence	22.22	5.59	18.13	5.53	2.91**
Discontinuity	21.57	5.76	18.13	5.60	2.39*
Current Thinking	35.31	9.94	28.13	9.38	2.91**
Historical Thinking	31.59	8.72	28.13	7.86	1.62
LSI-R					
Risk of reconviction	26.59	8.67	21.65	8.37	2.11*
Criminal history	6.20	1.93	5.50	2.52	1.19
Education/employment	5.90	2.85	4.85	2.70	1.38
Financial	1.29	.72	.80	.70	2.54*
Family/marital	1.59	1.36	1.45	1.28	0.37
Accommodation	1.12	.84	1.05	.89	0.31
Leisure/recreation	1.15	.82	.75	.79	1.79
Companions	2.22	1.49	1.75	1.25	1.21
Alcohol/drug	5.20	1.60	3.90	1.92	2.78*
Emotional/personal	1.22	1.35	1.15	1.87	0.17
Attitudes	.61	.77	.35	.81	1.21

*p < .05; **p < .005.

Table A3 Psychometric scores and primary desistance

	Persist		Desist		
CRIME PICS II	M	SD	M	SD	T score
General scale	47.96	8.96	38.84	6.18	5.14 **
A scale	15.11	3.88	12.56	3.01	3.15 ***
V scale	5.57	2.19	6.02	2.62	.76
E scale	13.64	2.78	10.82	2.65	4.34 **
P scale	35.54	10.21	27.82	9.02	3.38 **
PICTS					
Confusion	18.07	4.75	12.27	3.55	5.92 **
Defensiveness	14.04	3.27	17.11	4.10	3.35 **
Mollification	16.68	4.56	16.32	4.63	0.32
Cut-off	24.21	5.51	17.70	5.15	5.09 **
Entitlement	19.18	3.67	14.73	4.48	4.40 **
Power Orientation	18.00	6.04	14.48	4.87	2.72 *
Sentimentality	20.43	4.55	18.70	4.68	1.54
Super-optimism	20.86	4.63	17.25	4.51	3.27 ***
Cognitive Indolence	24.29	4.40	18.77	5.69	4.36 **
Discontinuity	23.86	5.56	18.32	5.07	4.35 **
Current Thinking	40.00	8.39	28.57	8.82	5.46 **
Historical Thinking	34.21	9.06	28.11	7.38	3.13 ***
LSI-R					
Risk of reconviction	30.25	6.73	22.39	8.63	3.57 **
Criminal history	6.75	1.86	5.59	2.19	2.04*
Educational/employment	6.50	2.35	5.10	2.95	1.86
Financial	1.35	0.67	1.02	0.76	1.63
Family/marital	1.80	1.44	1.41	1.26	1.07
Accommodation	1.40	0.82	0.95	0.84	1.98
Leisure/recreation	1.35	0.75	0.85	0.82	2.28 *
Companions	2.60	1.31	1.80	1.42	2.10*
Alcohol/drug	5.85	1.22	4.24	1.81	3.58**
Emotional/personal	1.70	1.56	0.95	1.47	1.84
Attitudes	0.85	0.81	0.37	0.73	2.34 *

*Significant at $p < .05$; **significant at $p < .001$; ***significant at $p < .005$.

Table A4 CRIME-PICS problems and primary desistance

Problem area	Total (n = 73)		Offenders (n = 28)	Desisters (n = 45)	t score
	M	(SD)	M	M	
Money	2.32	(1.19)	2.68	2.10	2.09*
Relationships	1.96	(1.08)	2.43	1.67	2.95*
Employment/prospects	2.35	(1.25)	2.96	2.02	3.38**
Controlling temper	2.00	(1.13)	2.71	1.56	4.52**
Excitement	2.19	(1.11)	2.54	2.02	1.96
Family	2.03	(1.22)	2.46	1.81	2.29*
Health	2.03	(1.10)	2.21	1.90	1.15
Boredom	2.65	(1.07)	3.11	2.42	2.82*
Housing	2.13	(1.31)	1.93	2.29	1.16
Drink/drugs	2.16	(1.26)	2.82	1.81	3.59**
Gambling	1.16	(0.52)	1.32	1.06	1.72
Depression	1.67	(0.98)	1.71	1.63	0.38
Feeling good about self	1.76	(0.91)	1.82	1.71	0.52
Confidence	1.93	(1.02)	2.18	1.83	1.41
Lots of worries	2.29	(1.14)	2.64	2.13	1.94

*Significant at $p < .05$; **Significant at $p < .001$.

References

Adler, F. (1983) *Nations Not Obsessed with Crime*. Littleton, CO: Rothman.

Ajzen, I. and Fishbein, M. (1980) *Understanding Attitudes and Predicting Social Behaviour*. London: Prentice-Hall.

Andrews, D. (1982) *The Level of Service Inventory: The First Follow-Up*. Toronto: Ontario Ministry of Correctional Services.

Andrews, D. (1995) 'The Psychology of Criminal Conduct and Effective Treatment', in J. McGuire (ed.), *What Works: Reducing Re-offending: Guidelines from Research and Practice*. Chichester: Wiley.

Andrews, D. and Bonta, J. (1995) *Level of Service Inventory – Revised*. Toronto: Multi-Health Systems, Inc.

Andrews, D. and Bonta, J. (2006) *The Psychology of Criminal Conduct*. Cincinnati, OH: Anderson.

Apter, M. (2003) 'On a Certain Blindness in Modern Psychology', *The Psychologist*, 16(9): 474–5.

Arnett, J. (2000) 'Emerging Adulthood: A Theory of Development from the Late Teens Through the 20s', *American Psychologist*, 55(5): 469–80.

Asay, T. and Lambert, M. (1999) 'The Empirical Case for the Common Factors in Therapy: Quantitative Findings', in M. Hubble, B. Duncan and S. Miller (eds), *The Heart and Soul of Change: What Works in Therapy*. Washington, DC: American Psychological Association.

Atkinson, D. (2004) 'The What Works Debate: Keeping a Human Perspective', *Probation Journal*, 5(3): 248–52.

Bacik, I., Kelly, A., O'Connell, M., *et al.* (1997) 'Crime and Poverty in Dublin: An Analysis of the Association Between Community Deprivation, District Court Appearance and Sentence Severity', *Irish Criminal Law Journal*, 7(2): 104–33.

Bandura, A. (1977) *Social Learning Theory*. Englewood Cliffs, NJ: Prentice-Hall.

Bandura, A. (1997) *Self-Efficacy: The Exercise of Control*. New York: W.H. Freeman.

Barber, J. (2002) *Social Work with Addictions (2nd ed)*. Basingstoke: Palgrave Macmillan.

Barnett, A., Blumenstein, A. and Farrington, D. (1989) 'A Prospective Test of a Criminal Career Model', *Criminology*, 27(2): 373–88.

Barry, M. (2000) 'The Mentor/Monitor Debate in Criminal Justice: "What Works" for Offenders', *British Journal of Social Work*, 30(5): 575–95.

Barry, M. (2007) 'Youth Offending and Youth Transitions: The Power of Capital in Influencing Change', *Critical Criminology*, 15(2): 185–98.

Baumer, E., Wright, R., Kristinsdotter, K. and Gunnlaugsson, H. (2002) 'Crime, Shame and Recidivism: The Case of Iceland', *British Journal of Criminology*, 42(1): 40–59.

Becker, H. (1963) *Outsiders: Studies in the Sociology of Deviance*. New York: Free Press.

Bellerose, D., Carew, A., Lyons, S. and Long, J. (2009) *Treated Problem Drug Use in Ireland: Figures for 2007 from the National Drug Treatment Reporting System*. Dublin: Health Research Board.

Berman, A. (2002) *Reconviction Outcomes Among Swedish Male Probationers: Pattern Analysis by Substance Use*. Stockholm: Centre for Health Equity Studies, Stockholm University/Karolinska Institutet.

Biernacki, P. (1986) *Pathways from Heroin Addiction: Recovery Without Treatment*. Philadelphia: Temple University Press.

Blumenstein, A., Cohen, J., Roth, J. and Visher, C. (1986) *Criminal Careers and 'Career Criminals'*. Washington, DC: National Academy of Sciences.

Bottoms, A. (2006) 'Desistance, Social Bonds and Human Agency: A Theoretical Exploration', in P.O. Wikström and R. Sampson (eds), *The Explanation of Crime: Context, Mechanisms and Development*. Cambridge: Cambridge University Press.

Bottoms, A. (n.d.) *The Sheffield Pathways Out of Crime Study* [online]. Available at: http://www.scopic.ac.uk/StudiesSPooCS.html (accessed 20 September 2009).

Bottoms, A., Shapland, J., Costello, A., *et al.* (2004) 'Towards Desistance: Theoretical Underpinnings for an Empirical Study", *Howard Journal of Criminal Justice*, 43(4): 368–89.

Braithwaite, J. (1989) *Crime, Shame and Reintegration*. Cambridge: Cambridge University Press.

Brannigan, A., Gemmell, W., Pevalin, D. and Wade, T. (2002) 'Self-Control and Social Control in Childhood Misconduct and Aggression: The Role of Family Structure, Hyperactivity and Hostile Parenting', *Canadian Journal of Criminology*, 44(2): 119–42.

Browning, K. and Loeber, R. (1999) *Highlights from the Pittsburgh Youth Study*. Washington, DC: Office for Justice Programs, Office of Juvenile Justice and Delinquency Prevention.

Burnett, R. (1992) *The Dynamics of Recidivism*. Oxford: University of Oxford, Centre for Criminological Research.

Burnett, R. (2004) 'To Re-offend or Not to Re-offend? The Ambivalence of Convicted Property Offenders', in S. Maruna and R. Immarigeon (eds), *After Crime and Punishment: Pathways to Offender Reintegration*. Cullompton: Willan Publishing.

Burnett, R. and Maruna, S. (2004) 'So "Prison Works" Does It? The Criminal Careers of 130 Men Released from Prison Under Home Secretary, Michael Howard', *Howard Journal of Criminal Justice*, 43(4): 390–405.

Bushway, S., Thornberry, T. and Krohn, M. (2003) 'Desistance as a Developmental Process: A Comparison of Static and Dynamic Approaches', *Journal of Quantitative Criminology*, 19(2): 129–53.

Bushway, S., Piquero, A., Broidy, L., Cauffman, E. and Mazerolle, P. (2001) 'An Empirical Framework for Studying Desistance as a Process', *Criminology*, 39(2): 491–515.

Byrne, D. (1998) *Complexity Theory and the Social Sciences*. London: Routledge.

Cann, J., Falshaw, L. and Friendship, C. (2004) 'Sexual Offenders Discharged from Prison in England and Wales: A 21-Year Reconviction Study', *Legal and Criminological Psychology*, 9(1): 1–10.

Case, S. (2007) 'Questioning the "Evidence" of Risk That Underpins Evidence-Led Youth Justice Interventions', *Youth Justice*, 7(2): 91–105.

Caspi, A., Moffitt, T., Silva, P., Stouthamer-Loeber, M., Krueger, R. and Schmutte, P. (1994) 'Are Some People Crime Prone? Replications of the Personality-Crime Relationship Across Countries, Genders, Races and Methods', *Criminology*, 32(2): 163–96.

Catalano, R. and Hawkins, J. (1996) 'The Social Development Model: A Theory of Antisocial Behaviour', in J. Hawkins (ed.), *Delinquency and Crime: Current Theories*. Cambridge: Cambridge University Press.

C'deBaca, J. and Wilbourne, P. (2004) 'Quantum Change: Ten Years Later', *Journal of Clinical Psychology*, 60(5): 531–51.

Central Statistics Office (CSO) (2007a) *Census 2006: Principal Demographic Results*. Dublin: Central Statistics Office.

Central Statistics Office (CSO) (2007b) *Garda Recorded Crime Statistics 2003–2006*. Dublin: Central Statistics Office.

Chaiken, S. (1987) 'The Heuristic Model of Persuasion', in M. Zanna, J. Olson and C. Herman (eds), *Social Influence: The Ontario Symposium*, (vol 5). Hillsdale, NJ: Lawrence Erlbaum Associates, Inc.

Colledge, M., Collier, P. and Brand, S. (1999) *Programmes for Offenders: Guidance for Evaluators. Crime Reduction Programme – Guidance Note 2*. London: Home Office.

Combat Poverty Agency (2001) *Against All Odds*. Dublin: Combat Poverty Agency.

Comiskey, C., Saris, J. and Pugh, J. (2007) 'Estimating the Prevalence of Opiate Use in Ireland and the Implications for the Criminal Justice System', *Probation Journal*, 54(1): 22–35.

Condon, J., Boyce, P. and Corkindale, C. (2003) 'The First-Time Fathers Study: A Prospective Study of the Mental Health and Wellbeing of Men During the Transition to Parenthood', *Australian and New Zealand Journal of Psychiatry*, 38(1): 56–64.

Côté, J. (1997) 'An Empirical Test of the Identity Capital Model', *Journal of Adolescence*, 20(5): 577–97.

Cottle, C., Lee, R. and Heilbrun, K. (2001) 'The Prediction of Criminal Recidivism in Juveniles: A Meta-analysis', *Criminal Justice and Behavior*, 28(3): 367–94.

Cox, G. and Lawless, M. (1999) *Where Ever I Lay My Hat: A Study of out of Home Drug Users*. Dublin: Merchant's Quay Project.

Cunningham, A. (2002) *One Step Forward: Lessons Learned from a Randomised Study of Multi-Systemic Therapy in Canada*. Ontario: Centre for Children and Families in the Justice System.

Cusson, M. and Pinsonneault, P. (1986) 'The Decision to Give Up Crime', in R. Clarke and D. Cornish (eds), *The Reasoning Criminal*. New York: Springer-Verlag.

Davis, C., Nolen-Hoeksema, S. and Larson, J. (1998) 'Making Sense of Loss and Benefiting from the Experience: Two Construals of Meaning', *Journal of Personality and Social Psychology*, 75(2): 561–74.

Dowden, C. and Andrews, D. (2004) 'The Importance of Staff Practice in Delivering Effective Correctional Practice: A Meta-analytic Review of Core Correctional Practices', *International Journal of Offender Therapy and Comparative Criminology*, 48(2): 203–14.

Dunkel, C. and Anthis, K. (2001) 'The Role of Possible Selves in Identity Formation: A Short-term Longitudinal Study', *Journal of Adolescence*, 24(6): 765–76.

Edgar, K., O'Donnell, I. and Martin, C. (2002) *Prison Violence: Conflict, Power and Victimisation*. Cullompton: Willan Publishing.

Eggebeen, D. and Knoester, C. (2001) 'Does Fatherhood Matter for Men?' *Journal of Marriage and Family*, 63(2): 381–93.

Evans, K. (2002) 'Taking Control of Their Lives? Agency in Young Adult Transitions in England and the New Germany,' *Journal of Youth Studies*, 5(3): 245–69.

Evans, L. and Delfabbro, P. (2005) 'Motivators for Change and Barriers to Help-Seeking in Australian Problem Gamblers', *Journal of Gambling Studies*, 21(2): 133–55.

Expert Group on the Probation and Welfare Service (1999) *Final Report*. Dublin: The Stationery Office.

Eysenck, S. and Eysenck, H. (1977) 'Personality Differences Between Prisoners and Controls', *Psychological Reports*, 47: 1299–1306.

Ezell, M. and Cohen, L. (2005) *Desisting from Crime: Continuity and Change in Long-Term Crime Patterns of Serious Chronic Offenders*. Oxford: Oxford University Press.

Fahey, T., Russell, H. and Whelan, C. (2007) *Best of Times? The Social Impact of the Celtic Tiger*. Dublin: Institute of Public Administration.

Farrall, S. (2002) *Rethinking What Works with Offenders: Probation, Social Context and Desistance from Crime*. Cullompton: Willan Publishing.

Farrall, S. (2004) 'Supervision, Motivation and Social Context: What Matters Most When Probationers Desist?', in G. Mair (ed.), *What Matters in Probation*. Cullompton: Willan Publishing.

Farrall, S. (2005) 'On the Existential Aspects of Desistance from Crime', *Symbolic Interaction*, 28(3): 367–86.

Farrall, S. (2006) *'What Is Qualitative Longitudinal Research?'* Papers in Social Research Methods Qualitative Series No. 11. London: London School of Economics and Political Science.

Farrall, S. and Bowling, B. (1999) 'Structuration, human development and desistance from crime', *British Journal of Criminology*, 39(2): 253–68.

Farrall, S. and Calverley, A. (2006) *Understanding Desistance from Crime: Theoretical Directions in Resettlement and Rehabilitation*. Maidenhead: Open University Press.

Farrington, D. (1997) 'Human Development and Criminal Careers', in M. Maguire, R. Morgan and R. Reiner (eds), *Oxford Handbook of Criminology* (2nd edn). Oxford: Oxford University Press.

Farrington, D. (2002) *What Has Been Learnt from Self-Reports About Criminal Careers and the Causes of Offending?* London: Home Office.

Farrington, D. and Hawkins, J. (1991) 'Predicting Participation, Early Onset and Later Persistence in Officially Recorded Offending', *Criminal Behaviour and Mental Health*, 1: 1–33.

Farrington, D., Loeber, R., Stouthamer-Loeber, M., van Kammen, W. and Schmidt, L. (1996) 'Self-Reported Delinquency and a Combined Delinquency Seriousness Scale Based on Boys, Mothers, and Teachers: Concurrent and Predictive Validity for African-Americans and Caucasians', *Criminology*, 34(4): 493–517.

Farrington, D., Coid, J., Harnett, L., Jolliffe, D., Soteriou, N., Turner, R. and West, D. (2006) *Criminal Careers Up to Age 50 and Life Success Up to Age 48: New Findings from the Cambridge Study in Delinquent Development*. London: Home Office.

Fischer, E. and Farina, A. (1995) 'Attitudes Towards Seeking Professional Psychological Help: A Shortened Form and Considerations for Research', *Journal of College Student Development*, 36(4): 368–73.

Fleischer, M. (1995) *Beggars and Thieves: Lives of Urban Street Criminals*. Madison, WI: University of Wisconsin Press.

Flood-Page, C., Campbell, S., Harrington, V. and Miller, J. (2000) *Youth Crime: Findings from the 1998/99 Youth Lifestyles Survey*. Home Office Research Study 209. London: Home Office.

Frankl, V. (1984) *Man's Search for Meaning*. London: Pocket Books.

Frazier, P., Conlon, A. and Glaser, T. (2001) 'Positive and Negative Life Changes Following Sexual Assault', *Journal of Consulting and Clinical Psychology*, 69(6): 1048–55.

Frude, N., Honess, T. and Maguire, M. (1994) *CRIME-PICS II.* Cardiff: Michael and Associates.

Furey, M. and Browne, C. (2003) *Opiate Use and Related Criminal Activity in Ireland 2000 and 2001.* Research Report No. 4/03. Templemore: Garda Research Unit.

Gadd, D. (2006) 'The Role of Recognition in the Desistance Process: A Case Analysis of a Former Far-Right Activist', *Theoretical Criminology*, 10(2): 179–202.

Gadd, D. and Farrall, S. (2004) 'Criminal Careers, Desistance and Subjectivity: Interpreting Men's Narratives of Change', *Theoretical Criminology*, 8(2): 123–56.

Ganem, N. and Agnew, R. (2007) 'Parenthood and Adult Criminal Offending: The Importance of Relationship Quality', *Journal of Criminal Justice*, 35(6): 630–643.

Garland, D. (2001) *The Culture of Control: Crime and Social Order in Contemporary Society.* Oxford: Oxford University Press.

Gendreau, P., Goggin, C., Cullen, F. and Andrews, D. (2000) 'The Effects of Community Sanctions and Incarceration on Recidivism', *Forum on Corrections Research*, 12(2) [online]. http://www.csc-scc.gc.ca

Gendreau, P., Little, T. and Goggin, C. (1996) 'A Meta-analysis of the Predictors of Adult Recidivism: What Works', *Criminology*, 34(4): 575–608.

Giordano, P., Cernkovich, S. and Rudolph, J. (2002) 'Gender, Crime and Desistance: Toward a Theory of Cognitive Transformation', *American Journal of Sociology*, 107(4): 990–1064.

Giordano, P., Schroeder, R. and Cernkovich, S. (2007) 'Emotions and Crime Over the Life Course: A Neo-Meadian Perspective on Criminal Continuity and Change', *American Journal of Sociology*, 112(6): 1603–1061.

Gladwell, M. (2000) *The Tipping Point: How Little Things Can Make a Big Difference.* London: Abacus.

Glaser, D. (1964) *Effectiveness of a Prison and Parole System.* Indianapolis, IN: Bobbs-Merrill.

Gleick, J. (1987) *Chaos: The Amazing Science of the Unpredictable.* London: Vintage.

Glueck, S. and Glueck, E. (1940) *Juvenile Delinquents Grown Up.* New York: Commonwealth Fund.

Gottfredson, M., and Hirschi, T. (1990) *A General Theory of Crime.* Stanford, CA: Stanford University Press.

Graham, J. and Bowling, B. (1995) *Young People and Crime.* Home Office Research Study No. 145. London: Home Office.

Greenwood, P., Chaiken, J., Petersilia, J. and Peterson, M. (1978) *The RAND Habitual Offender Project: A Summary of Research Findings to Date.* Santa Monica, CA: RAND Corporation.

Haase, T. and Pratschke, J. (2008) *New Measures of Deprivation for the Republic of Ireland.* Dublin: Pobal.

Haines, K. and Case, S. (2008) 'The Rhetoric and Reality of the 'Risk Factor Prevention Paradigm' Approach to Preventing and Reducing Youth Offending', *Youth Justice*, 8(1): 5–20.

Hall, S., Havassy, B. and Wasserman, D. (1990) 'Commitment to Abstinence and Acute Stress in Relapse to Alcohol, Opiates and Nicotine', *Journal of Consulting and Clinical Psychology*, 58(2): 175–181.

Harrison, L. and Hughes, A. (1997) *The Validity of Self-Reported Drug Use: Improving the Accuracy of Survey Estimates.* NIDA Research Monograph No. 67. Rockville, MD: National Institute on Drug Abuse.

Health Research Board (2003) *Trends in Treated Drug Misuse in the Republic of Ireland, 1996 to 2000.* Occasional Paper 9. Dublin: Drug Misuse Research Division.

Healy, D. (forthcoming) 'Betwixt and Between: The Role of Psychosocial Factors in the Early Stages of Change', *Journal of Research in Crime and Delinquency*.

Healy, D. and O'Donnell, I. (2005) 'Probation in the Republic of Ireland: Context and Challenges', *Probation Journal*, 52(1): 56–68.

Healy, D. and O'Donnell, I. (2008) 'Calling Time on Crime: Motivation, Generativity and Agency in Irish Probationers', *Probation Journal*, 55(1): 25–38.

Hindelang, M., Hirschi, T. and Weis, J. (1981) *Measuring Delinquency.* Sage Library of Social Research No. 123. Beverly Hills, CA: Sage Publications.

Hollin, C., Palmer, E. and Clarke, D. (2003) 'The Level of Service Inventory – Revised Profile of English Prisoners', *Criminal Justice and Behavior*, 30(4): 422–440.

Home Office (2002) *Probation Statistics: England and Wales.* London: Home Office.

Horney, J., Osgood, D. and Marshall, I. (1995) 'Criminal Careers in the Short-Term: Intra-individual Variability in Crime and Its Relation to Local Life Circumstances', *American Sociological Review*, 60(5): 655–673.

Hosser, D., Windzio, M. and Greve, W. (2008) 'Guilt and Shame as Predictors of Recidivism: A Longitudinal Study with Young Prisoners', *Criminal Justice and Behaviour*, 35(1): 138–152.

Huizinga, D., and Elliott, D. (1986) 'Re-assessing the Reliability and Validity of Self-Report Measures', *Journal of Quantitative Criminology*, 2(4): 293–327.

Irish Court Service (2008) *Annual Report.* Dublin: The Stationery Office.

Irish Penal Reform Trust (2007) *Public Attitudes to Prison.* Dublin: Irish Penal Reform Trust.

Irish Prison Service (2001) *Annual Report.* Dublin: The Stationery Office.

Jacobs, B. and Wright, R. (1999) 'Stick-Up, Street Culture and Offender Motivation', *Criminology*, 37(1): 149–173.

Jamieson, J., McIvor, G. and Murray, C. (1999) *Understanding Offending Among Young People.* Edinburgh: The Stationery Office.

Jung, C. (1968/1981) 'Aion: Researches into the Phenomenology of the Self', in H. Read, M. Fordham, G. Adler and R.F.C. Hull (eds), *The Collected Works of CG Jung*, volume 9(2). London: Routledge and Kegan Paul.

Jung, C. (1963/1995) *Memories, Dreams, Reflections*. London: Fontana Press.

Kahneman, D., Slovic, P. and Tversky, A. (1982) *Judgement Under Uncertainty*. Cambridge: Cambridge University Press.

Kaukinen, C. (2002) 'The Help-Seeking Decisions of Violent Crime Victims: An Examination of the Direct and Conditional Effects of Gender and the Victim–Offender Relationship', *Journal of Interpersonal Violence*, 17(4): 432–456.

Kazemian, L. (2007) 'Desistance from Crime: Theoretical, Empirical, Methodological and Policy Considerations', *Journal of Contemporary Criminal Justice*, 23(1): 5–27.

Kelman, H. (1958) 'Compliance, Identification and Internalisation: Three Processes of Attitude Change,' *Journal of Conflict Resolution*, 2(1): 51–60.

Kemshall, H. (2008) 'Risk, Rights and Justice: Understanding and Responding to Youth Risk', *Youth Justice*, 8(1): 21–37.

Kemshall, H., Marsland, L., Boeck, T. and Dunkerton, L. (2006) 'Young People, Pathways and Crime: Beyond Risk Factors', *Australian and New Zealand Journal of Criminology*, 39(3): 354–370.

Kennett, J. (2001) *Agency and Responsibility: A Common-Sense Moral Psychology*. Oxford: Clarendon Press.

Keogh, E. (1997) *Illicit Drug Use and Related Criminal Activity in the Dublin Metropolitan Area*. Templemore: An Garda Síochána.

Kershaw, C., Goodman, J. and White, S. (1999) *Reconvictions of Offenders Sentenced or Discharged from Prison in 1995, England and Wales*. Statistical Bulletin No. 19/99. London: Home Office.

Kilcommins, S., O'Donnell, I., O'Sullivan, E. and Vaughan, B. (2004) *Crime, Punishment and the Search for Order in Ireland*. Dublin: Institute of Public Administration.

Kroner, D. and Mills, J. (2001) 'The Accuracy of Five Risk Appraisal Instruments in Predicting Institutional misconduct and New Convictions', *Criminal Justice and Behaviour*, 28(4): 471–489.

Kvale, S. (1996) *Interviews: An Introduction to Qualitative Interviewing*. London: Sage Publications.

Kyvsgaard, B. (2003) *The Criminal Career*. Cambridge: Cambridge University Press.

Langan, P. and Cunniff, M. (1992) *Recidivism of Felons on Probation, 1986–9*. Bureau of Justice Statistics, Special Report. Washington, DC: US Department of Justice.

Laub, J., Nagin, D. and Sampson, R. (1998) 'Trajectories of Change in Criminal Offending: Good Marriages and the Desistance Process', *American Sociological Review*, 63(2): 225–238.

Laub, J. and Sampson, R. (2001) 'Understanding Desistance from Crime', in: M. Tonry (ed.), *Crime and Justice: A Review of Research*, vol. 28. Chicago: University of Chicago Press.

Laub, J. and Sampson, R. (2003) *Shared Beginnings, Divergent Lives: Delinquent Boys to Age 70*. London: Harvard University Press.

Lawlor, P. and McDonald, E. (2001) *Story of a Success: Irish Prisons CONNECT Project 1998–2000*. Dublin: Stationery Office.

Layton-MacKenzie, D., Browning, K., Skroban, S. and Smith, D. (1999) 'The Impact of Probation on the Criminal Activities of Offenders', *Journal of Research in Crime and Delinquency*, 36(4): 423–453.

LeBel, T., Burnett, R., Maruna, S. and Bushway, S. (2008) 'The "Chicken and Egg" of Subjective and Social Factors in Desistance from Crime', *European Journal of Criminology*, 5(2): 131–159.

LeBlanc, M. and Loeber, R. (1998) 'Developmental Criminology Updated', in M. Tonry (ed.), *Crime and Justice* vol. 23. Chicago: University of Chicago Press, 115–198.

Leibrich, J. (1993) *Straight to the Point: Angles on Giving Up Crime*. Dunedin: University of Otago Press.

Lemert, E. (1972). *Human Deviance, Social Problems and Social Control* (2nd edn). Englewood Cliffs, NJ: Prentice-Hall.

Lewis, M. (1998) *Altering Fate: Why the Past Does Not Predict the Future*. London: Guilford Press.

Lipsey, M. (1995) 'What Do We Learn from 400 Studies on the Effectiveness of Treatment with Juvenile Delinquents?', in J. McGuire (ed.), *What Works: Reducing Re-offending: Guidelines from Research and Practice*. Chichester: Wiley.

Little, M. and Steinberg, L. (2006) 'Psychosocial Correlates of Adolescent Drug Dealing in the Inner City: Potential Roles of Opportunity, Conventional Commitments and Maturity', *Journal of Research in Crime and Delinquency*, 43(4): 357–386.

Lloyd, C., Mair, G. and Hough, M. (1994) *Explaining Reconviction Rates*. Home Office Research Study No. 136. London: Home Office.

Loeber, R., Stouthamer-Loeber, M., Van Kammen, W. and Farrington, D. (1991) 'Initiation, Escalation and Desistance in Juvenile Offending and Their Correlates', *Journal of Criminal Law and Criminology*, 82(1): 36–82.

Longshore, D. (1998) 'Self-Control and Criminal Opportunity: A Prospective Test of the General Theory of Crime', *Social Problems*, 45(1): 102–113.

Loza, W. and Simourd, D. (1994) 'Psychometric Evaluation of the Level of Supervision Inventory (LSI) Among Male Canadian Federal Offenders', *Criminal Justice and Behavior*, 21(4): 468–480.

Ludwig, K. and Pittman, J. (1999) 'Adolescent Pro-social Values and Self-Efficacy in Relation to Delinquency, Risky Sexual Behaviour and Drug Use', *Youth and Society*, 30(4): 461–482.

Lyder, A. (2005) *Pushers Out: The Inside Story of Dublin's Anti-Drug Movement*. Victoria: Trafford.

MacDonald, R. and Marsh, J. (2005) *Disconnected Youth? Growing Up in Britain's Poor Neighbourhoods.* Basingstoke: Palgrave Macmillan.

Mair, G. (1997) 'Community Penalties and Probation', in M. Maguire (ed.), *Oxford Handbook of Criminology.* Oxford: Oxford University Press.

Mair, G. (2004) 'Introduction: What Works and What Matters', in G. Mair (ed.), *What Matters in Probation.* Cullompton: Willan Publishing

Mair, G. and May, C. (1997) *Offenders on Probation.* Home Office Research Study No. 167. London: Home Office.

Marcia, J. (1966) 'Development and Validation of Ego-Identity Status', *Journal of Personality and Social Psychology*, 3(5): 551–558.

Markus, H. and Nurius, P. (1986) 'Possible Selves', *American Psychologist*, 41(9): 954–969.

Maruna, S. (1999) 'Desistance and Development: The Psychosocial Process of "Going Straight"', in M. Brogden (ed.), *The British Criminology Conferences: Selected Proceedings*, vol. 2. British Criminology Conference, Queen's University Belfast, 15–19 July 1998 [online]. Available at: http://www.britsoccrim.org/v2.htm (accessed 27 January 2010).

Maruna, S. (2000) 'Desistance from Crime and Offender Rehabilitation: A Tale of Two Research Literatures', *Offender Programs Report*, 4(1): 1–13.

Maruna, S. (2001) *Making Good: How Ex-convicts Reform and Rebuild Their Lives.* Washington, DC: American Psychological Association.

Maruna, S. and Copes, H. (2005) 'What Have We Learnt from Five Decades of Neutralisation Research?', *Crime and Justice*, 32: 221–320.

Maruna, S. and Farrall, S. (2004) 'Desistance from Crime: A Theoretical Reformulation', *Kölner Zeitschrift für Soziologie und Sozialpsychologie*, 43: 171–194.

Maruna, S., Immarigeon, R. and LeBel, T. (2004) 'Ex-offender Reintegration: Theory and Practice', in S. Maruna and R. Immarigeon (eds), *After Crime and Punishment: Pathways to Offender Reintegration.* Cullompton: Willan Publishing.

Maruna, S., LeBel, T., Mitchell, N. and Naples, M. (2004) 'Pygmalion in the Reintegration Process: Desistance From Crime Through the Looking Glass', *Psychology, Crime and Law*, 10(3): 271–281.

Maruna, S., Porter, L. and Carvalho, I. (2004) 'The Liverpool Desistance Study and Probation Practice: Opening the Dialogue', *Probation Journal*, 51(3): 221–232.

Maruna, S. and Roy, K. (2007) 'Amputation or Reconstruction? Notes on the Concept of "Knifing Off" and Desistance from Crime', *Journal of Contemporary Criminal Justice*, 23(1): 104–124.

Maslow, A. (1954) *Motivation and Personality.* New York: Harper and Row.

Matza, D. (1964) *Delinquency and Drift.* New York: Wiley.

May, C. (1999) *Explaining Reconviction Following a Community Sentence: The Role of Social Factors.* Home Office Research Study No. 192. London: Home Office.

Mays, N. and Pope, C. (1995) 'Qualitative Research: Rigour and Qualitative Research', *British Medical Journal*, 311: 109–112.

McAdams, D. (1993) *The Stories We Live By: Personal Myths and the Making of the Self.* New York: Guilford Press.

McAdams, D. (1995) *The Life Story Interview* [online]. Available at: http://www.sesp.northwestern.edu/foley/instruments/interview/ (accessed 9 September 2009).

McAra, L. and McVie, S. (2007) 'Youth Justice? The Impact of System Contact on Patterns of Desistance from Crime', *Youth Justice*, 4(3): 315–345.

McGuire, J. (ed.) (2002) *Offender Rehabilitation and Treatment.* Chichester: Wiley.

McGuire, W. (1981) 'The Probabilogical Model of Cognitive Structure', in R. Petty, T. Ostrom and T. Brock (eds), *Cognitive Responses in Persuasion.* Hillsdale, NJ: Erlbaum.

McIvor, G. (2004) 'Getting Personal: Developments in Policy and Practice in Scotland', in G. Mair (ed.), *What Matters in Probation.* Cullompton: Willan Publishing.

McIvor, G. and Barry, M. (2000) *Social Work and Criminal Justice: The Longer Term Impact of Supervision.* Edinburgh: Scottish Executive Central Research Unit.

McNeill, F. (2006) 'A Desistance Paradigm for Offender Management', *Criminology and Criminal Justice*, 6(1): 39–62.

McNeill, F. and Whyte, B. (2007) *Reducing Reoffending: Social Work and Community Justice in Scotland.* Cullompton: Willan.

McNeill, F., Batchelor, S., Burnett, R. and Knox, J. (2005) *21st Century Social Work: Reducing Re-offending: Key Practice Skills.* Edinburgh: Scottish Executive.

Merrington, S. and Stanley, S. (2004) 'What Works: Revisiting the Evidence in England and Wales', *Probation Journal*, 51(1): 7–20.

Merton, R. (1938) 'Social Structure and Anomie', *American Sociological Review*, 3(5): 672–682.

Miller, W. and C'deBaca, J. (1994) *Quantum Change: When Epiphanies and Sudden Insights Transform Ordinary Lives.* New York: Guilford Press.

Mills, J., Kroner, D. and Hemmati, T. (2004) 'The Measures of Criminal Attitudes and Associates (MCAA): The Prediction of General and Violent Recidivism', *Criminal Justice and Behaviour*, 31(6), 717–733.

Milovanovic, D. (ed.) (1997) *Chaos, Criminology and Social Justice: The New Orderly (Dis) Order.* Westport, CT: Praeger.

Mischkowitz, R. (1994) 'Desistance from a Delinquent Way of Life?', in E. Weitekamp and H. Kerner (eds), *Cross-National Longitudinal Research on Human Development and Criminal Behaviour.* London: Kluwer Academic.

Moffitt, T. (1993) 'Adolescence-Limited and Life-course Persistent Antisocial Behaviour: A Developmental Taxonomy', *Psychological Review*, 100(4): 674–701.

Montez, L. (1858) *The Arts of Beauty; Or Secrets of a Lady's Toilet: With Hints to Gentlemen on the Art of Fascinating.* New York: Dick & Fitzgerald.

Moos, R. and Moos, B. (2006) 'Rates and Predictors of Relapse After Natural and Treated Remission from Alcohol Use Disorders', *Addiction*, 101: 212–222.

Morizot, J. and LeBlanc, M. (2007) 'Behavioural, Self and Social Control Predictors of Desistance from Crime: A Test of the Launch and Contemporaneous Effect Models', *Journal of Contemporary Criminal Justice*, 23(1): 50–71.

Morrison, S. and O'Donnell, I. (1994) *Armed Robbery: A Study in London.* Oxford: University of Oxford Centre for Criminological Research.

Mulvey, E., Steinberg, L., Fagan, J., Cauffman, E., Piquero, A., Chassin, L., Knight, G., Brame, R., Schubert, C., Hecker, T. and Losoya, S. (2004) 'Theory and Research on Desistance from Antisocial Activity Among Serious Adolescent Offenders', *Youth Violence and Juvenile Justice*, 2(3): 213–236.

Murray, M. (2003) 'Narrative Psychology', in J. Smith (ed.), *Qualitative Psychology: A Practical Guide to Research Methods.* London: Sage.

Nadesu, A. (2008) *Reconviction Patterns of Offenders Managed in the Community: A 48-Month Follow-up Analysis.* Wellington, New Zealand: Department of Corrections.

Nagin, D., Farrington, D. and Moffitt, T. (1995) 'Life Course Trajectories of Different Types of Offenders', *Criminology*, 33(1): 111–140.

Nagin, D. and Land, K. (1993) 'Age, Criminal Careers and Population Heterogeneity: Specification and Estimation of a Non-parametric, Mixed Poisson Model', *Criminology*, 31(3): 327 362.

Noble, C. and Walker, B. (1997) 'Exploring the Relationships Among Liminal Transitions, Symbolic Consumption and the Extended Self', *Psychology and Marketing*, 14(1): 29–47.

Nolan, B. and Maitre, B. (2007) 'Economic Growth and Income Inequality: Setting the Context', in T. Fahey, H. Russell and C. Whelan (eds), *Best of Times? The Social Impact of the Celtic Tiger.* Dublin: Institute of Public Administration.

Oberwittler, D. (2004) 'A Multilevel Analysis of Neighbourhood Contextual Effects on Serious Juvenile Offending: The Role of Subcultural Values and Social Disorganisation', *European Journal of Criminology*, 1(2): 201–235.

O'Dea, P. (2002) 'The Probation and Welfare Service: Its Role in Criminal Justice', in P. O'Mahony (ed.), *Criminal Justice in Ireland.* Dublin: Institute of Public Administration.

O'Donnell, I. (2004) 'Imprisonment and Penal Policy in Ireland', *Howard Journal of Criminal Justice*, 43(3), 253–266.

O'Donnell, I. (2008) 'Stagnation and Change in Irish Penal Policy', *Howard Journal of Criminal Justice*, 47(2): 121–133.

O'Donnell, I. and O'Sullivan, E. (2001) *Crime Control in Ireland: The Politics of Intolerance.* Cork: Cork University Press.

O'Donnell, I. and O'Sullivan, E. (2003) 'The Politics of Intolerance – Irish Style,' *British Journal of Criminology,* 43(1), 41–62.

O'Donnell, I., Teljeur, C., Hughes, N., Baumer, E. and Kelly, A. (2007) 'When Prisoners Go Home: Punishment, Social Deprivation and the Geography of Reintegration', *Irish Criminal Law Journal,* 17(4): 3–9.

O'Donnell, I., Baumer, E. and Hughes, N. (2008) 'Recidivism in the Republic of Ireland', *Criminology and Criminal Justice,* 8(2): 123–146.

O'Donovan, D. (2000) 'Ireland', in A. van Kalmthout and J. Derks (eds) *Probation and Probation Services: A European Perspective.* Nijmegen: Wolf Legal Publishers.

O'Mahony, P. (1997) *A Sociological and Criminological Profile of Mountjoy Prisoners.* Dublin: The Stationery Office.

Osborough, W. (1982) 'A Damocles' Sword Guaranteed Irish: The Suspended Sentence in the Republic of Ireland', *Irish Jurist,* NS 17: 221–256.

Oyserman, D. and Markus, H. (1990) 'Possible Selves and Delinquency', *Journal of Personality and Social Psychology,* 59(l): 112–125.

Palmer, E. and Hollin, C. (2003) 'Using the Psychological Inventory of Criminal Thinking Styles with English Prisoners', *Legal and Criminological Psychology,* 8(2): 175–187.

Palmer, E. and Hollin, C. (2004) 'Predicting Reconviction with the Psychological Inventory of Criminal Thinking Styles', *Legal and Criminological Psychology,* 9(1): 57–68.

Paternoster, R., Dean, C., Piquero, A., Mazerolle, P. and Brame, R. (1997) 'Generality, Continuity and Change in Offending', *Journal of Quantitative Criminology,* 13(3): 231–266.

Pawson, R. and Tilley, N. (1997) *Realistic Evaluation.* London: Sage.

Petersilia, J. and Turner, S. (1993) *Evaluating Intensive Supervision Probation and Parole: Results of a Nationwide Experiment.* Research in Brief. Washington, DC: National Institute of Justice.

Petty, R. and Cacioppo, J. (1986) 'The Elaboration Likelihood Model of Persuasion', in L. Berkowitz (ed.), *Advances in Experimental Social Psychology,* vol. 19. San Diego, CA: Academic Press.

Phillips, G. (2002) *An Empirical Study of the Intensive Probation Scheme in Cork.* Unpublished master's thesis, University College, Cork.

Piquero, A. (2004) 'The Intermittency of Criminal Careers', in S. Maruna and R. Immarigeon (eds), *After Crime and Punishment: Pathways to Offender Reintegration.* Cullompton: Willan Publishing.

Piquero, A., Blumstein, A., Brame, R., Haapenen, R., Mulvey, E. and Nagin, D. (2001) 'Assessing the Impact of Exposure Time and Incapacitation on Longitudinal Trajectories of Criminal Offending', *Journal of Adolescent Research,* 16(1): 54–74.

Plato (trans. 1955) *The Republic.* London: Penguin Books.

Pratt, T. and Cullen, F. (2000) 'The Empirical Status of Gottfredson and Hirschi's General Theory of Crime: A Meta-analysis', *Criminology*, 38(3): 931–961.

Presser, L. (2008) *Been a Heavy Life: Stories of Violent Men*. Chicago: University of Illinois Press.

Probation and Welfare Service (n.d.) *Strategy Statement 2001–2003*. Dublin: The Stationery Office.

Probation Service (2008) *Strategy Statement 2008–2010*. Dublin: The Stationery Office.

Prochaska, J. and DiClemente, C. (1984) *The Transtheoretical Approach: Crossing Traditional Boundaries of Change*. Homewood, IL: Dorsey Press.

Prochaska, J., DiClemente, C. and Norcross, J. (1992) 'In Search of How People Change: Applications to Addictive Behaviours', *American Psychologist*, 47(9): 1102–1114.

Raynor, P. (2003) 'Evidence-Based Probation and Its Critics', *Probation Journal*, 50(4): 334–345.

Raynor, P. and Vanstone, M. (1997) *Straight Thinking on Probation (STOP): The Mid-Glamorgan Experiment*. Probation Studies Unit Report No. 4. Oxford: Centre for Criminological Research.

Reddy, W. (1997) 'Against Constructionism. The Historical Ethnology of Emotions', *Current Anthropology*, 38(3): 327–351.

Rex, S. (1999) 'Desistance from Offending: Experiences of Probation', *Howard Journal of Criminal Justice*, 38(4): 366–383.

Rex, S., Gelsthorpe, L., Roberts, C. and Jordan, P. (2003) *Crime Reduction Programme: An Evaluation of Community Service Pathfinder Projects, Final Report*. RDS Occasional Paper No. 87. London: Home Office.

Robinson, G. and McNeill, F. (2008) 'Exploring the Dynamics of Compliance with Community Penalties', *Theoretical Criminology*, 12(4): 431–449.

Rottman, D. and Tormey, P. (1985) 'Criminal Justice System: An Overview', in Committee of Inquiry into the Penal System (the Whitaker Report), *Report*. Dublin: The Stationery Office.

Rumgay, J. (2004) 'Scripts for Safer Survival: Pathways Out of Female Crime', *Howard Journal of Criminal Justice*, 43(4): 405–419.

Rutter, M. (1990) 'Pathways from Childhood to Adult Life', *Journal of Child Psychology and Psychiatry*, 10(1): 23–46.

Rutter, M., Giller, H. and Hagell, A. (1998) *Antisocial Behaviour Among Young People*. Cambridge: Cambridge University Press.

Sampson, R., Raudenbush, S. and Earls, F. (1997) 'Neighbourhoods and Violent Crime: A Multi-level Study of Collective Efficacy', *Science*, 277(5328): 918–924.

Santrock, J. (1999) *Life-Span Development*. London: McGraw-Hill.

Savolainen, J. (2009) 'Work, Family and Criminal Desistance: Adult Social Bonds in a Nordic Welfare State', *British Journal of Criminology*, 49(3): 285–304.

Schmidt, F., Hoge, R. and Gomes, L. (2005) 'Reliability and Validity Analyses of the Youth Level of Service/Case Management Inventory', *Criminal Justice and Behavior*, 32(3): 329–344.

Schwartz, S., Côté, J. and Arnett, J. (2005) 'Identity and Agency in Emerging Adulthood: Two Developmental Routes in the Individualisation Process', *Youth and Society*, 37(2): 201–229.

Seymour, M. and Costello, L. (2005) *A Study of the Number, Profile and Progression Routes of Homeless Persons Before the Court and in Custody.* Dublin: The Stationery Office.

Shanahan, M., Porfeli, E., Mortimer, J. and Erickson, L. (2005) 'Subjective Age Identity and the Transition to Adulthood: When Do Adolescents Become Adults?', in R. Settersen, F. Furstenberg and R. Rumbaut (eds), *On the Frontier of Adulthood: Theory, Research and Public Policy.* Chicago: University of Chicago Press.

Shover, N. (1992) 'The Socially Bounded Decision Making of Persistent Property Offenders', *Howard Journal of Criminal Justice*, 31(4): 276–293.

Shover, N. (1996) *Great Pretenders: Pursuits and Careers of Persistent Thieves.* Boulder, CO: Westview Press.

Shover, N. and Thompson, C. (1992) 'Age, Differential Expectations and Crime Desistance', *Criminology*, 30(1): 89–104.

Smith, D. (2006) *Social Inclusion and Early Desistance from Crime.* Edinburgh Study of Youth Transitions and Crime Research Digest No. 12 [online]. Available at: http://www.law.ed.ac.uk/cls/esytc/findings/digest12.pdf (accessed 9 September 2009).

Smith, D., McVie, S., Woodward, R., Shute, J., Flint, J. and McAra, L. (2001) *The Edinburgh Study of Youth Transitions and Crime: Key Findings at Ages 12 and 13.* Edinburgh Study of Youth Transitions and Crime Research Digest No. 1 [online]. Available at: http://www.law.ed.ac.uk/cls/esytc/findings/digest1.htm (accessed 29 September 2009).

Smith, D. and McVie, S. (2003) 'Theory and Method in the Edinburgh Study of Youth Transitions and Crime', *British Journal of Criminology*, 43(1): 169–195.

Smith, N. and Jones, C. (2008) *Monitoring Trends in Re-offending Among Adult and Juvenile Offenders Given Non-Custodial Sanctions.* Contemporary Issues in Crime and Justice No. 110. Sydney: NSW Bureau of Crime Statistics and Research [online]. Available at: http://www.bocsar.nsw.gov.au/lawlink/bocsar/ll_bocsar.nsf/vwFiles/cjb110.pdf/$file/cjb110.pdf (accessed 9 September 2009).

Social Exclusion Unit (2002) *Reducing Re-offending by Ex-prisoners.* London: Social Exclusion Unit.

Steffensmeier, D., Ulmer, J. and Kramer, J. (1998) 'The Interaction of Race, Gender and Age in Sentencing: The Punishment Cost of Being Young, Black and Male', *Criminology*, 36(4): 763–798.

Tang, T. and DeRubeis, R. (1999) 'Sudden Gains and Critical Sessions in Cognitive-Behavioural Therapy for Depression', *Journal of Consulting and Clinical Psychology*, 67(6): 894–904.

Tarling, R. (1993) *Analysing Offending: Data, Models and Interpretation*. London: Home Office.

Taylor, R. (2000) *A Seven-Year Reconviction Study of HMP Grendon Therapeutic Community*. Research Findings No. 115. London: Home Office.

Tedeschi, R., Park, C. and Calhoun, L. (1998) *Posttraumatic Growth: Positive Changes in the Aftermath of Crisis*. Mahwah, NJ: Lawrence Erlbaum.

Tennen, H. and Affleck, G. (1998) 'Personality and Transformation in the face of Adversity', in R. Tedeschi, C. Park and L. Calhoun (eds), *Posttraumatic Growth: Positive Changes in the Aftermath of Crisis*. Mahwah, NJ: Lawrence Erlbaum.

Thomas, C., Benzeval, M. and Stansfeld, S. (2005) 'Employment Transitions and Mental Health: An Analysis from the British Household Panel Survey', *Journal of Epidemiology and Community Health*, 59: 243–249.

Thornberry, T., Wei, E., Stouthamer-Loeber, M. and Van Dyke, J. (2000) *Teenage Fatherhood and Delinquent Behaviour. OJJDP Juvenile Justice Bulletin (NCJ 178899)* [online]. Available at: http://www.ncjrs.gov/html/ojjdp/jjbul2000_1/contents.html (accessed 29 September 2009).

Triggs, S. (1999) *Sentencing in New Zealand: A Statistical Analysis*. Wellington: Ministry for Justice.

Trotter, C. (1995) 'The Supervision of Offenders – What Works?', in L. Noaks, M. Levi, and M. Maguire (eds), *Contemporary Issues in Criminology*. Cardiff: University of Wales Press.

Tucker, J., Vuchinich, R. and Rippens, P. (2004) 'A Factor Analytic Study of Influences on Patterns of Help-Seeking Among Treated and Untreated Alcohol Dependent Persons', *Journal of Substance Abuse Treatment*, 26: 237–242.

Turner, V. (1970) *The Forest of Symbols: Aspects of the Ndembu Ritual*. London: Cornell University Press.

Uggen, C. (2000) 'Work as a Turning Point in the Life Course of Criminals: A Duration Model of Age Employment and Recidivism', *American Sociological Review*, 65(4): 529–546.

Ulmer, J. and Spencer, W. (1999) 'The Contributions of an Interactionist Approach to Research and Theory on Criminal Careers', *Theoretical Criminology*, 3(1): 95–124.

Urban II Initiative Ballyfermot (n.d.) *Community Initiative Programme 2000–2006*. Dublin: Urban Ballyfermot.

Van Gennep, A. (1977) *The Rites of Passage*. London: Routledge and Keegan Paul.

Vaughan, B. (2007) 'The Internal Narrative of Desistance', *British Journal of Criminology*, 47(3): 390–404.

Visher, C. and Travis, J. (2003) 'Transitions from Prison to Community: Understanding Individual Pathways', *Annual Review of Sociology*, 29: 89–113.

Visher, C., LaVigne, N. and Travis, J. (2004) *Returning Home: Understanding the Challenges of Prisoner Reentry: Maryland Pilot Study, Findings from Baltimore.* Washington, DC: Urban Institute, Justice Policy Center.

Vittengl, J., Clark, L. and Jarrett, R. (2005) 'Validity of Sudden Gains in Acute Phase Treatment of Depression', *Journal of Consulting and Clinical Psychology*, 73(1): 173–182.

Walsh, D. and Sexton, P. (1999) *An Empirical Study of Community Service Orders in Ireland.* Dublin: The Stationery Office.

Walters, G. (1990) *The Criminal Lifestyle: Patterns of Serious Criminal Conduct.* London: Sage.

Walters, G. (1995) 'The Psychological Inventory of Criminal Thinking Styles, Part I: Reliability and Preliminary Validity', *Criminal Justice and Behaviour*, 22(3): 307–325.

Walters, G. (1996) 'The Psychological Inventory of Criminal Thinking Styles, Part III: Predictive validity', *International Journal of Offender Therapy and Comparative Criminology*, 40(2): 105–112.

Walters, G. (1998) 'Time Series and Correlational Analyses of Inmate-Initiated Assaultive Incidents in a Large Correctional System', *International Journal of Offender Therapy and Comparative Criminology*, 42(2): 123–131.

Walters, G. (2002a) 'The Psychological Inventory of Criminal Thinking Styles (PICTS): A Review and Meta-analysis', *Assessment*, 9(3): 278–291.

Walters, G. (2002b) 'Developmental Trajectories, Transitions, and Nonlinear Dynamical Systems: A Model of Crime Deceleration and Desistance', *International Journal of Offender Therapy and Comparative Criminology*, 46(1): 30–44.

Walters, G. (2002c) 'Current and Historical Content Scales for the Psychological Inventory of Criminal Thinking Styles', *Legal and Criminological Psychology*, 7(1): 73–86.

Walters, G. (2003) 'Changes in Criminal Thinking and Identity in Novice and Experienced Inmates', *Criminal Justice and Behavior*, 30(4): 399–421.

Walters, G. (2005) 'Incremental Validity of the Psychological Inventory of Criminal Thinking Styles as a Predictor of Continuous and Dichotomous Measures of Recidivism', *Assessment*, 12(1): 19–27.

Warr, M. (1998) 'Life-Course Transitions and Desistance from Crime', *Criminology*, 36(2): 183–215.

Webster, C., MacDonald, R. and Simpson, M. (2006) 'Predicting Criminality? Risk Factors, Neighbourhood Influence and Desistance', *Youth Justice*, 6(1): 7–22.

Weitekamp, E. and Kerner, H. (1994) *Cross-National Longitudinal Research on Human Development and Criminal Behaviour.* Dordrecht: Kluwer Academic.

West, D. (1963) *The Habitual Prisoner.* London: Macmillan.

West, D. (1969) *Present Conduct and Future Delinquency.* London: Heinemann.

West, D. and Farrington, D. (1977) *The Delinquent Way of Life.* London: Heinemann.

West, R. (2005) 'Time for a Change: Putting the Transtheoretical (Stages of Change) Model to Rest', *Addiction*, 100: 1036–1039.

Whelan, C., Nolan, B. and Maitre, B. (2007) 'Consistent Poverty and Economic Vulnerability', in T. Fahey, H. Russell and C. Whelan (eds), *The Best of Times? The Social Impact of the Celtic Tiger*. Dublin: Institute of Public Administration.

White, H., LaBouvie, E. and Bates, M. (1985) 'The Relationship Between Sensation-Seeking and Delinquency: A Longitudinal Analysis', *Journal of Research in Crime and Delinquency*, 22(3): 197–211.

Wikström, P.-O. (2006) 'Individuals, Settings, and Acts of Crime: Situational Mechanisms and the Explanation of Crime', in P.O. Wikström and R. Sampson (eds), *The Explanation of Crime: Context, Mechanisms and Development*. Cambridge: Cambridge University Press.

Williams, C. and Arrigo, B. (2002) 'Law, Psychology and the "New Sciences": Rethinking Mental Illness and Dangerousness', *International Journal of Offender Therapy and Comparative Criminology*, 46(1), 6–29.

Wilson, C. (1956) *The Outsider*. London: Phoenix.

Wright, J. and Cullen, F. (2004) 'Employment, Peers and Life-Course Transitions', *Justice Quarterly*, 21(1): 183–205.

Zamble, E. and Porporino, F. (1988) *Coping, Behaviour and Adaptation in Prison Inmates*. New York: Springer-Verlag.

Zamble, R. and Quinsey, V. (1997) *The Criminal Recidivism Process*. Cambridge: Cambridge University Press.

Index

Note: the letter 'f' after a page number refers to a figure; the letter 't' refers to a table.